This is a limited
edition of 200 copies.

H.M.A.T., A14. The "Euripides" on which the original Battalion embarked on the 8th May, 1915.

The Red and White Diamond
by SERGEANT W. J. HARVEY, M.M.

Authorised History of the Twenty-fourth Battalion A.I.F.

The Naval & Military Press Ltd

Published by
The Naval & Military Press Ltd
5 Riverside, Brambleside, Bellbrook
Industrial Estate, Uckfield, East Sussex,
TN22 1QQ England
Tel: +44 (0) 1825 749494
Fax: +44 (0) 1825 765701
www.naval-military-press.com
www.military-genealogy.com
www.militarymaproom.com

In reprinting in facsimile from the original, any imperfections are inevitably reproduced and the quality may fall short of modern type and cartographic standards.

LIST OF PLATES AND MAPS.

Frontispiece:—The "Euripides"
An Underground Tunnel Leading into the
  Front Line at Lone Pine 27
Snipers in Position at Lone Pine 27
White's Valley, Gallipoli.............. 30
Lieut. Col. W. E. James, D.S.O. and Bar 71
Col. W. R. Watson, C.B., C.M.G., V.D. 71
The Battalion on the Road to Pozieres—July,
  1916 88
The Hanging Virgin 91
Effects of Shell Fire 120
Bogged in the Mud 127
War and Winter 136
24th Battalion Memorial on Pozieres Ridge.. 167
Bellewarde Ridge 178
German Pill-boxes and Dug-outs 181
Broodseinde Operations 185
A Duckboard Trail 193
German Prisoners 198
Scene near Ville-sur-Ancre 238
Tanks going forward to Battle 263
Mont, St. Quentin 274
Lieut. Sedgwick and Party awaiting Attack .. 280
Lieut. G. M. Ingram, V.C., M.M. 297
Montbrehain 300
A Royal Inspection................. 316
"Pea Soup or Cocoa?" 137

Maps:

Pozieres and Moquet Farm 99
Bullecourt, May 3rd, 1917 (Hindenburg
  Line)....................... 148
The Battles in Flanders 174
Beaurevoir and Montbrehain: Scene of the
  Final Australian Infantry Attacks in the
  Great War 293

FOREWORD.

By GENERAL SIR WILLIAM BIRDWOOD, Bart., G.C.M.G., K.C.B.,

I welcome the publication of the history of the 24th Battalion as an interesting and detailed account of the achievements of a unit which so fully did its share in making and maintaining the magnificent reputation of the A.I.F.

My first association with this Battalion was on its arrival at Gallipoli, under the command of Colonel Watson, with the Second Australian Division, where it garrisoned one of our most difficult positions at Anzac, known as "Lone Pine."

The first heavy fighting in which the Battalion took part in France was at Pozières, and later it gained even greater distinction in the attack on Bullecourt on 3rd May, 1917, where, I regret, the Battalion suffered heavily. The Battalion fought there with unsurpassable bravery and determination.

With our other Australian Battalions, the 24th, under Colonel James, who had succeeded Colonel Watson in the command (which, I am glad to say, he retained to the last), was heavily engaged in the Passchendaele operations. There again it gave proof of its splendid fighting qualities, while it was also conspicuous in the epic advance from Amiens to the Hindenburg Line in 1918. It took part in our last fight of the war at Montbrehain, where the losses of the Battalion were heavy, particularly in officers.

The 24th Battalion may well look back with pride on its magnificent fighting achievements, in which our men displayed the highest qualities of manhood throughout five years of unprecedented struggle in the cause of right and liberty. The cost of such a record was inevitably great, and the Battalion suffered a total of 3420 casualties during the war.

No words of mine can do justice to the courage, cheeriness, and determination of my comrades in arms under conditions of the greatest severity. I shall always retain a proud and fond memory of my long and close association with them, and follow with interest the future of those whose services for Australia and the Empire will never be forgotten.

I am sure this publication will be a valued souvenir, not only to the members of the 24th Battalion, but to their comrades in other units of the A.I.F., and their relatives and friends in Australia.

W. R. BIRDWOOD,
General.

4th March, 1920.

IMPRESSIONS BY MAJOR-GENERAL SIR JOHN GELLIBRAND, K.C.B., C.M.G., D.S.O.

It is hard to imagine a more arduous duty of loving remembrance than the compilation of Regimental Records for a Battalion which took part in the Great War. To those who served with the unit a Calendar of Events and a Muster Roll suffice to recall to mind the details of the work as well as the character of the men they served with, and the conditions of mind and body at the time of each event. But to convey anything like an adequate impression of these matters to those who were not eye-witnesses in some enterprise—to make notes at the time of occurrence—demands ample leisure, and to my certain knowledge that commodity was a short issue to the 24th between 1914 and 1919.

I do not believe that any unit had a more hurried start than the 24th in Melbourne. Their training in Egypt was very restricted, both in scope and in time; their first real systematic training was at Le Transloy in 1917. Yet they succeeded from the first day of their active service on Gallipoli in establishing a shining example of cheerful, unselfish devotion to the Cause, of eager willingness to undertake, and steadfast endurance in carrying out what they undertook. To the last day of their service they kept the Red and White Diamond level with the best.

To describe the temperament of the 24th I know of no better words than Steverson used of the Mariners of the " Wager "—" They liked to do things nobly for their own satisfaction. They were giving their lives, there was no help for that; and they made it a point of self-respect to give them handsomely." Light-hearted the 24th certainly were, but underlying their gaiety of mind was a stern determination to see the matter out. Their business creed was to get the most out of life, and to demand the highest price from the enemy for their casualties.

At the risk of trenching on the narrative I cannot avoid referring to a few of the 24th by name. Scotty Lang, as chief gravedigger at Pozieres, seeking refreshment for Padre Durnford, and diplomatically "touching" the Staff-Captain and the Brigadier alternately for the wherewithal. Tommy Godfrey, barely able to stand on his feet after each heavy stunt, yet moving heaven and earth to avoid the turn of duty in England that would have given him a spell. Nicholas walking back into our lines with a Boche M.G. on his shoulder in broad daylight: "Just as well to make certain it won't be used again." Lloyd holding his conference in the Boche lines at Bullecourt to appreciate the situation of an "onion on a stalk a thousand yards long." Ball "bombing towards the Anzacs" at the unofficial battle of Le Transloy on a very wet night: and Savige succeeding in the impossible because he was trusted, and finding his reward as so many of his comrades did in the knowledge that he was trusted.

Of this I am certain, that any Battalion commanded by Colonel Watson or Colonel James could hardly fail to make history, but when that Battalion was composed of men like the 24th, the result could never be in question.

I do not remember any occasion which found me at variance with the 24th, except perhaps once when their tendency to manoeuvre their field kitchens in action like a battery coming into position frightened the enemy into shelling Brigade Headquarters. Also I should not care to umpire for the 24th at manoeuvres unless protected by a steel helmet. Their method of bombing through a ruined village with half-bricks will no doubt be remembered by many.

Since this history serves as a link between all who were associated with the Red and White Diamond, I wish it with all my heart a wide and successful circulation.

J. GELLIBRAND.

Hobart, 31st May, 1920.

PREFACE.

To what unit did you belong?

No soldier who was on active service with the A.I.F. is ashamed to answer that question.

The writer of this story sets out upon the record of the 24th Battalion of the Australian Imperial Forces with a firm conviction that the men who wore the red and white diamond are as proud of their colours as any regiment has been since the Celtic inhabitants of Britain stood up in arms to oppose the legions of Julius Caesar.

The world war of 1914-1918 has, like Waterloo and Trafalgar, passed into the realms of history, but the spirit of the men who made these glittering pages of history lives on. It is the nature of man to conquer the forces of opposition in every phase of life. Just as Britishers defended their country in the distant past, the race born of that strong blood went out in 1914 and the succeeding years of the war inspired by tradition and a worthy cause, and they won through in a test compared with which all former wars were as skirmishes.

What honour, then, have the men who carried their colours to victory in the fiercest, most colossal, protracted and determined struggle the world has known? Who can measure their valour?

Not because we glory in war (for we abhor the shedding of blood), not through any spirit of plunder (for we waged a war of defence), not wholly for ourselves (for we went out to stand by other worthy nations), not because we sought opportunity to display our strength of arms (for we were not skilled in war), but because our country was in danger, and our honour at stake, did we marshal an army and march to the beat of the war drums.

And this story of one small unit—one Australian Battalion—of the British armies is told, not for the purpose of glorying in the downfall of our enemies, not to boast of our achievements, not to reflect the horrors of bloody strife, but to perpetuate the spirit of comradeship which linked men together in the days of peril, and inspired them to serve with faithfulness, to strive, to endure, and to sacrifice even life itself, for a cause.

The reader of this story may possibly receive the impression that the long campaign was one of severe strain and great hardship. If that be so, the author gives his assurance that such an impression is not misleading. Any narrative giving a different conclusion might be pleasanter reading, but it would be less faithful as a history. There is no intention to complain. All ranks of the Battalion accepted the vicissitudes of active service with a true soldierly spirit, and the author hopes that the facts and sentiments set forth in this book will be found in sympathy with the memories of the men whose achievements and experiences he has endeavoured to record.

If this record falls short as a history of battles, but breathes the spirit of the Battalion in its ideals and its human elements; if it helps to bind together by the ties of memory the men who served under its colours; if it honours the men who rest in the graves on the battlefields; if it lives in the future as a treasured possession of our children and inspires in them the patriotism of their fathers, it will accomplish its purpose.

W.J.H.

1915.

FORMATION OF THE BATTALION.

It is doubtful whether any other unit of the Australian Imperial Forces was organised and equipped with such rapidity as that which marked the assembling of the 24th Battalion.

The intention had been to form three Battalions of the Sixth Brigade in Victoria, and to draw the fourth from the other States of the Commonwealth, but owing to the large number of recruits in Broadmeadows Camp at this time it was decided at the eleventh hour to raise the whole Brigade in Victoria. The result was that the 24th Battalion had to be organised, largely from raw recruits, and equipped for embarkation overseas on just over one week's notice.

The decision to draw the headquarters staff for this Battalion from New South Wales was adhered to. The commanding officer, the second in command, and adjutant came to Victoria a few days before embarkation to take over the unit.

The original Battalion was formed the first week in May, 1915, under Captain Frank W. Frawley.

On the arrival of the Commanding Officer, Lieut.-Colonel W. W. R. Watson, V.D., on 6th May, the Battalion was handed over in what was admittedly a disorganised state, for although Captain Frawley had accomplished much, the time was too short for the most experienced organiser to attain perfection in the equipment and establishment of a whole Battalion under the circumstances which prevailed at that comparatively early stage of the campaign.

The last night in camp was one of bustle and excitement. The work of issuing uniforms and kits went on until the small hours of the morning, and even then many of the men were not sure whether they had their full outfits; and those who were satisfied that they had as much as they could carry were at a loss to know how to arrange everything in such order that they might in some degree resemble soldiers. In addition to uniforms, fighting equipment and kits, many of the men struggled with a variety of articles bestowed on them by relatives and friends. Nothing could be left behind. They felt that the military authorities might at least have provided each man with a private luggage van.

EMBARKATION.

Early on the morning of Saturday, 8th May, 1915, the 24th Battalion marched out of Broadmeadows Camp and entrained for Port Melbourne. The knowledge that they were embarking for active service filled the troops with joy. Never did a keener body of men set out for the seat of war.

Lieut.-Colonel Watson being temporarily detained in connection with affairs at Rabaul, where he had already been on active service with the First Naval and Military Expeditionary Force, Major W. K. Fethers (second-in-command) took charge as acting C.O. Captain C. E. Manning was Adjutant, and the company commanders were—"A" Coy., Captain E. V. E. Neill; "B" Coy., Captain F. W. Frawley; "C" Coy., Captain W. E. James; "D" Coy., Captain G. R. Richardson.

The Brigade, consisting of the 21st, 22nd, 23rd, and 24th Battalions, looked a formidable force as it embarked, and the 24th Battalion, in spite of its hurried organisation, suffered nothing by comparison with the other units. The acting C.O. and the Adjutant, upon whose shoulders the main responsibility of turning out the unit for service had latterly rested, had cause to be proud of the Battalion.

Everybody was eager to reach the pier to get a view of the ship which was to convey the unit overseas. There were two transports at the Town Pier, Port Melbourne, and fortune favoured us at the outset, for we were allotted to the better of the two, namely, the "Euripides," a 15,000 ton Aberdeen liner, which was assigned to the 23rd and 24th Battalions, while the "Ulysses" conveyed the 21st and 22nd Battalions.

THE VOYAGE.

Our ship was the first to get away, and proceeded to Portsea, where we dropped anchor. During the night we were joined by the "Ulysses," and we passed through the Heads early on Sunday morning. Then our troubles began. For a few days seasickness quelled our exuberant spirits, and produced a feeling that wars should be fought at home.

The first port of call was Albany, where members of the Base Records and Pay Corps staff, who on account of our hurried departure had accompanied us in order to adjust records and paybooks, were disembarked.

On leaving Albany we had hopes of seeing the remains of the "Emden," but apparently it was thought advisable to give this renowned spot a wide berth, as, after steaming a long way out of the usual course, we arrived at Colombo.

At this port the troops on the "Ulysses" went ashore for a march to stretch their legs. When our men found that they were not to be accorded this privilege, a number of them scrambled off the ship into the native row-boats, and made off. A guard was posted to prevent others following their example, while one of the officers dashed up and down the decks, shouting threats and brandishing a revolver. In his excitement he dropped the revolver overboard, and his persuasive powers were thus considerably reduced.

Some men made a rush at the guard, and gained the gangway, but this success was nullified by the simple expedient of ordering the native row-boats to stand off from the ship, and as sharks were reported to be plentiful, even the most headstrong men hesitated to risk the swim. So the "mutiny," as some of the lads described the demonstration, was quelled, and only the most resourceful of the troops (who got away early) saw Colombo.

Two lady residents of Colombo (Mrs. Duff and Mrs. Fogarty) presented to Major Fethers a brass-mounted elephant, and for some reason it was considered appropriate to adopt this emblem as the Battalion's insignia on active service. Jumbo's image was accordingly printed on the unit's correspondence, with the motto, "No Surrender," which, as far as the troops could see, had no particular significance in respect to elephants, and savoured a little of vanity or presumption at that early stage of the campaign, however worthy of the distinction the unit might eventually prove. Consequently, it was not long before both the emblem and the motto were "struck off strength." The spirit of the motto was always maintained, but there was never afterwards any vaunted sign of the men's resolve to " stick it " in the face of the greatest odds.

A raid on a "two-up school" in the fo'c'sle was another incident which earned distinction for a number of defaulters. These offenders and the "tourists" who went ashore at Colombo atoned for their disobedience by "C.B.," which meant extra drills on deck for a week.

While at Colombo we were called upon to perform the sad duty of burying two comrades on shore, and before Suez was reached six others were buried at sea. The deaths were mainly due to pneumonia and the severe heat endured whilst passing through the tropics. It was reported that on our sister ship, the "Ulysses," seven deaths occurred.

During the voyage sports were held on board. Tug-of-war contests were most exciting. In the company competition the giants in "C" Company, including such hefty champions as Jim Ford, displayed so much strength that had they been ashore with the rope they might have pulled the ship uphill. The 24th subsequently challenged the 23rd, and gained a victory in the first trial. The 23rd reversed the honours in the second test, but it was discovered that their anchor-man had the rope encircling one of the ventilators. As this was considered a departure from the accepted rules in tug-of-war, it was disallowed in the third trial, and the 24th proved their superiority amid intense excitement.

Another feature of the voyage was the quantity of vaccine pumped into the troops to guard them against microbes whose activities were known to include attacks on soldiers. So often and so liberally were the boys inoculated that they believed themselves fortified for eternity against all germs and epidemics.

Submarine guard, drill, lifebelts, and "furphies"

(rumours) were other prominent features of a highly interesting trip.

With little delay in Suez Harbour we were allotted our turn to proceed up the Canal, to which stage of the voyage all looked forward with keen interest. We were fortunate in making the trip during the hours of daylight, thus obtaining an excellent view of the Canal defences.

At Port Said an interesting episode caused a delay of two days. One of the Canal service vessels, a small craft conveying heavy stone for the breakwater, collided head on with an Australian transport, which was swinging round in the basin, and within three minutes the Canal boat had disappeared, the result being that vessels which appeared to have been tied up to the side of the Canal for years had to be moved to permit of our passage into the open sea. Some three months afterwards we learned through the Egyptian press that a court martial had been held on the Austrian pilot in charge of the Canal service vessel, and it was discovered that this scheme had been planned prior to the outbreak of war.

On the run from Port Said to Alexandria "furphies" were rampant. The first rumour which had pervaded the ship was that the Brigade was going to India on garrison duty, but now that India had been left well behind some fresh intelligence had to be found to coincide with the altered prospects. The imagination of the "furphy kings" was equal to the occasion. Just at this time the first official reports of the casualties at the Dardanelles were issued, and these gave rise to the report that, owing to heavy losses, the Australians were not to be further " sacrificed " for some time, so the new units were going to England to be held in reserve for some months. Other rumours consigned the troops to Salonika, Greece, and to almost every part of the globe.

Some of the "wise heads," however, appeared to have a better idea of the truth, for at Suez they swam ashore and made their way to Cairo to await the arrival of the unit there.

During the voyage the stewardesses of the ship proved

themselves veritable "angels of mercy," for they had come to the aid of the boys under most trying circumstances when sickness was prevalent, and rendered invaluable services as nurses. This kindness was not forgotten, and now that the voyage was about to end the troops unanimously contributed to a practical testimonial as an expression of appreciation, with the result that each stewardess received a gift of £25.

EGYPT.

When the "Euripides" arrived at Alexandria and we received orders to disembark, there was a scramble for equipment. Men who had not bothered to make themselves acquainted with the art of putting their equipment together came to the conclusion that the easiest procedure was to take the outfits of those who had been possessed of that foresight. Naturally this for a time caused considerable confusion.

When the train which was to convey the unit to its destination was observed on the pier, no one looked forward with much pleasure to his trip in the rough conveyances. After a five or six hours journey in the train, with the temperature at 130 deg. in the shade, we were shunted into Helmiah siding, about eight miles from Cairo. It required another two or three miles march to bring us to our camping ground, near Heliopolis, and this march will never be forgotten. All ranks were wearing heavy uniform, and were encumbered with everything they possessed. The pace was fast, and the troops, as soft as butter after several weeks aboard ship, began to drop as if they had been under enemy fire. The discomfort and strain of such a tramp over heavy sand can hardly be understood without experience.

On arrival at the camp site we were shown our position, which was minus tents and water supply. But, with the Australian knack of fossicking, it must be said to the credit of our men that they were not long in satisfying the inner man by way of liquid refreshment. There was a general rush for the canteens. A piquet was immediately detailed to round the men up, and presently lusty voices were heard shouting in the canteens, " Any 24th men found in here after five minutes will be arrested." That threat was only the sergeant's way of effecting his purpose, and it had the desired result. A little bounce often worked wonders when used discreetly.

After a lecture on the snares and pitfalls of Egypt by Lieutenant-Colonel James Barrett (afterwards Sir James Barrett, K.B.E.), we were dismissed.

That night the order for sleeping accommodation was "every man for himself." Some slept on the forms in the mess huts of other units, and others had their first experience of a "doss" on the sand.

The position at Gallipoli at this time was so vital that we did not anticipate having much leisure. The next day's rising sun meant work. Tents gradually made their appearance, and the camp was established by degrees. Later a time-table was issued which gave the hour of reveille 5 a.m., "fall-in" 6 a.m., drill to 9 a.m., and then breakfast, after which lectures were delivered by platoon officers in the mess sheds until 12.30 p.m. We were free until 4 p.m. From 4 p.m. until 7 p.m. we were occupied with drill, musketry instruction, and route marches. We were thus relieved from outdoor duty during the hottest period of the day.

All our big manoeuvres took place during the evening, and towards the end of our sojourn in Egypt we were bivouacking or marching almost every night. Battalions opposed one another in practice warfare on the desert during the hours of darkness, and with the dawn of day began an attack which carried them back to their camps. They charged their objective all the more eagerly with the prospect of getting breakfast. In the Battalion's manoeuvres over the plains a tall chimney stack several miles distant was a favourite objective. A wag one day commented on this landmark, and asked, "Why not put a guard on the chimney and save the trouble of capturing it every day?"

The food supply was good (from an army point of view) in Egypt, as the allowance of 8½d. per day per man from the Egyptian Government added very materially to the quantity and quality of the rations.

The troops made the most of their leisure hours in Heliopolis and Cairo, and the 24th boys became experts in the art of breaking camp at times and under circumstances which were contrary to orders. As an example of the genuine spirit of comradeship which existed among all ranks, some of the young officers are known to have befriended men of the regiment whom they encountered making their way back to camp late at night and well overdue.

A successful ruse was to get an officer to fall the party in and march them past the sentries. When challenged, the officer would say, "Piquet returning from duty," and the sentry would reply, "Pass, piquet," even when it was plain that the men had been out on no military duty.

A few weeks after settling down at Heliopolis the junior officers and many of the N.C.O.'s of the Battalion were withdrawn and sent to a military school of instruction at Zeitoun, where they were supposed to learn the modern methods of warfare; but, to be candid, the majority of those who attended the school gained very little experience, as everything they were doing was already contained in the drill books and manuals. Imperial officers and N.C.O.'s, (mostly Ceylon tea planters) were allotted to the Battalion as substitutes for those withdrawn for the school of instruction, and the greatest compliment paid to our own officers on rejoining was the reception tendered them by the men. Although the Imperial men proved themselves "jolly good fellows," they were not the leaders under whom the troops were going into action, which made all the difference.

It was during the course of this school that Colonel Watson rejoined the unit and took over command.

The musketry course was carried out at the Abbassia rifle range. Several competitions were decided, the best aggregate being secured by Sergeant S. G. Savige ("C" Coy.). Other prize-winners on this range were Pte. Thompson (H.Q.), Pte. Briggs ("C" Coy.), Pte. C. Dean ("C" Coy), and Pte. R. Tuckerman ("C" Coy.). A field firing contest was won by No. 1 Section, No. 12 Platoon, "C" Coy., No. 7 Section, No. 2 Platoon, "A" Coy. being second.

During the early stages of our sojourn in Egypt the unit experienced a number of cases of sunstroke, but the subsequent issue of sun helmets, "shorts" and linen shirts tended to improve conditions greatly.

There is no doubt that the thoroughness with which the troops were trained in Egypt was largely responsible for the high standard of efficiency attained by the unit at Gallipoli.

The realities of active service were brought home to us very vividly on witnessing the number of hospital trains which nightly drew into the siding at the rear of No. 1 Australian General Hospital, Heliopolis. These trains were loaded with sick and wounded men from the Peninsula, whose reminiscences of their experiences gave us a strong desire to get to the scene of hostilities without delay.

Men who were with the Battalion in those days will clearly call to mind the sight of the Sixth Brigade on its numerous parades at the camp, with our C.O., Lieutenant-Colonel Watson, on his fine charger, " Bob," calling the Brigade to attention as the Brigadier (the late Colonel Linton) rode on to the parade ground. " The Brigade will come to attention and slope arms, with an excellent show of discipline.

And who will forget the day on which the C.O., as proud of his Regiment as any commander ever was, announced that the Battalion was about to depart for the front, the cheers that were given, and the excitement and delight which the news created?

The first draft of reinforcements for the Battalion had already arrived, and had been taken on strength to fill gaps which had resulted from sickness and other causes.

BOUND FOR THE FRONT.

On 29th August, 1915, the 24th Battalion moved out of camp at 1 a.m., and entrained at Helmiah siding for Alexandria. After another weary journey in open trucks, we arrived at our port of embarkation, and boarded the Royal Mail Steam Packet Company's s.s. " Nile," one of the fastest vessels of this line. The conditions on board were the best that could be expected for this short trip, but were certainly nothing to be compared with those on our old friend the " Euripides." The ship took a devious course to elude lurking submarines, and arrived at Lemnos Island at about 9.30 a.m. on September 2nd. Owing to reports of the sinking in the vicinity of a vessel with 2000 soldiers of the Imperial forces on board, we had an anxious trip, fearing a similar fate. Our convoy consisted of four troopships, three of which accomplished the voyage without mishap. An ex-German vessel, then named the "Southland," carrying Divisional and Brigade Headquarters staffs, the 21st Battalion, and some of the 23rd Battalion, was torpedoed. The troops displayed remarkable discipline, and the majority were safely taken off in the boats, while the ship itself was brought into Mudros Harbour and beached. Several volunteers from the officers and men aboard rendered valuable assistance in the stokehold and engine-room.

Thirty-three lives were lost in this unfortunate happening, and included in the number was Colonel Richard Linton, V.D., commanding the Sixth Brigade, a leader who was loved by all for his fine soldierly bearing and his courteous consideration for his subordinates.

Lieut.-Colonel Watson left us temporarily to take command of the Brigade pending the appointment of a successor to Colonel Linton.

After two days on board at Lemnos, where the time was spent pleasantly, including many enjoyable swims from the ship's side, the Battalion transferred to the small steamer "Abbassia," of the Khedival Line, which had already been under fire at Anzac, and still bore traces of shot and shell. Three days' rations and supplies of ammunition were issued to the men.

The big liner "Mauritania," with about 9000 British troops for Suvla Bay, was at Lemnos when we left that port.

The evening of 4th September saw us moving out through the boom at Lemnos Harbour without escort and without a light visible on board. Our thoughts were divided between submarines and the battlefield to which we were heading. In a few hours we would be on Gallipoli, whence we knew some of us would never return. There was hardly a man who did not give the address of a relative or friend to several comrades in case he should "go west." That was not superstition. These men were facing stern realities with soldierly resignation and loving thought for those at home. One of them, at the close of the war, wrote, "I can truly say that of more than twenty comrades with whom I exchanged addresses that night, I am the only one alive to-day. Some of them fell on Gallipoli, some in France, some in Belgium—all of them among the bravest and best."

When men are approaching a battlefield for the first time their faces may be lit up with smiles and their talk light and jocular, but their thoughts are deeper than outward expressions would indicate. Our unit was a typical body of Australian manhood, with a fair percentage of those reckless individuals often described as "hard doers." But who can judge a man's deeper nature by a casual acquaintance? After leaving Egypt, as we headed for Lemnos, some of these hard-living, and, apparently, hard-souled fellows, sat on the decks with the rest of the troops pondering over the pages of small Testaments which had been given to them by the church societies as they left for the field of action. Such a manifestation of a spiritual trait in human nature drew men closer together in the bonds of comradeship, and it shed a softening light on the dark days that crossed our path later.

About four hours' steaming brought us under the shadows of the Anzac heights.

The strength of the Battalion on that eventful night was 30 officers and 991 other ranks.

GALLIPOLI.

THE BATTALION'S BAPTISM.

In the early hours of Sunday morning, 5th September, 1915, the Battalion received its baptism of fire at Gallipoli.

The green lights of the hospital ships lying off the beach and flares from the front lines stood out conspicuously. British monitors were firing at the Turkish positions on the ridges, and the cracking of rifle fire along the whole sector, where a demonstration was in progress, told us plainly that we had arrived at the scene of action. Bullets from the Turkish lines, passing over the Anzac trenches, cut the water around us. It was a strange and uncanny sound, that whistle of flying lead, and its nearness aroused a suspicion that the enemy, who we knew was somewhere ahead in the gloom, had detected the arrival of the boats. The barges by which we were to land were lashed to the sides of steam pinnaces, and when brought alongside they rocked and bumped on the swell of the sea.

It may seem, to one who has not tried it, a simple thing to go down a rope ladder over a ship's side in the dark with the weight of a soldier's equipment and a rifle slung across the back, but it requires a certain amount of care, especially when it has to be accomplished with a total absence of noise. At the bottom of the ladder one felt his foot seized by the friendly hand of a "Jack Tar," who guided it to the edge of a barge and then reached up for the next man. Each barge, as it gained its complement, was taken by the pinnace to Watson's Pier, where the men disembarked. Every detail of this operation had to be performed noiselessly, quickly, and with perfect discipline, and it was daylight before the last bargeload of men reached the pier.

The troops, as they gained the land, proceeded quietly around Hell's Spit to Rest Gully. One of the first things to be distinguished was the cemetery, not a very cheerful sign for our initiation. As the troops arrived in Rest Gully they threw themselves down wherever they found space to repose. The Battalion stores, ammunition, etc., were all landed safely by the rear party under Capt. W. E. James.

Daylight, eagerly awaited, revealed Gallipoli—a scene resembling a vast mining camp.

The firing line appeared to be so close that everybody had the impression we were going straight into action.

Before us rose the ridges which had been scaled by the magnificent First Division in the face of determined opposition. As we gazed at the beach and the rugged battlefield, the question on every man's lips was, "How did they do it?" It looked impossible, but it was done, for those wonderful men were still there, holding doggedly the ground they had won.

The shabby and scant dress of these defenders, whose appearance reflected the hardships of the campaign, and contrasted so markedly with the spic and span uniforms of the new arrivals, appealed to us as something strangely humorous, and at the same time pathetic. The men who had been sticking it since the landing on the 25th April welcomed the arrival of fresh troops, and hearty greetings were exchanged on all sides. The "old hands" were almost unrecognisable at first. Their novel attire (in many cases only short knickers, boots and cap), their scrubby beards, sunburnt skins, and altogether rough appearance made the newcomers wonder what race of men these could be. Only men who realised they had set out on a difficult mission could have laughed at the condition of those pioneers of the Australian army. Every feature of the place was a signboard which said the job was rough and hard. Yet the men who had "carried on" there for four months were cheerful and undaunted, and the new arrivals were not perturbed by what they saw.

Part of the Battalion was sent round to "Shrapnel Gully," and here we sustained our first casualties. Several men who were overanxious to get a view of the Turkish line crawled up to the top of the hill to get a glimpse of this "promised land." Enemy snipers greeted them with bullets, and one of the inquisitive party came down with his arm pierced. "They're there all right," he said as he exhibited his wound.

The first positions of the 24th Battalion occupied in the

Snipers in position at Lone Pine.

An underground tunnel leading into the front line at Lone Pine.

trenches were "Courtney's," "Quinn's," and "Steele's" Posts, at the head of "Wire Gully," where we relieved the 8th Battalion on September 6th. The men, burdened with equipment and packs, struggled up the steeps through Shrapnel Gully to Wire Gully, which was about 1600 yards from the sea. Here they gained an insight into the nature of the defences and the work going on. It was a fairly quiet part of the line, with deep, well-made trenches. Compared with what we had anticipated, it was a "home."

Lieut.-Colonel Watson resumed command of the Battalion on the 7th September.

LONE PINE.

After 48 hours in the quiet sector referred to, we learned, with some concern, that the 24th Battalion was to take over the defence of the newly won "Lone Pine" trenches. This position had been allotted to the 21st Battalion, but, in the opinion of the staff, the men of that unit were too shaken after their trying experience on the torpedoed "Southland" to put them straight into this important and critical sector.

When the intelligence concerning "Lone Pine" got abroad and our boys began to question experienced Anzacs on the nature of this part of the line, the information they gathered was not calculated to reassure them respecting their fate. "Going into the Pine, are you? Poor————! You'll never come out of it. It's a ——— of a place!"

"Lone Pine," which was one of the most advanced parts of the Australian line, had been a former Turkish stronghold, and the enemy had quite recently been ousted from these trenches only after a desperate and costly battle. It was regarded as a key position, and it was anticipated that the Turks would make a determined effort to regain it at the first favourable opportunity.

It was on the 10th September that our companies first went into the "Lone Pine" trenches. They came out again on the 11th, as it was only intended then to initiate them into the mysteries of the position and the art of trench warfare.

"Lone Pine" was reached by underground tunnels, which had been excavated by the First Division. "A" and "B" Coys. entered by way of B8 Tunnel, and "C" and "D" Coys. through "Plateau Sap" and B5 Tunnel. Part of the section of the line held by "A" Coy. was known as the "Circus." On the right of "A" Coy. was "Piccadilly," held later by a garrison supplied by the 13th Light Horse, temporarily attached to the Battalion. Beyond this was "B" Coy.'s. sector, then "C" Coy., and at the dead end "D" Coy., where the distance between our line and that of the Turks was, at certain points, only about five yards. The nearness of the enemy's positions and the danger of attack without warning demanded the strictest vigilance on the part of our troops.

Facing us on the enemy's side was "Mule Gully," with "Battleship Hill" (often bombarded by our warships) looming up behind it. On the left were "Johnson's Jolly" and the "Chessboard," and on the right front what was known as the "Harem," a name bestowed by the First Division on account of the story that Turkish women were there. Our reserve trenches comprised a part of the old firing line in rear, together with the "Pimple" and "Brown's Dip," at the corner of "Gun Lane," usually occupied by a company from the Battalion out of the line.

It was in this famous sector of the firing line that we faced the Turks during the period of our activities on Gallipoli, which extended over 16 weeks. Our duties were shared by the 23rd Battalion (excellent soldiers and staunch comrades), with which unit we changed over every 48 hours.

Going back to "White's Valley" after our initiation, fatigue duty awaited us. The four companies moved round to the north beach to work on the construction of a light railway. Lieut. A. C. Fogarty had charge of the men while they carried on this important work.

At the first opportunity some of the boys went down to the beach for a swim, and had their initial experience with "Beachy Bill," the elusive Turkish gun whose special duty appeared to be the shelling of the beach whenever fatigue parties were at work, or when the troops were bathing in the sea. The shells sent the bathers helter-skelter in all directions, those who were in the water rushing out, and those who were out rushing in. Under shell fire one has a feeling that any place is preferable to the one he is in, and wherever he dashes for shelter the feeling pursues him. Bathing under shell fire is not a popular mode of seaside pleasure. Some of the parties adopted the novel procedure of posting one man on the land while the rest were in the water. The sentry, the instant he heard the gun fire, would shout a warning. In the brief period of several seconds before the shell burst, the bathers would all disappear like frightened fish. A little practice made the boys expert in the art of " ducking " at the critical moment.

" Beachy Bill " is credited with having inflicted over two thousand casualties on the Anzac forces.

Rain fell on the 13th, and after all the dust and heat of Egypt it was not an unwelcome change, though it did not add to our comfort in the rough shelters we had constructed without provision for wet weather.

" Abdul " strafed the beach vigorously on the 14th, when fatigue parties, particularly those with mules and carts, had a trying experience, while a heavy bombardment by our warships on the left indicated that there was " something doing " in that direction.

The first mail to reach us on Gallipoli from Australia arrived on the 16th, which, needless to say, was an auspicious day.

The Battalion was now doing regular garrison work in "Lone Pine," alternatively with the 23rd Battalion, and the nature of the duties and the monotonous regularity of " going in " and " coming out " of the line is indicated by the following brief record of operations:—

September 10th and 11th.—Holding " Lone Pine." Unit divided into four sections for garrison duty. Considerable fire from the enemy. Several casualties sustained.

12th.—Returned to " White's Valley."

14th and 15th.—" Lone Pine." Sniping and bombing activities. Six men wounded.

16th.—Back to "White's Valley." Shelled by enemy. Three men killed, five wounded.

18th and 19th—"Lone Pine." Sniping, bombing, and preparations to meet possible attack. Lieut. Tippet killed, six men wounded.

20th.—"White's Valley."

22nd and 23rd.—In "Lone Pine." Heavy machine-gun fire damaged our parapets. Three killed, seven wounded.

24th.—"White's Valley."

26th and 27th.—"Lone Pine." Mining and counter-mining. Enemy blew up tunnel in No. 2 section. New Turkish troops reported opposite our positions. Driving tunnels forward and forming galleries for offensive and defensive operations.

28th.—"White's Valley."

30th.—"Lone Pine."

This procedure was maintained throughout our Gallipoli campaign.

On the 23rd September we had what was termed our first "dust up" with the Turks. An artillery observer located a strong force of the enemy massed at "Johnson's Jolly," apparently ready to attack "Lone Pine." The artillery raked them with shrapnel, and must have inflicted heavy casualties and complete disorganisation. Our men, having just relieved the 23rd Battalion under shrapnel fire, got into the line in time to meet a heavier bombardment of the "Pine." The order was given to man the parapets to resist the expected attack. They sprang to arms and stood awaiting the assault, ready to meet for the first time in deadly hand-to-hand conflict a brave foe. Many of these troops were mere lads, yet none hung back. The light of battle was in their eyes, and their lips were set with that "do-or-die" expression. The parapets bristled with bayonets, flashing in the autumn sun. That display of steel on the top of the mauling which the Turks received from our artillery must have convinced them that it was better to leave "Lone Pine" to our safe keeping, for they did not launch their threatened assault.

Our casualties were small considering the lively nature of

WHITE'S VALLEY, GALLIPOLI.— Rest area for the 24th Battalion.

the stunt. Among the killed was Sergt. Finning, of "A" Coy.

Machine guns, which were used so effectively throughout the war, played an important part in the defence of the line. Five machine guns were posted in our sector, and several in rear of the forward positions. An 18-pounder field gun was a'so mounted close up in "Gun Lane" to support the line in case of attack. The machine-gun sections of the two Battalions were always in the trenches, day and night, doing two hours on post and having four hours off. These men became accustomed to the noise of rifle fire, bombs, and guns. Every night, after "carry on" had been given, the troops not on post would soon fall asleep, though explosives were bursting overhead. Broken rest and hard work were effective antidotes for battlefield insomnia.

At dawn and at dusk (the most likely hours of attack by the enemy) every man in the trenches "stood to," sometimes for half an hour, an hour, or longer. "Carry on" meant the resumption of normal duties, when men off post might put away their rifles, but on account of the nearness of the enemy no man while in the trenches was permitted to remove his equipment or boots. Everybody had to be ready to jump up, even from sleep, fully prepared for action.

On 1st October the second batch of reinforcements for the Battalion arrived, and these men were detailed at once for fatigue work on the beach as a process of initiation.

Sickness became more prevalent as the weather became colder, and numbers of men were evacuated to hospital.

The men had arrived on Gallipoli hopeful of engaging in decisive battles. They were well trained physically, and were ready for the biggest job that could be given them, consequently the monotony of the trench garrison work, with little alteration in the position from day to day, was a disappointment.

On the 4th October we had our first actual brush with the enemy. The Turks, after a brisk bombardment, made an attack on "C" bomb pit. A strong party hopped out of their trenches and rushed at the line, but only a few got close to the parapet, and the boys declared that not a single

Turk got away. The fight created quite a stir in the "Pine," and made the lads keener on their job. They found it exciting work shooting Turks at close range. The action lasted only about ten minutes, but it convinced the enemy that the men holding "Lone Pine" were excellent shots, and were not to be caught napping.

The 6th was another notable day, in a different way. A distribution of gifts—chocolates, cigarettes, etc., cheered all hands considerably.

A report on the strength of the Battalion on 13th October showed that to that date the numbers who had "gone sick" were 11 officers and 531 other ranks. Reinforcements (including the third draft) received up to the same date numbered 5 officers and 475 other ranks.

Towards the middle of October the Turks began to increase their shell fire on "Lone Pine," and they displayed greater activity in mining operations.

Fearing an attack they put up wire entanglements in front of their second and third line trenches. The nearness of the opposing lines provoked many daring and impudent feats on both sides. One night, when our men had been ordered to cut down the expenditure of ammunition, and the line consequently became much quieter, the Turks threw out grappling irons and dragged away the wire entanglements we had placed on "knife rests" in front of our line. They "anchored" the wire in front of their own line, and had it held so firmly that our men were not able to recover it.

A thunderstorm one night caused some amusement, and on that account somewhat relieved the discomfort it occasioned. Rain came down in sheets, and the wind blew with hurricane force. In "No-man's-land" tins rattled with dramatic effect. The Turks appeared to go mad, believing we were "over the top" and at them, for, while the storm raged, they blazed away in a frantic effort to defend themselves. The boys rather enjoyed the excitement in spite of the fact that they had to "stand to" in the drenching rain, with the trenches converted into creeks. We suffered no casualties, though "Abdul" expended much ammunition. Clothes, which we were unable to change, took a long time to dry.

Many of the dugouts were flooded, and some of the lads had to dive to recover their belongings.

We imparted a shock to the enemy on the 21st of October by exploding a mine containing 250 lbs. of ammonal in a tunnel driven out from L.P.8 sap. Our own parapet suffered slightly by the explosion.

Tunnelling was a special feature of the operations on Gallipoli. The entrenchments were so stoutly defended on both sides that infantry assaults were rendered exceedingly costly. So the opposing forces resorted to the laborious task of undermining one another and lifting sections of the ground up in clouds of smoke. What tales could be told of blistered hands and aching backs by men who honeycombed the hard ground to improve our positions and destroy those of the enemy! As a consequence of all this burrowing, the troops in the front line did not know the moment they might experience a sudden rise, and be blown off the face of the earth. But even the work of the tunnellers was not without its humorous side. To suddenly and unexpectedly break through into an enemy tunnel was not exactly humorous, but to find after you blocked up the gap that the Turk was stealing your sandbags was getting rather close to the funny side of things.

The possibilities attending this work were demonstrated when a party of our men were arrested in their labours by the sounds of picks in action from the direction towards which they were driving. They remained silent, as the other group appeared to be working towards them. Presently the sounds became plainer, and when only a few inches of earth remained, one of the men drove his bayonet through the thin partition. It was gripped on the other side! With feverish excitement the opposing tunnellers prepared for battle, and tore down the wall to get at each other with weapons more deadly than picks. When the partition collapsed two parties of our own men faced each other! They had started from different points, but had converged as they progressed. They laughed and swore at each other, and sat down to rest a while after their exertion.

An interesting exploit of a small party of " B " Coy. men

affords another example of the underground operations at
"Lone Pine." While tunnelling at L.P. 14 (reputed to be
the worst hole on the Peninsula), the sappers broke into
a Turkish tunnel. It was resolved to explore this tunnel
immediately. Captain Frawley secured four men for the
job. These were Corporal Hughes, Lance-Corporal Nicholls
(afterwards lieutenant), Private Cliff Ellis (afterwards
lieutenant), and Private Kelly, known to all 24th Anzacs as
the "kookaburra" of the Gallipoli hills on account of his
clever mimicry of the kookaburra's vocal powers. The "B"
Coy. men were having their evening meal when the orders
for the adventure were received. In his inimitable way
Captain Frawley called out his men in these words: "I
want four men to go down a bit of a tunnel. Come on, leave
your tea; you'll only be away a few minutes." Kelly was
detailed by an officer who thrust a revolver and ammunition
into his hands, and said, "Come with me," and thereupon
led him off. The men cast lots to decide which course they
would take in the enemy tunnel. Hughes and Nicholls went
to the left, and Ellis and Kelly to the right. An Engineer
officer who was supervising the exploration remained at the
mouth of our own tunnel to receive reports of the men's
discoveries. The two who went to the left came to a dead
end. The others discovered a manhole dropping down
several feet to another tunnel. Ellis and Kelly squeezed
through this hole, and proceeded along the lower tunnel,
which led towards the enemy's lines. Soon they arrived at
a fork, the tunnel dividing into two passages. One remained
on guard at this point while the other went back to report
the situation. The nerve required by a sentry at such a post
can be imagined. These underground tunnels were, of
course, in inky darkness. To remain alone a considerable
distance from all means of help in a weird underground pas
sage, guarding what appeared to be two approaches from the
enemy's positions, was a duty which only a brave man
would have undertaken. Progress through these tunnels,
particularly through the small manhole, was slow and difficult, and it would be half an hour before the man who went
back to report the situation could return or bring assistance.

The two men who had first gone to the left were guided to the point where the solitary sentry stood holding the tunnel at the parting of the ways. Lots were again cast, and the party advanced, two going right and two left. A dead end was this time encountered on the right, while in the passage on the left another fork was discovered. Again the four assembled at the parting of the ways. Ellis and Kelly, who now went left, came to a dead-end, but Hughes and Nicholls, in the right passage, found themselves in an open enemy trench a few yards from the Turkish front line. Again one went on guard, and one went back to report. When the rest of the party arrived, three took possession of the short trench, while one made his way back to the Engineer officer to notify him of the discovery. The position was then garrisoned permanently, and men who did duty there bombed the enemy with so much success that the locality became known as " Bloody Corner." The men who carried out this daring and successful adventure were engaged on the exploit somewhat longer than " a few minutes." They set out at about 5 p.m., and did not conclude their exploration until midnight.

A movement of the Turks along their trenches with fixed bayonets on the 27th caused us to stand to arms ready to meet an attack, but nothing transpired. " Abdul " had evidently imitated a ruse adopted by us some weeks earlier, when our guns bombarded his position along the whole front, and we made a demonstration by marching through the trenches in a circuitous route, with bayonets fixed and held up to his view, so that he might be led to believe an innumerable host was swarming in to attack him.

The trench mortars (sometimes described as the " drainpipe artillery ") at first used by our men to bomb the Turkish trenches had little effect on the well-protected lines of the enemy, but later, when we were supplied with a powerful Japanese mortar, we were able to force "Abdul " to invoke the aid of Allah as the big bombs fired from these guns crashed with deadly effect on his trenches. The only disadvantage attending these mortars was the very limited supply of ammunition, a circumstance for which the Turk had reason to be devoutly thankful. The enemy reciprocated our more effective trench mortar activities by using larger bombs than before. His "broomstick" bomb took a toll of our men, and gave us many unpleasant shocks. The bomb, to which was attached a stick five or six feet in length, and as thick as a man's arm, was fired (from a trench mortar) high into the air, and fell with a terrific explosion. When one of these bombs was sighted descending men about the spot where it was likely to fall found business elsewhere without delay.

Occasionally a siege battery of heavy guns attempted to break the strong cover over the Turkish trenches, but the close proximity of the opposing lines rendered artillery fire almost equally dangerous for the men holding our own line, and after one or two painful experiences we were better pleased when the siege battery devoted its attentions to more distant targets.

"Lone Pine," particularly "D" Coy.'s section, was more suitable for the use of hand grenades, and our troops and the Turks bestowed these explosives on one another with the utmost liberality. Private Gosset (later lieutenant R.N.R.) was "D" Coy.'s "bomb king," and he handled fuse bombs with such fine precision that his mates often got out of his way, fearing the bombs would explode before they left his hand.

At a point known as "Bloody Angle" in "D" Coy.'s section (where Corporal Dunstan and Captain Tubbs, of the 7th Battalion, had won their V.C.'s) our front line trench was protected by wire-netting against hand grenades thrown by the enemy a few yards away. Unless the fuses were well timed the bombs rolled off to a safe distance, or gave the men a chance to get out of their way before they exploded.

On 28th October our C.O. recommended the linking up of our positions with the 22nd Battalion on the left, and also with the Third Brigade, on our right, and plans were made by the Divisional Engineer officer for this work.

Our losses up to the end of October were:—Killed in action, 14; died of wounds, 7; wounded (in hospital), 66;

evacuated sick, 149. Of the sick and wounded 94 had returned to duty.

All through November the unpleasant work went on—mining, bombing, sniping, and the tiring, unceasing vigil. During a bombardment of our positions in the first week of this month, a number of casualties occurred. The shells used by the enemy on this occasion were mostly "75's."

Gales now began to sweep over the Peninsula, and the weather turned exceedingly cold. Work at the beach was hazardous and difficult. The small piers were damaged by the rough sea, and at times the landing of stores was delayed.

The end of November was marked by dark days for our garrison in "Lone Pine." Troubles were literally showered upon us by the elements, in addition to the attentions of the Turks. On the 27th a cold snap set in, and that night many an Australian saw snow for the first time in his life. Daylight on the 28th found the whole field under a thick mantle of white. Everything left exposed was buried, and material required for the day's activities had to be fossicked out from under the snow. The troops, impoverished by lack of nourishment and the rough existence, and many of them also lacking clothing suitable for such a pronounced atmospheric change, suffered intensely. The weaker men and men in poor health collapsed, and many were depressed by the cheerless conditions. Even men on heavy fatigue duty could barely keep themselves warm. The standpipes at the water points froze, and the condenser on the beach had been smashed by a blizzard, leaving the troops without water, and driving them to the necessity of melting the snow, which continued to fall all day on the 28th. Large flocks of migrating birds passed overhead on their way to a warmer climate, and men wished that they too could have taken wings to seek a more congenial land. The troops set themselves to make whatever provisions were possible against the severity of the weather, but in the absence of timber and iron the work of improving the crude shelters was seriously handicapped.

The intense cold caused acute physical pain, and we thought that our cup of unhappiness was filled to overflowing, but friend "Abdul" had something more severe in store for us in the form of a terrific bombardment with heavy howitzers. This for the time banished all thoughts of chilled bodies.

AN INTENSE BOMBARDMENT.

Up till this time there had been evidence that the Turk was in low spirits over his inability to dislodge the comparatively small Allied force which had invaded his country, and which was holding on so tenaciously. One day the Turks had thrown to our men in the "Lone Pine" trenches a note with this very significant message, "We can't advance; you can't advance. What are you going to do?" But Bulgaria's recent entry into the war on the side of Germany had enabled the latter to dispatch to the Turks a number of heavy howitzer guns, which were about to be put into use against our entrenchments.

On the evening of 28th November the largest shells so far sent over by the enemy landed into "Brown's Dip." Eight or ten rounds were all that were fired on this occasion, and these were evidently "sighters" for his artillery to range on our lines. At dawn those in the front line discovered that the Turkish trenches were marked by red flags, placed in position, no doubt, to distinguish our line from theirs, and to direct their gun fire.

On the morning of the 29th the 24th Battalion was ordered to relieve the 23rd Battalion at 9 o'clock. While the relief was in progress the enemy commenced to shell the position, and the bombardment grew in intensity until 11 a.m., during which time every conceivable form of explosive the Turk possessed was hurled at us, and it was not before the early afternoon that the strafing ceased. Armour-piercing naval shells, which plunged deep into the ground, and lifted huge masses of earth into the air, were plentiful in the destructive deluge. The enemy's artillery included 12-in. guns. Communication trenches and tunnels were blown in, men and materials buried, and the whole sector plunged into chaos. " D " Coy., holding No. 1 section, and " B " Coy., holding No. 3 section, suffered most severely, " B " Coy.'s front line being in places entirely obliterated. Naturally, our casualties on this day were the heaviest so far experienced. Two officers (Lieuts. Chris. Fogarty and W. S. Finlay), 11 N.C.O.'s, and 30 men were killed, while there was a long list of wounded. The wounded included Major C. E. Manning, Lieut. Gordon Beith, 2nd Lieuts. J. H. Fletcher, P. G. D. Fethers, and C. M. Williams. All ranks were suffering badly from shock. Three N.C.O.'s and 8 men were reported missing.

The severe weather was responsible for the loss of many lives, as exposure proved fatal to numbers of the wounded.

While the bombardment proceeded in its fury there were many instances of gallantry and faithfulness on the part of those who escaped injury and were able to carry on. The men toiled with feverish eagerness to rescue their comrades, and but for the bravery of all ranks our losses must have been much heavier.

This' bombardment demonstrated that deep trenches and tunnels were death traps under the fire of howitzer guns, whose shells, fired at a high angle, dropped with deadly precision into the earthworks, and buried more men than they killed or wounded. It also proved that the Allies at that time could have successfully operated against the Turks only by employing similar guns. The fire of the war ships, on which we largely depended, was not sufficiently effective against entrenchments, the trajectory being so flat that many of the enemy positions lay in " dead " ground.

The strength of the 24th and 23rd Battalions was so reduced after that day that men of the 21st Battalion and a whole battalion of the Seventh Brigade were called in to clear up the lines and strengthen the position.

It has been estimated on good authority that at least 2000 Turks were massed against our position on that occasion, and the reason they did not attack after such a bombardment remains a mystery.

The question has often been raised by the troops—" Would the Turks have captured the ' Pine ' had they attacked after that bombardment?" Whatever the issue might have been, one cannot but admire the spirit of one of the men, who writes thus of the critical situation :—

" I say without a doubt that the Turks would have failed, " for never have I seen more determined men than the rem- " nant of the Battalion which went into the trenches that " morning. Many of the men were ill. For the past week " they had lived on scant rations—half a small pannikin of " tea for breakfast, nothing to drink for dinner, and again at " tea time half a small pannikin of tea, and usually only " bully beef and biscuits to eat. Yet at the word of command "they sprang to the parapets without a sign of wavering. " They knew that if the attack came they would be facing " overwhelming odds. But for the sake of the comrades " who had fallen around them, and the name of Anzac, they " were ready to fight to the last man. On all sides one " could hear such defiant expressions as ' Let them come!' " or ' If Abdul comes he will get what he is looking for!' " For all they knew, ' Lone Pine ' was isolated. They be- " lieved the communication trenches and tunnels had all been " blown in. But B8 was open, and, what was more, the " splendid 7th Battalion (rested for two months at Lemnos) " was ready to dash in to the aid of the line."

On the day following the bombardment General Holmes and staff inspected our positions, where the men were working strenuously repairing the trenches. General Birdwood thoughtfully sent a message of encouragement to the troops.

With the exception of half an hour's shelling by the enemy on 4th December, the week following the bombardment was comparatively quiet. Many men were suffering from frost bite, but otherwise the health of the troops was improving.

On the 12th December a patrol was sent to "Owen's Gully," but there was no sign of the enemy. Our 17th Siege Battery returned the fire of the enemy's big guns, and the " heavies " on both sides were active during the following days.

In consequence of reports that the Turks were being supplied with more batteries of heavy guns, the troops received orders to " dig in." Everybody looked forward to a lively time, and although " digging in " was not a particularly pleasant task, the prospect of being " dug out " by Abdul's shells was decidedly less agreeable.

Warnings were received from the Turk, whose spirits were now considerably brightened, that unless we took our departure he would " blow us into the sea." Had we been strongly supported by suitable artillery, with plenty of ammunition, instead of a painfully limited supply, we might have defied the boastful Turk. But the odds were decidedly in his favour, and had we remained he would at least have convinced us that it was an extremely unhealthy country.

RATIONS.

The feeding of the men on Gallipoli always constituted a difficult problem, and the quartermaster, Lieut. John Anderson (afterwards captain), and his able assistant, R.Q.M.S. Selleck (afterwards captain, M.C.), had their resourcefulness tested severely. There were periods when only 1½ pints of water per man per day was the allowance, and at no time during the occupation of Gallipoli by the Second Division was water obtained except as a strictly checked ration. The water was brought from the islands in huge tank barges, and pumped into tanks on the beach. It was then carried in cans by mules (when they were available) to other tanks in the gullies, and finally conveyed by fatigue parties into the trenches. Strong guards were always maintained on the water tanks.

The company S.M.'s, who had to detail men for water fatigue every night, were silently cursed by the troops at first, but when the boys found that water fatigue meant a " baksheesh " pint of the precious liquid they felt there was some compensation for their hard labours.

In view of the scarcity of fresh water a theory of domestic economy was evolved which led to experiments by the cooks, who were instructed to use 50 per cent. of salt water in the making of bully beef stew and in the cooking of vegetables. The theory did not survive the first day's experiments, however.

On one occasion the padre, Chaplain-Captain Goidanich, became possessed of the " dinkum oil " that foodstuffs could be purchased on the Island of Imbros, about 12 miles distant. He set off on a quest for supplies, and caused much merriment on his return two days later with a rooster under his arm and another on a string. The roosters were tied up outside the colonel's dugout, and it is safe to say that no roosters ever found themselves in a stranger environment than those two had on Gallipoli. The presence of the two crowing cocks was a novelty which appealed strongly to the humour of the troops, and as the morning calls of the birds were answered by " Kicker " Kelly from the top of the hill with excellent powers of mimicry, one might have imagined, as the roosters doubtless did, that some game cockerel had advanced dangerously close to the battle line.

It is held by some of the troops that the " poultry farm " belonged to the C.O., while a certain member of the Battalion, popularly known as " Tonto," avers that the Headquarters staff cut the combs of the roosters with the object of causing them to produce eggs. It is certain, however, that the Headquarters officers, with those two small birds and plenty of imagination, had a poultry dinner, and the bones were picked till they were as dry as the stones of the desert.

During a storm the regimental aid-post was blown down. " It is an ill-wind that blows nobody good," even in war. The collapse of the medical quarters revealed stocks of Red Cross goods, including tinned chicken, maizena, cocoa, and other luxuries, and some of the boys got away with sufficient to provide themselves with a dainty meal.

When the troops were in the front line trenches rations were transported by mules from the 16th A.S.C. dump to " Brown's Dip " along narrow and precipitous pathways. The first half-mile of this journey was through a communication trench along the foreshore and at right angles to the Turkish positions at Gaba Tepe, and the ration parties, often enfiladed by " Beachy Bill," had a strenuous task. Sixteen mules were required daily to transport the Battalion's rations.

At " Brown's Dip " the rations were distributed to the

company quartermaster-sergeants, who had them conveyed by carrying parties to the trenches, and handed over to the platoon sergeants for final distribution to the men.

The rations usually consisted of bully beef, hard biscuits, desiccated vegetables, rice, jam, and, occasionally, bread and fresh meat. Up to the end of November the bread ration averaged ¾ lb. per man twice a week. Fresh vegetables in very small quantities were sometimes received.

Whenever the rough fare was relieved by bread and fresh meat the men considered the occasion worthy to be recorded in their diaries, even if they felt constrained to add their suspicions that what was issued as mutton was in reality the flesh of some tough old donkey they had ridden round Cairo.

The men of the Hindoo Mule Corps received a daily ration of fresh vegetables, curry powder, and Indian corn, and many an Aussie bartered his personal possessions for a meal at the cookhouse of the Hindoos.

Resourceful cooks made porridge by grinding army biscuits into meal, and when flour (half a pound per man) was issued on rare occasions the troops experimented with it by making pancakes, with the result that many of them were henceforth much more sympathetic towards the cooks. It was a great stretch of imagination to call these creations pancakes, but they were a treat for the men who lived on the hard fare in that campaign, and meant to them a veritable birthday. If fortune happened to add to the auspicious occasion the great joy of a letter from home, the day was regarded as one of riotous pleasure.

IMPRESSIONS.

The outstanding memories of this campaign savour rather more of the unlovely than the picturesque. To men who appreciated the beautiful in nature, however, the glory of the sun setting behind the Island of Imbros, when viewed from a hilltop across the miles of intervening blue sea, provided a magnificent picture, and formed a striking contrast to the immediate surroundings.

On the other hand, to an observer on the beach, the hills and valleys of Gallipoli presented a different spectacle. The hungry-looking slopes, devoid of vegetation save for the straggling, stunted scrub, and intersected with well-worn tracks, winding up from the gullies, had been excavated into a succession of terraces on the side which offered shelter from enemy fire. One above the other from the bottom of the valleys almost to the top of the ridges, these terraces were crowded with shelters cut into the earth and fortified with sandbags, and at night they glimmered with the lights of candles or slush lamps, by which the troops contrived to read a precious bit of literature or indulge in a game of cards in an occasional hour of leisure.

Slush lamps were made by filling with fat or grease empty jam tins or the empty cases of "cricket ball" bombs, in which were inserted wicks improvised from cloth or pieces of sandbag. A party of Egyptian labourers, who one night found a *live* " cricket ball " bomb, mistook it for one of these patent lamps. While seated round, they lit the fuse!!

Like every battlefield, Gallipoli afforded many instances of miraculous escapes from death. One example may appear to some to have special significance. The padre, after service in " White's Gully " one Sunday morning, administered Holy Communion to a number of the men. The party had only moved a few paces off the spot where the service was held when a huge shell from the fort at the Narrows landed where the emblems of the sacrament and the men had been grouped. Had this shell caught the party it would have been difficult to find a trace of them. It seemed fitting, especially to those with religious sentiments, that those men should have thus been providentially preserved.

The antiquated bombs used on Gallipoli were exploded by means of fuses, one variety, known as the " jam tin," being crudely made by parties on the beach by filling empty jam or milk tins with explosive and inserting a fuse. Such were the primitive weapons of offence and defence by which the troops were handicapped. To light these fuse bombs " slow matches " (pieces of cloth or bag rolled into the form of a wick and soaked in oil) were kept hanging in the trenches. The use of hand-grenades, it can thus be seen, was carried on in a most crude fashion compared with later methods. The Mills bomb did not make its appearance until late in the campaign, and was then only issued as an expensive emergency weapon to the troops who formed the rearguard at the evacuation. In those days the Mills bombs, it was stated, cost 17/6 each. This grenade was regarded as such a precious possession that a dozen of them were placed in a specially constructed dugout, and the R.S.M. was required to report daily on their safe keeping.

The troops had other enemies than the Turks. Vermin never infested the habitations of soldiers in greater numbers than they did on the Peninsula, while for size and biting capacity these "Anzacs" had no rivals in any country. On a sunny day it was a common thing to see men in various stages of undress squatting about in scores, hunting " chats " in the folds of their garments and perpetrating the wholesale slaughter of these tantalising enemies with the keenest satisfaction, and with hopes of a brief respite from torture when the raid had yielded a numerous catch.

The washing of clothes was a problem. No fresh water was available for this purpose, and the use of salt water rendered the process difficult and the results far from satisfactory. Therefore no garments ever came into contact with water before their time for ablution was well overdue. A shave was a luxury indulged in only when a man felt inclined to sacrifice a little of his cold tea or precious water. Fuel for the cook-houses had to be brought by boat from overseas, for there was no timber inside the British lines, the hills being productive of nothing more than stunted scrub, which the men gathered for their own small fires. The occasion of the first rum issue was regarded as a red letter day, and thereafter rum jars became objects of special interest to all fatigue parties who got near ration dumps or quartermasters' stores. The safety of the large jars marked "S.R.D." (which the men subsequently interpreted as meaning " Seldom reaches destination " or "Soldiers' rum diluted") occasioned the troops painful anxiety when "Beachy Bill" or "Annie from Asia" was shelling the Anzac positions. Still, it was never conclusively proved that these guns had been brought into action specially to destroy the supplies of rum.

The 11th October was our first pay day on the Peninsula, and we saw the colour of money only on one other occasion during our sojourn there. A private found himself in possession of the fabulous sum of about 20/-, which could be spent by giving orders for goods obtainable at Mudros and trusting to luck for the fulfilment of the orders. Writing paper was as scarce as all other good things.

SANITATION.

With such large numbers of men confined in a small area and occupying the same locality month after month, it can be understood that the question of sanitation was a serious and vital one. That sickness was not more prevalent was mainly due to the individual cleanliness of the troops, who had been trained to be particular in all things pertaining to the welfare of one another in a situation which was fraught with difficulties in its every aspect. The inoculation of the men also undoubtedly proved a very effective check on epidemics.

Dysentery was common, but, owing to the need for men on the field, only the worst cases could be evacuated. Others were treated at the beach hospital, and some were obliged to carry on, although they were unfit for their work. Jaundice was another complaint from which the men suffered. Towards the close of the campaign a "trench cough" was a common possession. The exertion of climbing the hills set many of the troops "barking" as if they were in a chronic stage of consumption. The Turks suffered from the same irritation, and on a quiet night in the front line the enemy soldiers could be also heard coughing violently.

Soldiers have never regarded fatigue duty at the front as a light or desirable occupation, but the carrying of supplies to the trenches on Gallipoli was as strenuous an undertaking as men ever encountered. Hill climbing involves a strain without backs and shoulders heavily burdened, and with the loads the troops staggered under there it was an agonising task. Men preferred duty in the trenches any time, and, consequently, some of them considered that the period of supposed "rest" when out of the firing line was often the most strenuous part of the campaign, and they ironically spoke of going back to the trenches for a "spell."

The whole of the Battalion was scarcely ever privileged to occupy the sheltered position of Brown's Dip or White's Gully at the same time, for as soon as the companies left the firing line, parties would set out for different localities where other duties awaited them.

Aeroplanes were not numerous on Gallipoli. The Allied aerodrome was at Imbros, where perhaps half a dozen seaplanes were kept and sent out to observe the enemy's activities. The Turks had about an equal number of German "Taube" machines. One of the British anti-aircraft gunners, who had his gun in position at the corner of Gun Lane, gave exhibitions of expert shooting when the enemy machines were on the wing.

In a record of our experiences on Gallipoli a word should be said of the honourable manner in which the Turks waged war. Our hospital ships and our Red Cross stations were never wilfully fired upon, though our men often remarked that the contiguity of our dumps to Field Ambulance stations, due to the limited area available, and the anchoring of other vessels in line with hospital ships at times might have provided reason for a breach of the rules of warfare had the enemy been less scrupulous. The Turk was a fair fighter, even though he was not a Christian. He even took the trouble to warn our command of the advisability of removing one of the supply dumps from its dangerous proximity to a Field Ambulance, as it was likely to involve the Ambulance in shell-fire.

If an artist had to paint the most typical picture of a soldier "on post" in Lone Pine he would surely depict him looking at the enemy's lines through a periscope. But for this instrument how many of our men would have done their duty as observers and lived? Of all the souvenirs of the war, probably none is more prized than the little mirrors out of the periscopes used on Gallipoli. Snipers' bullets smashed many of the periscopes, but glass was cheaper than soldiers' heads, and men were seldom anxious to dispense with the substitute.

There is one word inseparably associated with Gallipoli. That word is "rice." The men ate rice (for want of something better) till they talked rice in their sleep, and imagined they could taste it in their tobacco. And they wondered whether, with all the rice that was carted to Gallipoli, China's millions were going short of food. The lads vowed they would never be able to look a Chinaman in the face again. Rice was a nightmare!

One of the worst features of Gallipoli was its utter loneliness. Held up by overwhelming numbers of Turks on the hills in front, and cut off from the world by the sea at their feet, the men realised how isolated they were. This isolation was made the more apparent by the absence of news from the outside world or from the other theatres of war. And sometimes the men wondered whether they had been forgotten—whether the armies on other fronts had finished their jobs and gone home.

The cemeteries, growing larger as the days passed, made men think hard in their quiet moments. Every pal who went under left a man more lonely and with less interest in life. The thoughts of the boys often strayed back to home. Even on fatigue duty a man might be seen gazing, transfixed, at a hospital ship pulling out from the pier, his foot and arms resting on his shovel, and his mind far away. He would stand in that attitude till he was, in very reality, miles away from everything around him. Then a pal would tap him on the shoulder and remind him of the job in hand, and he would come back to earth—on Gallipoli.

THE EVACUATION.

The evacuation of Gallipoli had been decided upon after Lord Kitchener's visit of inspection, when it was apparent that all hopes of advancing had vanished, a deadlock having been reached. This decision necessitated, on the part of the Higher Command, various strategical discussions and experiments in preparation for the withdrawal, for it was realised that to remove an army from such a situation was a task hardly less difficult than the capture of the Peninsula itself. The Allied forces were holding a long rugged strip of country fringing the coast and only about a mile in depth, with a strong enemy army looking down upon them from commanding positions, and in some places the opposing lines were only a few yards apart. The plan decided upon was to withdraw gradually and quietly while making a pretence of preparing for more aggressive operations.

The principal preparatory feature of this strategy was a succession of silent "stunts" which began in November. For three days all fire was to cease, and all signs of our presence in the trenches to be veiled from the enemy. This silence was repeated at intervals, and for varying periods in December. The object was to mystify the Turk. At the same time it puzzled our own troops, who until the last few days were kept entirely in the dark regarding the proposed evacuation. So well was the secret preserved that when an instruction was given some days before that officers' kits were to be packed and conveyed to a certain dump it merely gave rise to the rumour that the Second Division was about to be withdrawn for a spell in the same way as the First Division had been rested and brought back to the front.

"Abdul" was unmistakably perturbed by the silence, and resorted to many tantalising tricks to draw our fire. Occasionally, during these periods, inquisitive enemy patrols crawled close up to our line, and some even peered through the loopholes. Needless to say, that was the last act they performed in this world. Prying Turks had to be shot if they came too near, and it was these shots alone which broke the silence on our side, though the enemy kept up intermittent sniping.

While our trenches remained perplexingly quiet, vessels in the Aegean Sea were lifting and lowering their anchors at night and creating as much noise as possible with the object of leading the Turks to believe we were landing numerous reinforcements. Actually, guns, stores and ammunition were being stealthily removed. During the day, when hostile planes were overhead, bodies of men were marched about and every activity displayed, and, to further deceive the Turkish airmen, when a gun or other noticeable object was removed, it was replaced by a dummy. To add weight to the idea that a forward move was intended, patches of coloured cloth, which were fixed to the backs of the tunics in an attack to enable the men to distinguish their comrades at night, were issued to several battalions, causing much speculation as to when and where the attack would be launched. The policy of the staff was to encourage such rumours, so that any spies within our lines would be misled as to the real intention.

It was hoped that the enemy would become used to our eccentric behaviour, and that eventually when the evacuation was in progress his suspicions would not be aroused. The wisdom of this strategy was demonstrated by the complete success with which the whole of the Anzac line was evacuated on the 19th and 20th December.

It was necessary to burn some of the less valuable stores without raising any doubts in the minds of the enemy. An opportunity was therefore awaited until "Beachy Bill" shelled the dumps. The Turkish gunners, no doubt, were congratulated by their commander on their good work in destroying our supplies. At all events, the plans worked admirably.

Orders for the withdrawal were promulgated on 17th December. It was significant that the Turks began to range on our communications with the heaviest guns yet employed against us. The shells were 12 inch, and were fired from the Goeben, lying in the Straits. To the troops the Peninsula had become the beginning and end of all things, and many a man had given up hope of ever getting away from those uninviting shores. Imagine the excitement and speculation which ensued concerning the possibilities of an evacuation. It subsequently transpired that the first estimate by the staff was that the movement would entail a 20 per cent. loss in casualties. This was, after careful consideration, reduced, as an absolute minimum, to nothing less than 10 per cent. of the whole garrison. In the event of being hard pressed, the rearguard had orders to leave any wounded to a party of volunteers from the A.M.C. The wounded and the A.M.C. men would thus be left to the mercy of the enemy. Two hospital tents were allowed to remain for their accommodation.

On the 18th December the whole of the Lone Pine front was taken over by the 24th Battalion, under the command of Lieut.-Colonel Watson. The unit was divided into groups to be drawn equally from each company sector. A timetable, as under, was arranged for the withdrawal of the various parties, which were to rendezvous in "Gun Lane" and be checked, prior to moving down to the beach.

	Departure.	Arrive at Pier.
First party (Capt. Godfrey, Lieuts. Harriott and Ellwood, and 137 other ranks)	6.30 p.m.	8 p.m.
Second party (Lieuts. Fletcher, Anderson, and Ahern, and 118 other ranks)	2.30 a.m.	4 a.m.
Night of 19-20th December (last night on Gallipoli)—		
B1 party (Capt. Frawley, Lieuts. Kerr and Marchant, and 200 other ranks)	9.30 p.m.	11 p.m.
B2 party (Capt. Parkes, Lieuts. Akeroyd, Hyndes, Jones, Clark, and Drummond, and 186 other ranks)	11 p.m.	1 a.m.
C1 party (Major Fethers, Capt. Cole (M.O.), Lieuts. Carr and Needham, and 26 other ranks)	2 a.m.	2.30 a.m.
C2 party (Lieuts. Tatnall and Bennett, and 34 other ranks)	2.15 a.m.	2.45 a.m.
C3 party (Lieuts. Brinsmead, McIlroy, and Savige, and 34 other ranks)	3 a.m.	3.20 a.m.

Parties of the 23rd Battalion were to remain for a time as supports in "Brown's Dip."

The N.C.O.'s with the party were: Sgts. F. McCooey and N. V. Dyte, Cpls. G. D. Pollington, M. Butcher, R. Kirk, J. Harrington, A. Mundell, L.-Cpls. A. C. Dixon, S. J. Patman, L. Almond. Sgt. A. R. Keith was in charge of the signallers. (The names of the men, unfortunately, are not available).

The following order was issued to the rearguard parties:— "All movements will be made expeditiously and in silence. The utmost care will be taken to maintain the appearance of a normal night. No lights or smoking will be permitted. Talking will not be allowed, and orders will be given in an undertone. There must be no use of the word 'retire'."

Each battalion in the line worked to a similar timetable, so that simultaneously groups of men from all sectors would be converging towards the points of embarkation. It will be seen from the table that more than a third of the garrison at Anzac, already sadly depleted by sickness, wounds, and death, was removed on the night of the 18-19th December. It was from then on that the situation grew precarious, for if "Abdul" once suspected our intentions it would go hard with the remainder if he attacked in force. Much concern was caused during the day of the 19th December by the enemy ranging with very heavy artillery on the communications in rear of our line. Knowing from past experience that this ranging was the preliminary to a more severe bombardment and attack, the garrison had an anxious time towards dusk. Fortunately nothing occurred to disturb the plans for the evacuation, though to indicate how fortune favoured us, rumour has it that a terrific barrage was laid down on Lone Pine at daylight next morning.

On account of the proximity of the enemy trenches, elaborate care was taken to prevent any noise which might arouse suspicion. Strips were torn from blankets and bound round the feet, and the bottom of the trenches was carpeted with blankets. Mess tins and any article of equipment likely to rattle were likewise covered. The stealthy and noiseless movements of the men as they glided in and out of the shadows caused by the bright moonlight lent a weird aspect to the scene. Commands were given in hoarse whispers, smoking was prohibited, and strict adherence to the scheduled time was absolutely necessary.

Several schemes were devised for maintaining an intermittent fire after the garrison had departed, one being an arrangement whereby weights attached by strings to the triggers of rifles fixed in position were released by the ignition of time fuses set for varying periods. The length of fuse regulated the time of firing, so that, with yards of fuse attached, some rifles would be fired when the troops were well at sea. It was discovered late in the day that the required fuse had been dumped, through an oversight, into the sea with a quantity of other material. Lieut. Gilchrist, therefore, dived into the water persistently until he had recovered enough fuse to carry out the scheme. However, on account of the bright moonlight, it was feared that the smoking fuse would draw the enemy's attention, and the invention was not put into use. Another excellent device was the "water drop," worked by a can of water placed above an empty can, both being attached by a string to the trigger of a fixed rifle, and the water allowed to drip through a small hole into the bottom can, which, when sufficiently weighty, pulled the trigger and fired the rifle.

On the departure of the Brigadier of the Sixth Brigade, Lieut.-Colonel Watson was appointed C.O. of all the parties of this Brigade left to cover the withdrawal of the main body, and he also commanded the "C" parties of the Fifth Brigade. With Lieut.-Colonel Watson, as Brigade staff officers, were Major Goucher and Lieut. Aram. Everything was carried out with the utmost coolness and with excellent discipline, and the success of the plan earned distinction for all who took part in the closing acts of the Gallipoli campaign.

The departure of the different parties at the appointed times and the embarkation of the troops on the barges at the beach went on smoothly and without a hitch. Gradually the little garrison was reduced to a mere handful, until everybody had gone but the last party. Lieut. Brinsmead was in charge, and, with the assistance of three signallers kept in touch with the beach by 'phone. Lieut. G. S. McIlroy and Lieut. S. G. Savige, with 31 men, were holding the whole of the Brigade sector at Lone Pine, and were spread out at wide intervals to keep up a pretence of normal activity. Lieut. Savige's party was on the right flank, and A and B sections, under Lieut. McIlroy, were posted on the rest of the sector.

Each man had several firing posts to guard and fire from, passing quickly and silently from one to another, all the time keeping up the delusion that the whole line was manned as usual.

It is difficult to describe the feelings of the men who composed that gallant rearguard. The whole of the Allied line was held by only a few hundred men. The army had gone. It was realised by the command and by the troops who undertook the perilous task that there was a strong probability of the little band being left to a sad fate. The men knew when they volunteered to stay till the last that if the necessity arose they were intended to be sacrificed to safeguard the retirement of the main body. Yet they were thrilled with the prospect of a last desperate struggle—a deadly combat against fearful odds before the end came. They were all picked men—selected from the numerous volunteers who had coveted the distinction. Their plans were carefully made, and they were prepared for all possible developments. Their orders were to hold the line at all costs until 3 a.m. If attacked they must fight to the last man—there must be no retirement before the appointed time.

In the calm moonlight rifles cracked along the line in lazy warfare to all appearances as far as the enemy knew. Yet in our trenches the isolated men hurried from post to post discharging their arms and watching with keen eyes for the slightest sign of alarm.

From the firing line deep communication trenches and tunnels led back at different points to the valleys nearer the beach. In the event of an attack at any point by the enemy the breaking of the line was to be signalled by the firing of a flare straight overhead, and the men were to fall back through the communication lines and make a stand at the other ends of the exits. Here one man at each trench could better hold up the attackers, and the little garrison was to do or die at these vantage points.

While the men watched and fired their rifles the officers and sergeants passed along inquiring, in subdued voices, if all was well. The boys were in great heart, and all as cool as if they were amusing themselves at a shooting gallery. "Everything's as right as pie," "It's a soda," or "We've got them fairly tricked," they would say cheerfully.

But presently the Turks were reported by 'phone to have broken through in force on another sector, and were said to be pushing up Johnson's Jolly. The situation now looked hopeless indeed. The fatal hour had apparently come, but it was decided to keep this bad news from the men until further developments occurred. The wisdom of this was justified, as a later message came through advising that the first report was not confirmed. It was only a rumour born of the grave possibilities of the moment.

When one is conscious of the nearness of danger, especially when that danger is shrouded in the mysteries of night, one is beset on every side by phantom forms and eerie shadows, which in the sensitiveness of the imagination have the appearance of deadly reality. So it was in that last hour on Gallipoli. In fancy there came stealthy Turks with bayonets from the weird and empty places of those bloodstained trenches and pits, crouching figures with deadly bombs in the shadowy recesses, and mysterious noises which the unusual quiet magnified a thousand times.

Yet the resolute band did not allow the imagination free rein, and none of these fears found reality, the job being performed as if they were rehearsing for a play. At 1 a.m. Lieut.-Colonel Watson gave orders to the artillery to destroy the remaining guns. The evacuation proceeded so satisfactorily that it was found possible to order the withdrawal of the rearguard at 2.40 a.m., 20 minutes earlier than the appointed time.

The last hour had been full of anxiety for those in charge, but as the time of departure approached hopes began to rise rapidly with the vision of getting safely away. Yet when the order came to quit, there was a tinge of regret that the last desperate struggle had not come. It was, in the high pitch of the men's resolution, hopes and fears, a sort of disappointment. The great task had been accomplished too easily. And yet the danger was by no means past. It was a long way to the beach, and once the line was deserted there was no time to be lost.

Ordering the men away on the tick of 2.40, the officers went along the line to see that all was clear. At one post Lieut. McIlroy saw a figure crouching on the parapet. Covering him with a revolver, he challenged him quietly, and to his astonishment found one of his own men having, as he said, "just one more pot at them." This man was "Johnnie" Worrall (afterwards lieutenant), who was killed in Belgium in 1917. Then the sounds of bombs exploding caught the officer's ear, and hurrying to another post he found another of his party, all alone, bestowing the new Mills bombs on the enemy as a parting gift. "It's a pity not to use them," he said in explanation; "they're great." That man was Jim Egan (afterwards killed in France).

In the shadow of the trench near the dressing station the men were checked and reported all present, and Lieut. Brinsmead led the way at a brisk march to the beach. Just as the last man was disappearing round the first bend the officer in the rear, who was keeping a sharp lookout for any appearance of the enemy, saw what he thought to be two Turks emerging from the mouth of B8 Tunnel. Calling quietly to Sgt. Dight, who was just passing out of view, he decided, as no other enemy forces appeared in sight, to ambush these two scouts. Crouching on the shady side of "Gun Lane," they awaited their arrival. "Don't shoot," said the officer; "use the butt of your rifle—a shot might bring reinforcements." Ready to strike, they awaited their chance.

"A bonzer night," said one of the supposed Turks. "It's a pity to leave the old joint." They were two "B" Coy. men, who, on their way through the trenches, lost their direction, and having found it, were sauntering towards the beach as though they had hours to spare, oblivious of the fact that only 20 minutes was allowed for the party to reach the jetty and that they stood a fair chance of being left on a deserted shore.

Groups of men were now making their way quickly and quietly to the beach from all parts of the line. When our party passed the deserted dug-outs in White's Valley it was noticed that candles had been left burning in these shelters to give the place its accustomed appearance in case enemy planes were on the wing.

Before the beach was reached several men were overcome by fatigue and sleepiness after their strain of the past 48 hours, and they dropped exhausted on the ground, indifferent to everything. Kicks and punches had to be employed to induce them to push on.

One of the spots on the way to the boats was the cemetery. In the bright moonlight the burial ground with its numerous crosses stood out conspicuously, and the picture sent a sudden pang of regret to the hearts of the men as they turned their backs on the place where comrades had laid down their lives in a struggle which had apparently yielded such doubtful results. It was hard to give up the ground in any case, but it would have been easier to say farewell if the sacrifices of the dead had found the reward of success as well as the glory of noble effort. That the job had to be left uncompleted was no fault of the troops, yet it pained them to give up the task. As the men boarded the barges they were checked off to ensure that nobody had been left behind.

As our party was nearing the beach a huge mine, which had been laid under the enemy's trenches at "Russell's Top," was fired by an electric connection from the beach. The Turks, taking the explosion as a sign that they were about to be attacked, opened a frantic fire, which soon extended along the whole front.

But the Anzacs had gone!

"Beachy Bill" missed his last great opportunity. When day broke the beach was all silent and still, save for the action of the restless sea. Scarcely had the rearguard drawn away when the calmness of the night gave place to boisterous elements, and angry waves drove in upon the shore. Two hours later it would have been impossible to launch the boats by which the troops moved off to the transports.

What of the 10 per cent. casualties? One man wounded by a shell splinter, and a Light Horse man shot through the arm, after boarding the boat, by the accidental discharge of a rifle! The apparently impossible had been achieved.

Some of the earlier parties were conveyed on warships to Imbros, the remainder being taken to Lemnos.

It was just an instance of the irony of war that the men who were the last to leave the battlefield—men who had volunteered for what had been regarded as a forlorn hope—appeared to have been forgotten after the job was completed. Even their packs were left for them to carry, and, after disembarking at Lemnos, they marched, five or six miles and crawled into camp as if they had done nothing worthy of a word of commendation. Bully-beef, bread and jam, and a few questions from soldier pals were all that marked their arrival. Thus ended the campaign on Gallipoli.

The complete success of the unit's share in the evacuation reflected the greatest credit on Lieut.-Colonel Watson and his staff, and also upon the officers, N.C.O.'s, and men of the Battalion, particularly the rearguard. The manner in which the operations were carried out, following upon the good work at "Lone Pine," earned for our C.O. a highly meritorious honour—Companion of the Most Honourable Order of the Bath. In connection with this distinction General Birdwood later wrote to Lieut.-Col. Watson saying that the good work of the Battalion had been thus recognised.

The total casualties suffered by the Battalion on Gallipoli, in addition to sickness, were about 100 killed and died of illness, etc., and close on 100 wounded.

While on the Peninsula the Headquarters staff was composed as follows:—

C.O., Lieut.-Col. W. W. R. Watson, V.D.; Second in Command, Major W. K. Fethers; Adjutant, Capt. C E. Manning (succeeded by Lieut. K. Dawson); M.O., Capt. G. E. Cole; Q.M., Lieut. John Anderson; O.C. Signallers, Lieut. R. H. Jones; M.G.O., Lieut. John Needham; Padre, Chaplain-Capt. Goidanich; R S.M., W.O. R. Cunningham;

R.Q.M.S., F. P. Selleck. The company commanders were:—
"A" Coy., Capt. E. V. E. Neill (evacuated 20/9/15), succeeded by Capt. F. Parkes; "B" Coy., Capt. F. W. Frawley; "C" Coy., Capt. W. E. James (evacuated), succeeded by Capt. G. W. Akeroyd; "D" Coy., Capt. G. R. Richardson, succeeded by Capt. W. G. A. Lovelle.

The troops were now in a shabby condition. Many of them were lean and worn, numbers in bad health, and all reduced in weight and strength. If they had been marched through Melbourne as they left Gallipoli they would have provided a striking contrast to the imposing body of men that left Australia eight months earlier.

The Battalion spent Christmas at Mudros. Mails from Australia had been held up here owing to the impending evacuation, and parcels from home provided an abundance of good things to celebrate the season amid these happier surroundings. Some of the Christmas billies forwarded to the men were ornamented by a wrapper which, it was evident, had been designed before the evacuation was contemplated. A picture of a kangaroo ousting a Turk from the Peninsula, illustrative of the words of a popular song, " This Bit of the World Belongs to Us," was hardly a true representation of the situation. Nevertheless, the artist meant well. So had the troops, and they laughed, regretting at the same time that circumstances had not enabled them to earn the compliment.

On 8th January, 1916, the Battalion embarked on H.M.T. Minnewaska for Alexandria, en route for the new Australian base at Tel-el-Kebir.

The considerable portion of this story devoted to Gallipoli has given the author space to record many details and impressions that were typical of the spirit of the Battalion during its long period of active service. It will not be possible to describe so fully all our experiences of war, but if the reader carries through the story the impressions of our first campaign, the imagination will supply the necessary atmosphere for the correct understanding of all the vicissitudes of active service. Gallipoli was a unique phase of the war, and the distinction of having served on the field where the original Anzacs gained so much fame is considered good reason for the prominence given in this history to the battlefield where the original members of our Battalion and the early reinforcements received their baptism of fire and where they served so faithfully and endured so many hardships.

BACK FROM SALONIKA.

It fell to the lot of a party of our men to go to Salonika as members of the second line transport of the 30th Brigade, 10th Irish Division. This Division, which had been withdrawn from Gallipoli and reorganised, was sent to the relief of the Serbians. A party of 50 men and two N.C.O.'s from the Brigade (under 2nd/Lieut. W. M. Trew of the 24th Battalion) had been detailed for duty at the Dardanelles as the packhorse transport of the Sixth Australian Brigade, but at Lemnos they were detached for service in Salonika. Acting-Sergeant R. L. Williams, of the 24th Battalion, was the senior N.C.O. of the party. The voyage to Salonika was uneventful, and the men went into camp at Lambeth. At this time the Greek army was being mobilised, and the Australians were keenly interested in the methods of the Greek Mountain Artillery, which carried its mountain guns packed on small ponies, two beasts being required for every field piece. The "Aussies" were not slow in mastering the art of packing guns and all kinds of material on ponies, donkeys or horses, and as their duties consisted mainly of work of this nature they soon proved their value to the units to which they were attached. The Irish troops, whose units included Dublins, Munsters, Leinsters, and Connaught Rangers, found the Australians most sociable comrades and exceedingly resourceful. A large number of donkeys were required. Lieut. W. M. Trew (who had been promoted at Lemnos) and an Australian veterinary officer were deputed to purchase suitable beasts from the surrounding country, and the Australian troops were to collect them and bring them into the transport lines. Needless to say, the boys overlooked none of the purchases, though they would not have been prepared to swear that a few "baksheesh" donkeys were not gathered in. If, by some mysterious means, donkeys disappeared, it was sufficient to mention the fact to an Australian, and the loss was soon made good, even if the transport lines of adjacent "Tommy" units suffered correspondingly.

The drafting place was at Bogdainci, from which depot the animals were sent out to different units of the Irish Division. Another grouping place was Gheveille, and eventually the transport section pushed forward and billeted in Dedili.

At this time some anxiety was occasioned by the advance of the Bulgars, who were reported to have broken through. Consequently preparations were made to fall back at an hour's notice.

By the end of November, however, when thick snow covered the country, the Bulgars had been checked and a number of prisoners taken by the Allied forces. The Australians were appointed to guard these prisoners, and they soon had them trained so well that they rendered good service in the camps and cookhouses. The captives included two Turkish women, who were guarded very closely.

Eventually the British force had to fall back owing to loss of men through frostbite and cold, and a French Division moved up to fight a rearguard action. The transport unit rendered excellent service on the long forced march in the face of terrible difficulties. A distance of 72 miles was covered in four and a half days.

Two fresh divisions engaged the enemy forces and held them. Early in December the Australians arrived back at Salonika with about 200 donkeys. They received orders to rejoin their own forces, and on 22nd December they embarked on the minesweeper Folkstone, and sailed for Lemnos, taking with them several spies, whom they guarded with the utmost vigilance.

General Sir Bryan Mahon thanked the Australians, before their departure, for the excellent work they had performed, and complimented them on their exemplary discipline and cheerful comradeship while associated with the Irish Division.

1916.

TEL-EL-KEBIR.

It does not rain often in Egypt, but it rained at Tel-el-Kebir the night the 24th Battalion arrived there. A number of tarpaulins had been dumped on the sand, but as yet there was very little sign of a camp.

Reinforcements (the 4th and 5th), who had come from Heliopolis the day before, had erected tents for themselves, but no accommodation was available for the men just off the Peninsula. The Anzacs, used to hard life, soon made the most of any material at hand. The scene was one typical of active service in those days. Officers and N.C.O.'s wandered about with lamps endeavouring to help the troops find their blankets, which had been carted there from the railway and dumped on the sand. Blankets were always a mysterious quantity when a unit shifted camp. However many blankets the troops handed in, there was always a shortage when they were distributed again. It was a case of first in, lucky, and last in—well, shall we say unlucky, to be polite?

There was little rest for the men that night, and everybody was glad when daylight came and enabled the work of pitching tents to be proceeded with.

It was good to be back in Egypt on that clean, healthy desert, but the day had its difficulties. Just when a company had rigged its tents under the direction of its officer, someone of higher rank would come along and order the whole "show" to be removed and put up in conformity with the general plan of the camp. Then the men would adopt a "go slow" policy to give the staff time to change their minds again before too much energy was expended on fruitless labour. When, eventually, the camp began to assume ordered shape and permanency, the Anzacs had to be issued with new clothes, and also equipment wherever there were shortages.

Active service does not mean idleness at any time. Training was entered upon without delay. Route marches and imaginary battles were carried out on the desert, day and night.

The allotment of leave to Cairo was much too small to satisfy the hopes of the troops, who were burning to get back again to the city where they had enjoyed themselves before their departure for Gallipoli. Consequently scores of them made off without permission, and to these men the trip, with piquets and the military police en route, was one with a decided element of adventure. They enjoyed it all the more on that account, for if caught half way on their first attempt and brought back, they started out again immediately they were released. The credits in their pay-books, which had swelled to handy sums on Gallipoli, *had* to be wiped out, and Cairo was just the place where money could be spent. When the cash was gone they came back to camp, and answered the defaulters' call four or five times a day till their sins were atoned for—at least so far as the army was concerned. Every time the bugle sounded that call a cheer went up over the whole camp, and men who had not broken camp shouted to their penalised mates, "Go on, you tourists—get out and take your medicine!"

Picture Captain Frawley, O.C. "B" Coy., dealing with defaulters at the company orderly-room:—

"Well, ——, how long have you been away?"

"Four days!"

"Had a good time?"

"Yes, sir."

"Seven days C.B. And don't go away again. Give somebody else a chance!"

Frank had a lenient heart towards good soldiers.

Likewise Major Parkes, O.C. "A" Coy., whose pride in his men was as pronounced as his personal rotundity. For many years to come the men of that company will in fancy hear the popular Major shouting " 'A' Company" with that distinctive inflection of voice which the lads delighted to imitate.

General Sir Archibald Murray reviewed the First and Second Australian Divisions at Tel-el-Kebir.

This desert camp will be remembered as the place where the old games of "two-up," "crown and anchor," and other speculative amusements flourished in all their glory. For the whole length of the camp — about two miles — by the side of the railway, the "schools" were carried on every night by the light of slush lamps and candles, and the merry voices of the men could be heard inviting patrons to put down their money: "A hundred wanted in the centre." "Heads are right." "Put 'em on thick and heavy." "What's the old mud hook done?" The scene resembled a huge open-air bazaar, and even men who were not disposed to stake their money were glad to gather there and watch the players, because they had nothing else to do. Others played cards in the tents, but the "schools" always held the crowd.

ON THE DESERT.

The beginning of February brought orders for a move to the desert east of the Suez Canal, which was again threatened by the Turks. Train to Ismailia, across the Canal by ferries and on pontoon bridges, and a weary tramp over the sand with full packs brought us to a spot where a prominent sandhill named the Sphinx marked our camp, about twelve miles from the Canal.

The whole of the First and Second Divisions were spread along a wide front covering the threatened locality, and for a month we dug trenches and watched for Turks, who never came close enough to allow us to renew our acquaintance with the Sultan's forces, though we patrolled the confusing valleys and plains and lost our ways in the search.

Although we went looking for Turks, as a matter of fact we never expected to find them. We went out in utter carelessness. Men will always take risks; it must be their nature. It was a crime to start off on patrol at night with so much as a lighted cigarette, which would have been quickly observed by an enemy patrol. Yet one party of five men under a corporal went out several miles and there sat down, smoked cigarettes, and struck matches to see the time!

Camels brought rations and water to us over the sand, and though we went unwashed we lived well and healthy in the dry atmosphere of the lonely desert, where sports were carried on under difficulties, and sandstorms buried our equipment and filled in our trenches just when we had completed a work which was done with characteristic Australian thoroughness. With March came news that we were going to France, and a new outlook filled the troops with great expectations.

Handing over the Canal defences to the New Zealand Mounted Rifles, we dragged our burdened frames back over the sand to the Canal. Of all the strenuous marches accomplished by the Battalion whilst on active service, surely this journey over the heavy sand, on a day marked by desert

heat of a most oppressive nature, must have pride of place.
Carrying full kits and blankets, men began to drop out
before two miles had been covered. Water bottles were
emptied in the first half hour, and with no means of re-
plenishing the supplies, the troops tramped on till the column
became a line of stragglers. Half-way on the journey we
came upon some horse troughs, and men stuck their heads
down and drank like the beasts, defying the officers who for-
bade them to touch this polluted water. When "Ferry Post"
was reached at night the water tanks of other units there
were besieged and almost emptied in defiance of all attempts
to check the thirsty men. The weaker men came drifting
into the camping area till daylight next morning. Our
thoughts turned to the story of Napoleon's retreat from
Moscow, and we wondered whether Russian snows were
worse than desert heat.

Next day the Battalion crossed the Canal and pushed on
through Ismailia to Moascar, where we began preparations
for our departure for the Western Front. Lectures on
France and much imaginary information concerning that
country kept us eager and expectant.

A number of changes and promotions in the ranks of the
officers had taken place. Major Fethers had left us to join
the staff at Brigade Headquarters. (Later Major Fethers
was promoted Lieut.-Colonel, and commanded the 23rd Battalion.) Captain Manning was promoted major and appointed second-in-command of the 24th Battalion. Captain
Parkes, also promoted major, was appointed to the Training
Battalion. Captain T. H. Plant had succeeded Captain G.
E. Cole as our medical officer, the latter having been transferred to the Artillery. Captain H. C. Brinsmead was
adjutant, and the company commanders were:—"A" Coy.,
Captain G. S. McIlroy; "B" Coy., Captain G. M. Nicholas;
"C" Coy., Captain T. C. Godfrey; "D" Coy., Captain W. M.
Trew. Captain Frawley was now Q.M., and Captain C. M.
Williams Machine Gun Officer.

H.R.H. the Prince of Wales and General Birdwood inspected the Australian Divisions before we embarked for
Europe. The young Prince had an enthusiastic reception

from the troops, who cheered him everywhere they met him. That was the first time we saw His Royal Highness as a soldier. In France later we often saw him in the field as a staff officer, sometimes going about his duties with only a single attendant, pushing his way through the bustling traffic on the muddy roads, and just "carrying on" with less ceremony than many a subaltern.

BOUND FOR FLANDERS.

The night of 20th March found us rocking in rough trucks on the railway to Alexandria, and on the 21st we "imshied" from Egypt and steered across the Mediterranean for Marseilles, dodging submarines on the voyage and suffering the agony of seasickness once more as part of our duty to our country.

Part of the unit travelled on the steamer "Lake Michigan," part on the "Magdalena," and part on the "City of Edinburgh." On the voyage the "Magdalena" passed the "Minneapolis," which had been torpedoed a few hours earlier, and which eventually went down.

In the hold of the "Magdalena" the Battalion Band, under Bandmaster R. L. Pogson, practised diligently, and we were able at Marseilles to march from the wharf to the station to the strains of martial airs. The Battalion band had never been strong, and the few players who had pumped wind into the brass in Egypt had, as stretcher bearers on Gallipoli, been so reduced in numbers that at Moascar the band was re-organised.

Although we could speak "English, Australian and Arabic," we had few French scholars, and in France, where pretty girls shouted greetings at every station on the long railway journey from Marseilles to Flanders, we found more satisfaction in their smiles than their words, however affectionate the latter may have been.

Two days in the trains, and only eight or nine from torrid Egypt, carried us into a snow blizzard, and the boys, cold but happy, snowballed one another with greater zest than they had thrown hand grenades at the Turks.

Our first disappointment in France was experienced when the trains turned off 12 miles from Paris and carried us past that fair city by a back route. We resolved then to see Paris or die. Alas, many of those brave men met death before they had an opportunity of seeing Paris.

The rail trip through France was marred by a fatal accident to one of the men who fell whilst attempting to board the moving train. He was buried in the town where the accident occurred, and the C.O. subsequently received a touching letter from a lady resident, in which she undertook to tend our comrade's grave. This practical manifestation of French sympathy was deeply appreciated by the unit.

Our destination by train was the quiet village of Thiennes, near Aire-sur-la-Lys (where we arrived after three days on the railway), and we marched some miles to our first billets in the village of Robecq.

The cold morning of April Fool's Day—our first day in Robecq—was not an ideal one for an early reveille, but some practical joker robbed us of an hour's sleep on our beds of straw by putting on the bugler's watch. The C.O. was among the victims, but everybody took the joke in good part, and when Bugler Sgt. McKenzie blew the call again at the proper hour he explained to the questioning troops that the first call was given to rouse the village girls in order that they might be up early to greet the boys.

COL. W. W. R. WATSON, C.B., C.M.G., V.D.

LIEUT.-COL. W.E. JAMES, D.S.O. and BAR.

THE WESTERN FRONT.

FLEURBAIX.

The Australians were allotted to the Armentieres sector of the line in Flanders, and on the 7th April we set out towards that part of the field.

At Aire-sur-la-Lys Marshal Joffre took the salute of our Battalion as we marched in column of route, and we were satisfied that a highly favourable impression was made on the French commander. The inhabitants of Aire gave us an enthusiastic reception.

Resting that night at Havesque, we continued to march next day. The miles of cobblestones on the long journey were hard after the soft sand in Egypt, and sore feet were common property. We marched through Merville and Estaires on the 8th, led by the band. The people flocked into the streets to see the new troops. It was easier to march with a full kit when smiling girls lined the route, and the men were in great heart during these interesting stages.

Haverskerque, on the banks of the Lys, was our billeting area until the 10th April, when we moved off to go into the line in front of Fleurbaix. The band put away their instruments, and we had the noise of guns as music for the last stage of the march.

A few days in supports and fatigue duty in the trenches gave the men an idea of the conditions prevailing on the front, and on 15th April we took over a section of the front line at Fleurbaix, the Brigade relieving a regiment of Royal Scots. It had been a quiet part of the front for many months, but the arrival of the Australians, especially the artillery, was the signal for more activity. The difference became so marked in a few weeks that the inhabitants of Armentieres and the villages in rear began to complain that the Australians had turned quiet days and restful nights into periods of noisy and dangerous conflict, forbidding sleep and drawing shellfire.

The firing line was a continuous wall or breastwork of sandbags built up above the level of the ground, for this section of Flanders was usually too marshy for trenches.

These sandbags had been there since the end of 1914, and the rats, which were in occupation of the whole system, were numerous enough and big enough to defend the position without the aid of men. Ravenously hungry, the rats were more annoying than the Huns, for while the men slept in sandbag shelters the vermin raced over their faces, and even stayed to nibble noses and fingers.

The approaches to the front line comprised long winding communication trenches, with duckboards laid along the bottom. In some stretches of these trenches there was water several feet deep under the duckboards, and these parts, especially at night, had to be negotiated carefully.

The most eventful period of the week in the line at Fleurbaix was the night on which we were relieved. That was Good Friday. It had rained heavily all day, and the duckboard tracks were in places submerged. In the dark the men slipped and sprawled in all directions, and on the long trail out through the communication saps a false step often meant total immersion. Men groused as they had not done since they gave up fatigue duty on Gallipoli, but in spite of the ordeal there was more laughter than bad language. Trailing through the slush back to the village—or the remains of the village—the men threw off their wet clothes and slept soundly in the partly demolished houses.

On Easter Monday the men had a good day on "fizz" at five and six francs a bottle, the beverage being retailed by some of the few remaining inhabitants of the ruined town. A fatal accident occurred at this place. While Captain H. C. Buckley (22nd Batt.) was instructing a party of men in the use of hand grenades a bomb exploded in his hand. The captain and one of the men were killed and nine were wounded.

GAS ALARMS.

What atrocity of the war was more dreaded than the use of poison gases? This horror had already been used by the Boche when we arrived on the Western front, and at that time, not having the effective defensive equipment which was supplied later, we almost trembled at the thought of the deadly fumes, for we had heard all about the torture they inflicted, of the cemeteries in the Ypres sector full of their victims, and the general confusion a gas attack created. The small gas respirators with which we were issued were little more than suffocating masks, and the effects of perspiration and the chemicals which saturated the cloth of which the masks were made were bad enough without gas. Many a man had his face well blistered, though no gas came near him. Yet we cherished these crude masks as a miser clings to his gold. We knew that at any moment they might be all that stood between us and death.

Who of the men at Fleurbaix on the night of the 23rd April, 1916, will forget that startling gas alarm which sounded over the trenches, back through the supports and along the streets of the battered village?

It had been a stagnant war on that part of the front for months, and on this night—at least till 11 o'clock—there was an unusual calm. The dancing lights of German flares along the line, and the occasional rat tat tat of a machine-gun were all that could be seen or heard of the war.

The troops billeted in the remains of the village and the few civilians who had drifted back to do business with the soldiers had settled down for the night in their rough shelters.

With a thrill a hundred times more sensational than the cry of "Fire," the shrill blast of the siren burst upon the air, followed by the clanging of numerous gongs and the excited shouts of men on guard, who yelled with all the strength of their voices, "Gas! Gas! Gas!" In an instant everybody was astir. The village was only a mile or two from the trenches, and the German front line, from which the gas would be discharged, was only a few hundred yards further. The distance was short, and there was no time to be lost.

Everybody was supposed to sleep with a gas mask ready so that it could be slipped on quickly, even in the dark. But like the Pompeians who took the risk of building their homes at the foot of Vesuvius, so will human nature always take chances. On this night many persons, including not a few soldiers, had no idea where their masks were. They rushed about in alarm and confusion; and that is just what they should not have done. Calmness is the greatest essential in a gas attack. Yet who could blame them? To be caught by gas without any means of defence is something like being imprisoned in a burning building without a way of escape. Even with gas masks on we were in the greatest state of agitation. It was our first experience with the gas fiend. We had no fear of Huns, but gas was something a man could not grapple with.

A moment after the first sound of the alarm officers and N.C.O.'s were shouting the order, "Stand to." Civilians might flee, but soldiers must stand to arms, gas or no gas. With masks adjusted, clothes thrown on hurriedly, equipment and arms secured, the troops fell in quickly on the streets and roads. The gas attack would probably be followed by an infantry assault, and the whole of our forces in the sector were marshalled to meet this possibility.

Another feature which heightened the excitement was an outburst of artillery fire simultaneously with the alarm. Exploding shells had been found effective in breaking up gas clouds, which at that time were emitted in visible form from cylinders in the enemy's front line, and drifted along like a fog. Therefore our batteries put down a heavy fire in No-man's-land with the object of lessening the denseness of the gas by scattering it, for its natural tendency was to travel low. Being heavier than air, the poisonous fumes clung to the ground, and depended upon a favourable wind for their progress.

It was only a matter of moments before troops in support and reserve began to move up to reinforce the front line. The effect of the gas alarm on the men was noticeable by the nervousness they exhibited. Rifles were accidentally going off along the roads where the troops were hurrying to the trenches, and there was questioning and shouting such as soldiers would never be guilty of under any other circumstances. Excited and perspiring, and breathing heavily into those stifling head-"bags," the men soon had the eyepieces of their helmets so befogged that nothing was visible through them. They stumbled forward in intense darkness, gasping for breath, burning to take off the masks, yet clinging to them as one cast into the sea would cling to a life-belt. The enemy's guns had also become busy by this, and the communication saps and tracks were now being shelled.

For an hour the excitement continued. Then it was discovered that the gas had been released six or seven miles further north, and the "alarm" had been extended to our sector, where the "alert" would have been sufficient. But gas could not be regarded indifferently, and it was always wise to be on the safe side.

This initiation into the mysteries of gas attacks was serious enough for us, nevertheless. We were cooler and better prepared for it afterwards. We had several alarms in that locality. Even in respect to the dreaded gas the old proverb "Familiarity breeds contempt," was found as true as ever, for on the occasion of the third alarm the officers had difficulty in persuading many of the men to rise from their bunks and place their masks in the "alert" position. "There's no gas," said one man; "it's a smoke cloud. Those German; are smoking cheap tobacco. Their pipes are like farm-house chimneys."

THE ARMENTIERES SECTOR.

At the end of April we left Fleurbaix and marched to L'Halle-o-Beau, south-west of Armentieres, where we were billeted for four weeks in wooden hutments on the bank of the Lys.

There was much work to be done on that part of the front in the improvement of the defences. It appeared that very little had been accomplished in that direction. Probably it was left for the Australians. At all events, the Australians were called upon to do it, and they did it. There were new trenches to dig, communication cables to lay, gun screens to erect, barbed wire entanglements to put up, and a variety of strenuous labour. Fatigue parties marched miles to work every night, and tramped back in the early hours of the morning.

One particular job, which will be well remembered by the troops, was the laying of a cable from Artillery Headquarters at Armentieres to the support lines. The cable had to be put down six feet in the ground, and the work done at night, under cover of darkness. The "Pick and Shovel Brigade," as the lads contemptuously named themselves for the time being, had an early tea of bread and jam, and set off at about 5 p.m., carrying picks and shovels as well as full fighting equipment. They moved in platoons as far as the Erquinghem bridge over the Lys, then in small sections through Erquinghem and Armentieres, over several miles of cobble stones to the place of toil. As soon as darkness fell the men, in single file, would steal on to the job. A white tape laid by the engineers indicated where the trench for the cable was to be dug. Each man was allotted a certain share of work every night. It was no Government stroke stunt. There were shrapnel shells and bullets flying about; but there was another incentive to speed. The quicker the allotted task was done the sooner the men would get back to the billets. It was always late enough when they returned—generally daybreak—and as they were out almost every night, they needed all the rest they could get, which was not excessive, as there were parades as well. It was hard life; and there were other fatigue duties at times worse than this particular job. This fatigue duty had its humorous side, as almost everything in the army had, because the men, in their irrepressible cheerfulness, refused to become downhearted.

Picture that long line of men (or rather men and boys, for the youth of Australia was there) swinging those heavy spades and picks in the dark, straining their muscles to beat the next hand man, and then, as the trench was finished, sitting down while the engineer in charge placed the telephone cable in position. Then, at two or three a.m., the order "fill in" would be given, and the loose earth seemed simply to leap back again, so swiftly did the spades move. The only thing that provoked complaint was delay in leaving for "home." Sometimes the engineer would not be at hand when he was wanted to lay the cable. Then uncomplimentary "messages" respecting engineers would pass up and down the line. "Pass the word along that the engineer has been killed in action," someone would say; or "the engineer is dopey," or "the engineer is asleep in a shell hole."

The greatest task the officers had on that job was to account for all the picks and shovels used each night. The men would carry the tools to the work, but many of them could not see the force of carrying them away every morning, and such a distance too. Where did those tools go? Every man started off with a pick or shovel, and was supposed to put it in the appointed place on returning to the billets. The long grass, the gutters and the hedges along the route could have revealed many a pick and scores of shovels. It was easy to drop them in the grass or throw them into a gutter. Only the man immediately behind would see the deed, and he would say nothing, for it was more than likely that he had already done the same, and if he had not, he would be grateful for the example. When inquiries were made during the day, every man, of course, was certain he did not leave his pick or shovel behind.

Waste? No. Someone else would find those tools. There were thousands of troops moving about there, and what one party lost another would find. The art of discovering discarded property is known in the army as salvage work, and is a very important branch of the army's operations. A battlefield is littered with all kinds of material, some damaged, some in good order, some left by men who have become casualties, and (the greatest source of salvage) the material left by a retreating force.

The almost immeasurable stacks of war material to be seen at the front every day gave one the impression that a few hundred picks or shovels could not be missed. And then there were so many dumps—huge piles of all kinds of stores —that shortages could easily be made good, not according to regulations, of course, but by the unofficially approved method of taking things without asking for them. This army method, if practised in civil life, would be described plainly as theft. But it is professional practice on active service to steal a thing if you cannot get it any other way. The only condition of this unwritten law is that you must confine your appropriation to army property. It was a common thing to hear officers, even of high rank, say to men who were short of certain equipment, "You must get it somewhere, but go out of your own camp to get it." Motor bicycles were "stolen" with less compunction than a boy would evince at stealing an apple, while push bicycles were picked up and discarded as if they were so much waste paper. A soldier was never sure of preserving to himself even his own clothes, and his fighting gear was his only while he had it under his eyes. It was of little avail to complain, for if a fellow, for instance, should say, "Some —— has pinched my rifle," another would reply indifferently, "Well, he must have wanted it, or he wouldn't have taken it." The philosophy of the army is wonderful.

Demonstrations and threatening activities on the part of the enemy had us "standing to" occasionally, but we handled picks and shovels more than rifles during the month of May.

Brigadier-General Gellibrand, commanding the Sixth Brigade about this time at Erquinghem, was wounded. This village, only a few kilometres from the firing line, was often bombarded by the Germans, and the residents were exposed to the shell-fire. During one of these bombardments the General was endeavouring to get some of the people to places of shelter, and was hit by a piece of shell. Brigadier-General Brand took over the Brigade during the absence of Brigadier-General Gellibrand.

On 28th May the Battalion moved to Bois Grenier, where, in addition to hard work day and night, we supported the line at that point.

The Prime Minister (Mr. W. M. Hughes) and the Australian High Commissioner in London (Mr. Andrew Fisher) visited the front at this time and inspected the Australian Divisions then in the field. The Sixth Brigade paraded at L'Halle-o-Beau, where Mr. Hughes and Mr. Fisher addressed the troops, who were assembled under the trees in an orchard in order that they would not be seen by enemy airmen.

Casualties during these days were light, but shocks were numerous. Enemy guns shelled the billets from time to time, and we never knew when Fritz was going to open fire on any particular object. On 11th June we moved into the Armentieres salient, going at first to billets on the eastern side of the town, and into the front line at Chapelle Armentieres on the 23rd.

The whole front was becoming more active every day. Raids were organised and carried out successfully, gas attacks were resorted to by both sides, and the artillery displayed a stronger inclination to knock things about. The British offensive on the Somme was to commence on 1st July, and the whole front showed signs of increased energy. Our guns and trench mortars bombarded the German positions frequently, provoking Fritz to return the compliment. Aeroplanes were numerous. Large squadrons of battleplanes from the British aerodromes steered over the lines and above the city of Lille to bomb enemy stores, railways, and camps. It was here that we first witnessed the thrilling spectacle of an observation balloon on fire. A British plane, in one brilliant swoop over the German positions, fired three German balloons. The sight so delighted the boys that even in the front line they cheered loudly. The loss of the three balloons and the sounds of cheering threw Fritz into a violent rage. He shelled us viciously, and we stood to arms expecting an attack. "D" Coy., in a sharp salient on the left of the Battalion sector, was in a hot corner, and the 22nd Battalion was in a similar position on our right. The artillery duel lasted till 2.30 a.m. Our stretcher bearers were busy that night. German searchlights, star shells, and signals made a spectacular display. Next morning the C.O. inspected the front line, and was so pleased to find everything satisfactory that he promised a coffee ration and extra rum.

Our snipers tantalised the Boche next day by putting up dummy figures above the parapet and imitating the movements of men. Fritz wasted many rounds of ammunition on those dummies. If he did not guess that he was being fooled he must have believed either that he was killing scores of Australians or that he was a decidedly bad shot

A RAID.

The 24th Battalion took a prominent part in a highly successful raid by the Sixth Brigade on 29th June. This was the second assault made by Australians on the German positions on the Armentieres sector. The raiding party comprised about 200 troops, each of the four Battalions supplying about 50, or 12 from each company, and one officer. The raid commander was Capt. A. R. L. Wiltshire (afterwards Lieut-Colonel, C.M.G., D.S.O., M.C.) of the 22nd Battalion. Lieut. J. B. N. Carvick was in command of the 24th Battalion party, with several N.C.O.'s in charge of the respective groups. The raiders were selected from volunteers, which, in other words, meant practically the whole Brigade, for almost every man of the four Battalions was eager to join the assaulting force. The 24th Battalion's quota included some of our finest Anzac troops—such men as J. L. Scales, W. G. Scales, Maurice O'Neill, Simon O'Neill, Steve and Claude Newton, Ould, Morcom, Forbes, Neill, two Kellys, Duggan, "Johnnie" Worrall, Norman Guest, Cpl. Watson and other thoroughly reliable soldiers. Lieut. A. J. Kerr was in charge of the scouts.

When the raiding force had been selected and assembled, the men were provided with special billets and granted special rations, during which time they trained zealously for their task. The preparations and organisation were directed by Colonel Brand (acting Brigadier and afterwards General), under whose keen and enthusiastic supervision the picked force attained a high standard of efficiency.

On the afternoon of the 29th the raiders assembled behind our lines and "made up" for the tragic performance of the approaching night. The object of the raid was to impart a shock to the enemy on that part of the front and to secure prisoners and booty for intelligence purposes. The enemy's line was to be entered at three points. The attacking troops were divided into sections, with varied and specified duties.

The distance across No-man's-land was about 300 yards. The preparatory artillery and trench mortar barrage opened at 11.58 p.m. The raiders were lying silent and ready 50 yards from the Hun parapet. At 12.1 a.m., when the barrage lifted, our men rushed the enemy line, quickly overcoming the German troops, who were bombed and bayonetted with so much despatch that the raiders soon found themselves in complete possession of the position. While one of our men was getting over the enemy parapet a big Hun pinned him there by thrusting at him with his bayonet, which passed through the fleshy part of the Australian's leg and then into the bags. Our man shouted the worst of curses at the Boche. "Hush," said another Australian, "you'll give us away."

"Well, this ——— has stuck me." Then, to the Boche, "There, take that," as he caught the German a heavy blow on the head with his iron club. Then he pulled the bayonet out of his own leg, and hobbled along to a large dugout, where he had further revenge by throwing bombs down the steps at the occupants.

Another of our men took a fancy to a youthful Boche. At least he decided to take him prisoner instead of killing him—a favour to the fellow, certainly. But the youth was terrified at the black skin of his captor, for the raider had made up like a full-blooded aborigine. The German intelligence service, with the idea of preventing their troops surrendering, had communicated to them the interesting but alarming information that the Australians were cannibals and would make a feast of all Germans carried off as prisoners. This young Boche, with the evidence before him, was convinced of the truth of the statement, and was terrified beyond measure. The Australian guessed the cause of his prisoner's fears, and rubbed some of the black off his own dark face, revealing the white skin. It was a wonderful revelation to the German boy. He went along willingly after that.

The raiders had to wade through a creek to reach the enemy's lines, and again as they returned. A man escorting a German prisoner through this ditch got bogged. The Boche seized the opportunity and made off. Everybody was busy with his own job, but at least a few were not too busy to hear the escort, almost submerged, shouting, "Shoot the ———. Shoot the ———. There he goes. Stop him!" And just as the German reached his own parapet a rifle bullet laid him out. Five prisoners were required for purposes of information, and the 24th party had the honour of producing the specified haul of human material.

An interesting and suspicious incident marked this adventure. One of the raiding party disappeared. The word "Bunk" was to be the signal to retire in case of an outflanking movement by the Boche. Scarcely had the raiders gained the enemy line when that order was passed along. The men immediately fell back, as they had been instructed to do. Nobody knew who had given the order, and it was quickly realised that an act of treachery had been perpetrated. The order was at once given to re-enter the German position, and the men dashed over the parapet again to complete their job, which they did with marked success. The man who had disappeared was never seen again, and inquiries led to the conclusion that this individual, whose nationality was afterwards doubted, was responsible for the unexplained interruption of the proceedings.

In spite of this attempt to frustrate the enterprise the raid was thoroughly successful. The 24th Battalion claimed to have killed about 50 Germans (Saxons). A quantity of material and papers was secured, and the five prisoners safely handed over. Our casualties consisted of five killed (including Cpl. Watson) and several wounded. Lieut. Carvick was awarded the M.C., L.-Cpl. Grieve (signaller) the D.C.M., and others the M.M. Lieut. A. J. Kerr, scouts officer, rendered highly commendable service.

General Birdwood wrote to the C.O. the day after the raid: "All evidently did excellently last night. I think the bringing "back of the men who were killed (whose deaths I deeply "regret) was a very fine performance."

This was our first assault on the Hun. It gave our men confidence, for it showed them that they had nothing to fear from the boasted fighting qualities of the German soldier.

Activities increased as the days passed, and the necessity arose for improving and strengthening the decaying breastwork and shelters. The resourcefulness of the Australian soldier was early demonstrated in this direction. Holes were dug under the firing steps and duckboards behind the sandbag walls, and in these recesses all men not on duty were placed during enemy bombardments. These precautions were so effective that on one occasion when the Hun fired some thousands of shells at our positions only three casualties were sustained.

THE FLEMISH PEASANT.

Before we left Egypt we were told that in France we would be billeted in the houses with the civilians. The prospect was held up before us as a bit of good news. We pictured ourselves dining at tables with a charming mademoiselle beaming upon us. How polite we would be!

The reality hardly harmonised with our imaginations. The troops found themselves in the sheds and barns. Straw was plentiful, and though the men often had to steal it, it relieved their discomfort. Even the officers, who lodged in the houses, were by no means stylishly accommodated.

In Flanders we found people with varying degrees of patriotism. The children whose fathers and brothers were serving with the French army quickly became close friends with us, and the wives and mothers of worthy men cheered us on our way with brave words.

We were passing through Erquinghem one evening on our way to the trenches at the back of that village when we saw a striking example of womanly patriotism. Our lads were in a particularly happy mood. Swinging along on the cobbles of the main street, where the few remaining civilians stood at the doors of the sandbagged houses, we sang, whistled, and shouted greetings to the people.

The Huns were shelling the village at that moment, and the residents were somewhat excited. One old lady, cheering the troops as they passed her door, was also shouting in the French-English phraseology in which the people talked to us: "Allemand no bon! Allemand beaucoup brigand!"

One of our lads, in a highly jocular spirit, replied, "Allemand tres bon."

The taunt was too much for the old lady. Seizing a heavy broom, she dashed at the soldier and struck at his head.

The soldier was sorry for what he had said, and to assure her of this we burst into a unanimous denunciation of our common enemy. Indeed, one man shouted, "Allemand no ——— bon!"

We did not know whether it was his emphatic tone or his strong language that appealed to the aggrieved woman, but there was no doubt that his judgment on the Boche pleased her most. Perhaps the woman would have been prepared to use strong language herself. She had reason to do so. We learned later from her that two of her soldier sons had been killed in action, and a once happy group of grandchildren had been left fatherless. Their homes had been laid in ruins, and the woman and children were now glad of any shelter they could find.

ON THE WARPATH.

A few pages from my diary will best describe the experiences of the troops for the next two weeks.

July 4.—A brisk bombardment during the day, mostly counter battery work. We are to be relieved at night. A raid on the German lines on our right is timed for midnight. We must have the "change over" complete before that hour. To be caught in the communication trenches by the enemy guns that will burst forth at the call of his S.O.S. would mean heavy casualties.

The success of a change over depends mainly on the relieving forces. They must man the positions before the outgoing troops can "stand down" and take their departure.

Some of the relieving companies are late through blocks in the traffic. The communication trenches are narrow, and companies going in and out on different duties hinder one another. Having to squeeze past each other with their heavy loads of equipment and material, progress is slow. Men become irritable through delay; grousing is general; the language takes on a lurid expression. In a few minutes hell will break loose. The last platoons are still squeezing and doubling along the saps.

A big gun booms; a battery roars; in an instant the dark, quiet earth becomes a volcano. The country is lit up by the flashing of fire, and the smoke of explosives rises like clouds in a storm. Shells are screaming and bursting. We have half a mile further before we are out of the danger zone, so we hustle with our loads, tripping, falling, and cursing as we go.

In the early hours of the morning we are trudging through the ruins of Armentieres. Our destination is La Creche, 12 miles away. We march or plod on in groups all the rest of the night. Daylight finds us scattered on the roads. Some have pressed on, others are done up and are resting. Some are looking for food at a friendly house here and there on the way. Children sell us cakes and chocolates.

Up till 8 a.m. the stragglers keep drifting into the rendezvous, while the company cooks, who had gone ahead, keep the fires burning and the breakfast going for the late comers. Blistered feet, sickness, or heavy loads are the causes of some men's slowness in reaching the billets.

July 5.—Hunger appeased, the troops quickly fall asleep on their beds of straw. Everybody is dog tired. It is a day of inactivity save for necessary duties. Active service never permits everybody to rest at the same time.

July 6.—There is work to do. Fatigue parties are called out early for construction work on defences and roads. One party sets out with fighting equipment, picks and shovels, for a job near the Belgian border. The officer in charge takes the wrong road, and marches "off the map." The party arrives at the work in time to start back to the billets.

July 7.—Many of the men go on leave to Bailleul in the afternoon.

July 8.—The Division is on the move. We march to Strezeele and billet there for the night.

July 9.—We are off again. The weather is warm. Our packs are heavy, for we are carrying blankets as well as all our other gear, including 120 rounds of small arms ammunition. We plod along the railway all the way. Trains pass us frequently. Why cannot we ride? Much honest sweat is lost. Many of the troops fall out, unable to keep up. We camp for the night at Ebblinghem. At our billet the old Flemish farmer makes a fuss because some of the men bathe their sore feet in his duck pond. The lads threaten to raid his orchard if he does not display a little more hospitality. The old man puts his son on guard in the barn to prevent the troops smoking cigarettes on the hay. He might as well use his hat to extinguish a bush fire.

The soldiers, exceedingly fatigued, "turn in" early, and the rumble of the guns they have left behind lulls them to sleep—excepting at one particular farm, where a company of our infantry and some engineers fight for the possession of a rough barn in which a dog would not consider himself stylishly housed.

July 10.—On again—to Wardrecques. On the strength of the news that we are to entrain next day, the men make merry. There are some lively scenes in the estaminets.

Our blankets, which we have carried for three days on the hard roads, are now taken from us. (This and other hardships do not please us.) Arguments arise in the billets through the bad temper of the men. Anzacs fight with reinforcements. Several heads are bandaged.

July 11.—We march to Arques and entrain. Whither are we going? There is general ignorance on this important subject. Only the senior officers know. "Furphies" are rampant. Everybody has some "good oil." First we are going to Calais to embark for Ireland—Garrison work. That is a great idea. Visions of colleens and Irish homes set us singing songs of Shamrock themes. Another "furphy" is that we are going to rest at Boulogne or Etaples for a month or two.

As the slow train drags on we rock in the rough trucks. Calais dies away in the distance. Boulogne looms up and fades from view. It must be Etaples, for the Australians have a large training base here. The train pulls up right at the depot. We are awaiting orders to detrain.

Then we are aroused from our dreams. The train is moving. The truth dawns upon us in a flash. The Somme Push!

These men are too brave to allow any sudden change of feeling to manifest itself. Jests and song continue. But gradually the gaiety is subdued by the thoughts of home and the possibilities of the near future. But these thoughts, too, soon pass. Abbeville, with its cheering populace, sees our boys a few hours later flushed with the idea of battle. They are noisier than ever.

The railway yards at Amiens show us long trains of wounded from the Push. These wounded men—French, English, Scotch, Algerian—all smiles and good humour, cheer us past. In a few days we may be on one of these hospital trains, or perhaps—!

But, there, why think of that? We must take our chances.

We are vainly searching for that mythical army quantity—the unexpended portion of the day's rations—when the train pulls up at a siding outside Amiens, and we hear our officers shouting orders. The only fear we have is that there may be another route march. Alas! how fully our fears are realised, for soon we are on the road again, struggling with packs and heavy fighting equipment. When we start we know not when we are going to stop. These long tramps are a delightful pastime! They are the nightmare of a soldier's life.

What a drumlike roll of guns!! What a chain of observation balloons! What a haze of smoke! And we are over 20 miles from the battle front.

At midnight we are still marching. The troops are given more frequent spells. At 2 a.m., after marching for five hours we arrive at St. Sauveur, a town through which the train had taken us seven or eight hours earlier!

July 12.—The troops are searching the town for bread and other articles of food to supplement their rations. The transport columns, guns, troops, and all the general paraphernalia of war, are moving in every direction; and on the railway in the valley trains are passing back from the front with loads of wounded. Hospital barges, carrying the worst cases, glide smoothly down the canal to Rouen.

July 13.—Our Division practises an attack. We will soon be in the " Big Push." Ailly-sur-Somme, a village a few kilometres along the river, is the popular rendezvous of the Australians in the evening. The whole Division appears to be there; the place is jammed full of troops. Two days are spent in preparations for action.

July 16 (Sunday).—While the church bells are ringing for morning worship we move off towards the front. We march through Bertangles, and camp for the night at Raineville. This village is well named—it is raining torrents. The noise of the battle does not seem far away. But still the church bells ring, and the women wend their way along the slushy roads to evening worship. The only Frenchmen in sight are aged and feeble. France is at war, and that means all fit men to the colours.

At Raineville a woman declares she has been robbed of 400 francs. A whole Battalion is lined up for the possible identification of the supposed thief, but the woman fails to recognise anyone. The men are dismissed. The authorities doubt whether she ever had 400 francs, but they give her the benefit of the doubt and pay her that sum.

July 17.—An English Division, which has already been through the " Push " once and has been back reorganising for a second turn, is passing through our village to the battle. The men show signs of strenuous marching. An English Bantam Unit is also encountered. One of these men, in characteristic " chum " language, remarks—" We met the Prussian Guards at Contalmaison. We hopped over at the ———, and the ——— gave us ———."

July 18.—On again, to Toutencourt—" A day's march nearer hell." Here we meet the 29th British Division, which was associated with the Anzacs at the Dardanelles.

THE BATTALION ON THE ROAD TO POZIERES.—July, 1916.

They also are in the "Push." The night is intensely cold. Our men, having no blankets, cannot sleep. They are forbidden to light fires, for lights would be observed by enemy aeroplanes. It is a trying time. One company lights a fire, and the fire guard turns out. The offenders are promised that they will be punished. The boys sing and whistle till they exhaust their repertoire of tunes. Then everybody gets miserable. Thoughts of home are hard to keep out of one's mind at such times. One man finds a stretcher and throws himself upon it. A mate remarks, "You need to be careful. Those stretchers are so comfortable that men have died on them." We shiver all night, and welcome the relief daybreak brings.

July 19.—We are informed of the methods we will adopt in an assault on the enemy as soon as our turn comes to "go in." We practise a charge with the different units in their allotted positions.

July 20.—We are off again, this time to Varennes. Our next move will be into battle. We are able to appreciate with more feeling than inspired the poet the words, "Far flashed the red artillery," for at night the northern skyline is illuminated by the continuous glare of flashing guns and bursting shells, the locality of the battle being vividly indicated by the more lurid reflection.

Every day fresh batches of German prisoners are being brought from the front and placed in prison camps near Varennes. Our boys go over to have a look at Fritz. The Huns are sullen, and have evidently had a rough time.

One of our men, looking at a Hun through the barbed wire, asks, "What do you think of the British lion now, Fritz?" He hardly expected a reply, as he doubted whether any of the prisoners could speak English. Imagine his surprise, and also his wrath, when the German promptly answered in perfect English, "He is like you—all mouth!"

Our man wanted to fight that Hun, but the guard hunted him off.

We waited anxiously for our call to the fray, every day being occupied with the most careful preparation. For instance, the medical officer advised all the men to have their hair cut as short as possible, so that head wounds could be more easily dressed. Some of the lads, who were more than ordinarily proud of their locks, refused to be "clipped." So, for the sport of the performance, organised parties of hefty men captured them, dragged them to the "shearing shed," and removed their lovely curls. There were exciting chases after boys who bolted to evade the barbers. If a man struggled much, he would be held till the barber ran the clippers once across his head, from the forehead to the back of the neck, leaving a bare track like a path through a wheat crop. He would then be released. The disfigurement, of course, drove him to submit to the completion of the job.

THE HANGING VIRGIN.—*Effects of the enemy bombardment on the Cathedral at Albert.*

POZIERES.

The British offensive, known as "the big push of 1916," had been launched in the vicinity of Albert on the 1st of July, and when the Australian Corps entered the field here about three weeks later the Boche had been driven back to Pozieres, a distance of about four miles from the starting point. When it is considered that the hammering had been practically incessant, the severity of the struggle and the stubborn resistance of the enemy can be gauged to some extent by the comparatively small area of country regained.

The 24th Battalion moved off from Varennes on the 26th at about 4 a.m., and marched to the brickfields on the outskirts of Albert.

Prior to the 1st July the opposing lines skirted Albert on the north, the town being within the territory held by the British forces. It had received more than a fair share of attention from the enemy gunners, and we found it in ruins and deserted as far as the civilian population was concerned. The chief feature was its battered cathedral with the famed statue of the Virgin and child hanging from the ruined tower. The current superstition was that when the statue fell to the ground hostilities would cease, and on that account expectant eyes were often turned in its direction. However, it transpired that nothing short of a direct hit by the artillery would bring about its downfall, British engineers having firmly secured the statue to what was left of the tower.

While we awaited orders to move into action, our surplus kit was handed over to the quartermaster, letters and messages entrusted to the padre, and final touches made to our fighting outfit, leaving us in battle array.

The First Division had attacked the village of Pozieres on the night of 23rd-24th July, and after stubborn fighting had ousted the enemy from well-fortified positions. The Second Division was now relieving the First, and the broken units which had been through the first Australian engagement on this front were dribbling back past our rendezvous. First-hand information was eagerly sought by our men as to how things were going at the front. There was little need for questioning, however, as the wornout appearance of the men and their reduced numbers supplied sufficient evidence of the nature of the battle.

On the afternoon of the 26th the Battalion left the brickfield and started for the line. The route lay through the deserted town and over the chalk ridges beyond. A short distance out of Albert we passed the crater formed by the mine exploded under the enemy's line on 1st July. This had been the signal for the commencement of the first attack in the offensive. The crater was about 80 yards in diameter and 50 feet deep, and on this summer day gave forth unpleasant evidence of the number of Germans caught in the eruption. Smashed trenches and defences ran in all directions, but the fact that the Boche had recently been ejected from them was a source of much satisfaction. On all sides the ground was littered with the refuse of a modern battlefield and torn by shells, while numerous wooden crosses bore mute testimony to the struggles and sacrifices of the preceding days.

At dusk we reached Sausage Gully, a valley about 400 yards wide and half a mile long, on the rise at the head of which ran the Contalmaison road. The gully, in addition to being the main avenue for traffic to and from the battle zone at this part of the front, was packed with artillery of every calibre, which kept up a continuous fire on the enemy. It was to this busy spot that the wounded were borne from the front line by the stretcher bearers and transferred to horse and motor ambulances. The movement of men and transport gave the gully a scene of indescribable activity, and the German artillery fire made it as unhealthy as it was busy.

Here we learned that the Sixth Brigade was to relieve the Second Brigade, the 22nd and 24th Battalions taking over the firing line. The Brigade sector extended for about 1000 yards in an irregular north-west line from the Pozieres-Bapaume road. On the right of the road the

RED AND WHITE DIAMOND.

Fifth Brigade were in position, the South Wales Borderers supporting them on the right, while Warwickshires held the line on the left of the Sixth Brigade.

About midnight guides who had been sent down from the units we were relieving reported to take our companies into position, the route being along the Contalmaison road, then turning to the left along a smaller road past the Chalk Pit, across the Pozieres-Bapaume road into Kay trench, then to the allotted positions. The blackness of the night, brightened only by occasional flares over the firing line in the distance, rendered progress over the debris-strewn and shell-pitted roads slow and laborious. Gas shells falling along the route kept the men putting on and taking off their masks during the first stages of the journey, and as we got nearer the fighting area several casualties were sustained by shell and rifle fire. Fortunately, the enemy fire slackened for an hour or two while the relief was in progress. Nevertheless, the utmost difficulty was experienced by the companies in reaching their respective stations.

The disposition of our companies was as follows:—" A " Coy. (Captain McIlroy), front line from the cemetery to the orchard, linking up with the 22nd Battalion on the right. " D " Coy. (Captain Trew), front line on the left of " A " Coy., right flank near the village cemetery, left flank on the Courcellete road. A gap between " A "' and " D " Coy. was covered by Vickers machine guns secreted in the cemetery. " B " Coy. (Captain Nicholas) in supports. " C " Coy. (Captain Godfrey) in reserve. Battalion Headquarters were at " Gibraltar " and the aid-post in a sunken road in rear of the village.

" A " and " D " Coys. struggled forward in the dark, and they completed the relief of the troops in the front line before daybreak. The 8th Battalion, which the 24th relieved, had a half-dug trench close up to the German line, and the men of " A " and " D " Coys. had to start on its completion immediately. The Battalion had scarcely got into position when the German 5.9 shells began to crash about us with that ear-splitting sound so well known to all men at the front. The call for stretcher-bearers began with the first shell.

It was daylight before " B " Coy. was in position in Kay Trench, where " B " Coy. of the 22nd Battalion was also posted.

Owing to the nerve-shattered state of the troops going out little information could be gained from them as to the nature of the situation. They had carried out an attack the previous day and had ejected the Hun from the last of his defences in the village. The enemy had retired to a ridge about 350 yards away, and was now occupying a new line of trenches overlooking ours. The only point on which the Second Brigade men laid much emphasis was the probability of strong counter attacks during the day.

Daylight revealed a scene of desolation. The village of Pozieres was no longer in existence, churned-up earth, heaps of powdered masonry and blasted tree stumps alone marking the site. The only structure which had withstood the bombardment was " Cement House," also known as " Gibraltar," a former German dugout with a concrete observation post surmounting it, and situated at the entrance to Kay Trench near the Pozieres-Bapaume road. All the surrounding country was in a similar state of upheaval, and was strewn with wreckage, with which was mingled the bodies of many dead.

The enemy did not spare us after daylight revealed our whereabouts. His batteries, which were in great strength on that sector, opened a bombardment on the whole of the Australian positions, and maintained a withering fire for 36 hours. Kay Trench, where our " B " Coy. and also " B " Coy. of the 22nd Battalion were crammed in so tightly that men scarcely had room to move, was in a painfully exposed position. The troops suffered heavily, whole sections being killed, buried or wounded. "A" Coy.'s position was less exposed, and they had the advantage of the newly dug trench, which was narrow and winding and therefore a more difficult target for the German gunners, though the first shell to fall on this line killed Lieut. A. J. Kerr. " D " Coy. also suffered heavily.

All day the men were being buried by shell fire and extricated by their comrades. According to Brigade records, at one period of the day casualties on the field were occurring at the rate of 60 per Battalion per hour. The ordeal of holding those ghastly trenches, which appeared to be merely waiting for death, threw many of the men into a shell-shock stupor, and stretcher-bearers who struggled with the wounded had to kick the dazed men to induce them to move out of the way.

The troops hung on only by spurring themselves with all the gallantry and force of will which British blood could command. In Kay Trench, where the troops had no other duty but the utterly painful one of remaining at their post prepared for action in case they should be needed, the braver men displayed their contempt for death by squatting down and playing cards while the earth-shaking explosives fell fast around them; and every time the cards were shuffled, the strength of the platoons dwindled away. It seemed as if those men, as they played their cards in defiance of fate, were gambling, not for money, but for things which on that field appeared to be infinitely cheaper—the stakes of life and death. An officer, passing along that trench in the afternoon, sickened by the sight of the dead and wounded, saw the body of a sergeant which had been lifted out of the trench above the spot where four men were dealing their cards. "You've lost your sergeant, I see," remarked the officer to the group. "Yes," replied one of the men with a voice which failed in its attempt to conceal the speaker's emotion; " he was playing cards here with us a few minutes ago when he was hit."

Another man had taken the sergeant's hand of cards, and the brave men played on, hardly knowing what cards they dealt, but struggling against their feelings and trying, by a display of apparent coolness, to steady the nerves of others around them.

And when the officer came back the four had played their last hand, and had lost. Death had won.

Oh, Pozieres, resting place of heroes!

Retaliation was given by our artillery on the enemy's

front line, but this did not appear to affect the persistency of the German gunners.

For most of the time our front line was practically isolated, runners and carrying parties finding it extremely difficult to get through, and it was useless to rely on the telephone, for as fast as our gallant signallers repaired the lines they were broken again by shell fire.

The vicinity of "Gibraltar" was a terrible death trap. It lay right on the route of all movement to and from the lines, and as the shells crashed in salvoes around the structure, men fell right and left. Every track over the remains of the village changed shape a dozen times a day under the deluge of shells that fell there, and men went past "Gibraltar" and down "Death" road at the double. Stretcher-bearers with wounded were swallowed up in the inferno, and fatigue parties sometimes had half their numbers cut down getting through.

As a matter of fact, when allotting fatigue parties, the staff counted upon one-third of the men becoming casualties, so that if two-thirds got through, the required quantities of rations and ammunition would be safely delivered at the firing line.

Every foot of the ground was churned over and over by shell fire, and smoke and fumes blurred the field day and night. It was hell in very reality, and men who served there proved that their valour and faithfulness were beyond measure. The Battalion's A.M.C. section rendered faithful service throughout that trying period. The M.O. (Captain T. H. Plant) worked untiringly for two days attending the wounded. Stretcher cases poured in upon the aid post, and walking wounded painfully made their way to the dressing station in a steady stream. Private Kirby (afterwards promoted A.M.C. sergeant and awarded the D.C.M.) was an inspiration to the troops in the line. Whenever he could leave the aid-post he was in the trenches cheering the lads and applying dressings. Another man who distinguished himself at that critical period was Private (afterwards lieutenant) E. L. Forbes, of "A" Coy., who was as busy as a General, while the unruffled Sergeant Ball

THE RED AND WHITE DIAMOND.

("Tonto") kept up his droll jokes and provoked men to smile when the concussion of bursting shells was taking away their breath.

Pozieres provided our regimental stretcher-bearers with a task utterly beyond their powers. Each Battalion went into action with 16 bearers (four per company.). On that field a hundred bearers per Battalion would have been more in keeping with requirements. On the second day only four of our 16 bearers remained in action, the others having being killed or wounded. In the forward trenches the wounded waited hours for removal. Many of the company men helped with the work of rescue, and when our transport section heard of the plight of the troops in the line they immediately volunteered for duty as stretcher-bearers. Although some of them were included among the honoured dead before their task was done, the rest never wavered. Every trip to the aid-post left the bearers fewer in numbers, but they carried on their heroic work with coolness and faithfulness, dressing the wounded under hellish fire, and then carrying them away with all possible care. Even when shells fell so close that the debris was thrown over them, they went on calmly, having only one thought, namely, the safety of their wounded patients.

The work of regimental stretcher-bearers is not only dangerous, but also the most strenuous duty on a modern battlefield. Some of the bearers at Pozieres, after many hours of unceasing toil, had the muscles of their hands so strained that they could not grip the stretcher handles. Later in the campaign the bearers worked in parties of four and six, and carried the stretchers on their shoulders, but at Pozieres they were fortunate if they could maintain two men per stretcher.

Even the ambulance bearers, who took over the wounded after the regimental bearers had brought them back from the forward positions, found their task almost more than they could cope with.

One of our transport men who had been killed while stretcher-bearing had been the owner of a mascot monkey, whose antics always drew groups of delighted children around "A" Coy.'s cooker, on which he rode when the Battalion was passing through the towns and villages behind the front. " Jacko " appeared to be painfully conscious that his master was dead. He fretted for many days, and later he, too, was buried on the field.

Orders had been issued on the 27th for an attack to be carried out by the 22nd and 24th Battalions on the night of the 28th-29th July in conjunction with the Seventh Brigade. The objectives of the Sixth Brigade units were the enemy positions along the Courcellete road on our left and running almost at right angles to the line we then held, while the Seventh Brigade was to capture the trenches to the right of the point where the Courcellette road intersected the enemy lines on the ridge.

The hostile artillery fire did not abate until the afternoon of the 28th, and the 22nd and 24th Battalions were then found to be so badly shaken and so depleted in numbers that it was decided to entrust their part of the attack to the 23rd Battalion. Two companies of the 24th Battalion ("C" and " D ") and three companies of the 22nd Battalion were detailed to act as reserves.

The attack was timed for midnight, and prior to that hour the 23rd Battalion took over the line, our " A " and " B " Coys. withdrawing to Sausage Gully. Before dawn " D " Coy. was also ordered to retire, and on the night of the 30th " C " Coy. joined the other companies in the gully. Our Lewis-gunners remained to support the attack.

Our adjutant, Captain H. C. Brinsmead, had been wounded and evacuated, and Captain W. M. Tatnall was appointed to succeed him. (Captain Brinsmead subsequently became chief staff officer for Aviation at the A.I.F. Headquarters in London, with the rank of Lieut.-Colonel).

Unfortunately the attack by the 23rd Battalion and the Seventh Brigade was not the success desired. The 23rd Battalion gained all its objectives in the face of strong opposition, but through being unable to penetrate the barbed wire entanglements the Seventh Brigade was held up, thus leaving the 23rd Battalion's right flank in the air. Our comrades of the red and brown hung on, in a typically Sixth

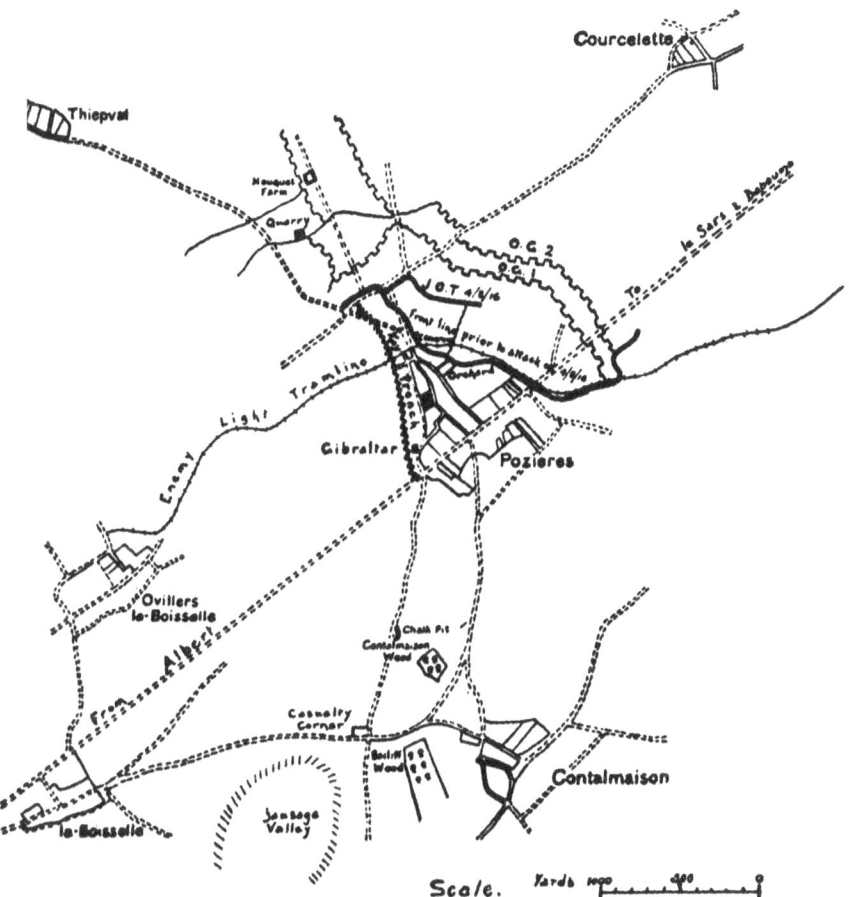

Pozieres and Mouquet Farm.

Brigade manner, to most of what they had gained, though the position was almost untenable, subjected as it was to fire from all angles. It was therefore necessary to organise another attack on the German positions.

Our sojourn in Sausage Gully was officially described as a period in which we were to "rest and reinforce." The term "rest" was a misnomer. We lived in shell-holes and battered trenches under the muzzles of countless guns, which blazed away day and night, while Fritz added to the general confusion with frequent bursts of shell fire. In addition, fatigue parties, carrying material and rations to the units in the line, and stretcher-bearing squads had to be continually supplied, with the result that many casualties were sustained, among those killed on this duty being Lieut. A. G. Goodson.

While we were in the Gully about 200 reinforcements arrived and were allotted to the companies, but many of them, being sent forward immediately with the fatigue parties, became casualties before the platoon commanders had time to include them on their rolls.

ATTACK ON POZIERES RIDGE.

Orders were issued for another attack on the Pozieres ridge, the objectives being the two German lines (officially designated O.G. 1 and O.G. 2) running to the right from the Courcellete road. The 22nd and 24th Battalions were allotted the left sector of the attack, the Seventh Brigade co-operating on the right. Elaborate preparations were made for the assault, which was to be delivered at 9.15 p.m. on 4th August. A continuous bombardment had been maintained on the objectives for two days to ensure that on this occasion the wire entanglements would be effectively destroyed and the trenches reduced as far as posible to an indefensible condition.

As this was the enemy's last hold on the Pozieres system, it was rightly assumed that his defence would be stubborn. On the other hand, the capture of the position was deemed imperative by our command, as in the event of success there were strong probabilities of the cavalry attempting the break through so much desired.

The Engineers and Pioneers had achieved wonders in preparing new communication trenches to the forward area, and though the Hun did not take long to locate these avenues and pound them with his shells, they proved a boon to the troops moving to and from the front line. The principal trenches were "Dinkum Alley," from the Contalmaison road near Sausage Gully to the Chalk Pit; "Centreway," beyond the Chalk Pit and running through the village to the trenches on the other side of it.

In the plan of the attack the 22nd Battalion was to form the first and second waves, and the 24th Battalion the third and fourth waves.

The company commanders in the assault were:—" A " Coy., Captain G. S. McIlroy; " B " Coy., Captain G. M. Nicholas; " C " Coy., Captain T. C. E. Godfrey; " D " Coy., Lieut. J. B. N. Carvick, M.C.

Every man was well supplied with bombs and ammunition, and carried as well as his usual fighting gear sandbags for rebuilding the enemy trenches when captured, and either a pick or shovel to assist in the work of consolidation.

At about 5 p.m. on the 4th August the 22nd Battalion moved out of the Gully, followed by the 24th Battalion, the two units numbering well over a thousand men. The route was by way of "Dinkum Alley," "Centreway," and Kay Trench to the jumping off position, which was a trench dug by working parties during the preceding nights and running from the Courcellette road parallel to and about 150 yards from the German front line.

Such a movement of troops in broad daylight could hardly escape observation by the enemy. We had not got far on our way when we were greeted with a heavy barrage, which temporarily disorganised operations. This was most disconcerting to the commanders, who realised it was essential that the troops should be at the jumping-off points in time to follow our own barrage, which would be launched on the tick of 9.15 p.m. Time was flying, and very little progress seemed to have been made. Contradictory orders of all descriptions were passing up and down the line as we waited in " Dinkum Alley," pressed on a few yards, halted, turned about, retired a few paces, went forward, halted, and repeated this performance until the men were in a bad temper. This was apparently caused by the barrage holding up the head of the column, which was already suffering casualties.

Darkness had fallen before we reached Kay Trench, which was being lashed with a tornado of "whizbangs." Who of those who participated in that engagement and have survived it will ever forget the dash along that notorious trench? Some idea of the physical and mental strain of that night may be gained when it is considered that the men, each carrying about 70lbs. of equipment, were pushing through a tempest of shells, and stumbling over the dead and wounded and all manner of obstacles.

The result of the confusion was that we were late in arriving at the jumping-off points, with the platoons and companies very much mixed. There was no time for sorting out, and as groups of utterly exhausted men rushed into the trench they were organised there and sent out " over the top " towards the objectives, while others in the rear were still struggling over the debris and groping their way in confusion and under heavy fire.

It was a night of terrible suspense and agony. The faithfulness of the troops in pushing on in spite of all opposition and uncertainty of direction and the excellent work of officers and N.C.O.'s in directing the men, won success out of a situation which might easily have resulted in failure.

So painful was the situation at times that men of weak nerve buried their faces in the dirt and clawed the soft ground as if trying to hide themselves, while stouter hearts climbed over them and went on towards the enemy. Some groups lost direction, and worked too far to the right or too far to the left, but they soon got their bearings and found their way to O.G.1. The men of " A " and " D " Coys. reached O.G.1. about the same time that the 22nd Battalion entered O.G.2., and they then assisted in ejecting the enemy from the second objective, where the Hun was making a determined stand. In this work Lieut. F. R. H. Hays, who was killed the next morning, played a very commendable part, having gallantly led the first two platoons of "A" Coy. in the attack.

The troops immediately commenced the work of mopping up, that is, disposing of the enemy in the trenches, clearing the dugouts, and passing prisoners to the rear. Sergeant E. H. D. Edgerton played a gallant part in this work. The method of clearing the dugouts was simple and effective. A phosphorous bomb was thrown down the steps, and any Germans below were thus smoked out. One dugout to which this treatment was applied unfortunately took fire, and blazed furiously through the night. This was a loss to us, as there were only two of these deep dugouts which had not been demolished by our bombardments, and the other one was full of badly wounded Germans.

At about 1 a.m. the 22nd Battalion reported that they had secured O.G.2, and the Seventh Brigade on the right advised that they had also gained all their objectives. This news of the complete success of the attack was very heartening, and the men at once set about consolidating the line in preparation for the certain artillery retaliation and probable counter-attacks.

Our artillery fire had been most effective, for the trench, as a trench, was almost unrecognisable, while the numbers of enemy killed and wounded testified to its deadliness.

The remaining hours before dawn were spent strenuously in the work of re-forming the trench and rebuilding the parapets with sandbags; and when daylight came good progress had been made.

About this time the enemy made an effort to deliver a counter-attack. Out of the morning mists and battle haze parties of Germans were observed pressing forward, but our fire scattered them before they reached our lines, and those who later reached our trenches came in as prisoners.

The success of the operations was largely due to the personal efforts of Brigadier-General Gellibrand, who had gone forward to the line and remained there directing the units of the Brigade in the consolidation of the captured positions.

As O.G.1 appeared to contain more men than it was necessary to expose to heavy enemy shell fire, it was decided to reduce the garrison, and a number of the men were moved back to the old jumping-off line about 150 yards in rear. This subsequently proved a very prudent move.

When the morning mists had cleared away we anxiously scanned the country from our new position. The view extended across a wide valley towards the ruined village of Courcellette, and on the far side of the valley groups of retreating Huns could be plainly seen, indicating that our assault had resulted in a severe defeat for them. Here and there batteries of enemy guns were drawn up in the open with the horses standing by ready to pull them out quickly should a further advance be attempted on our side. This seemed a favourable opportunity for the cavalry to attempt the expected break through, but it was not availed of, and the Hun soon pulled himself together. His guns began a heavy bombardment of our communication lines and the newly won positions, and further efforts were made by the German infantry to regain the Ridge, but their advances were repulsed. The new line was firmly held.

Naturally we suffered severely in this heavy fighting, and our next care was to remove the wounded, for whom there was no shelter in the battered trenches.

It was customary in an engagement of this description for parties of men from units not in action to assist the regular regimental stretcher-bearers in removing the wounded. The heavy hostile fire, however, made it extremely difficult on this occasion for any movement to or from the line, and the bulk of the work fell on our own bearers, assisted by volunteers from the transport section and the companies. These bearers worked magnificently, carrying through the continuous shell fire and never resting so long as a wounded man remained in the front line. Later in the day parties of the 21st Battalion rendered assistance in this work.

The number of enemy wounded was also considerable. One dugout was found to contain over 50 badly wounded

Germans. It was discovered that this dugout had been used as a front line hospital, and a German doctor informed us that they had been unable to shift their wounded for several days owing to the intensity of our artillery fire. The fact that all of these wounded enemy soldiers were removed from the line speaks well for the humanity and impartiality of our stretcher-bearers.

The German doctor, who spoke English fluently, volunteered to remain in the firing line, and he carefully attended to our own wounded. Orders subsequently came up to pass back all unwounded prisoners, and he left the line. We heard with much regret that he, with others, had been killed by a shell on the way out.

During our advance on the night of the 4th-5th our troops suffered heavy casualties from machine-gun fire which enfiladed them from the left. Observations during the following day led to the discovery of a strong German post in that direction. Our " B " Coy., in supports, and part of the 23rd Battalion developed a keen interest in the Hun at this point. Arrangements were made for the bombardment of the post by trench mortars. Our men watched with the utmost satisfaction the havoc wrought by the mortar bombs as they crashed upon the enemy. Terrified Huns made off in all directions, some crawling, and some dashing from shell hole to shell hole, but most of them came under the fire of our waiting riflemen, who exposed themselves in the excitement of " potting " the discomfited Germans.

Then Captain Nicholas, O.C. " B " Coy., called his N.C.O.'s together and informed them that the enemy post had to be captured. A party composed of half-a-dozen N.C.O.'s and men was formed for the attack, which was to be made in the afternoon. It was a daring venture to attack a machine-gun post in broad daylight, but it was typical of " B " Coy.'s commander. Captain Nicholas, with Corporal Barnard, led the party, which included Sergeant Bob Nicholls and Sergeant Cliff. Ellis. The attackers, armed with bombs and rifles, " went over the top," and straight for the enemy post. A trench leading to the enemy's position was found and followed up.

Fortunately for the party the trench mortars had done their work thoroughly, and the post was full of German dead. In a radius of 40 yards from the strong-post there were fully 50 Huns who had been killed by the trench-mortar bombardment.

Captain Nicholas took possession of a German machine-gun, and conveyed it back to Headquarters, and Lieut. Hughes was sent up to take charge of the captured German post.

Sergeant Ellis was then detailed to explore the trenches in this locality, and find their connection with the forward positions captured by our troops during the preceding night. This duty he successfully carried out.

About an hour before dusk on the 6th "B" Coy. was ordered to reinforce the 22nd Battalion in the front line. Captain Nicholas sent his men forward over the open. After a brisk sprint they landed in the firing line. That was another daring manoeuvre, but it was a successful one, for the men reached the forward trench without a casualty.

On the morning of the 7th the Germans made another attack on our line, but the men stood up to them with coolness and deliberation, and scattered them before they reached our positions.

In earlier operations the airmen had experienced great difficulty in accurately locating the positions captured by the attacking troops. On this occasion a polished tin disc was fixed to the back of each man's tunic. It was believed that the reflection of the sun on these discs would indicate to the airmen our situation, and the artillery would thus be correctly advised of our whereabouts. Results proved that the idea was not quite sound. The reflection of the sun on the discs was so strong that the enemy gained as much advantage from it as our own artillery. Even at night the light of the flares reflected the presence of our troops. The discs courted enemy fire wherever they glittered in the rays of the light, and they were soon discarded.

Our Lewis gunners, who included such excellent soldiers

as Sergeant A. A. Ball, W. Graham, Walter West, and M. M. L. Dobbie, were a tower of strength to the Battalion. Lieut. Walter Godfrey, M.C., who had charge of a trench mortar gun until badly wounded, also greatly inconvenienced the enemy. Lieut. J. Clark, a popular young officer of " D " Coy., was killed in the attack.

The N.C.O.'s killed in action during the operations from 26th July to 7th August included Coy. Sergeant-Major A. G. Hawkins, Sergeants A. K. Roebuck, A. Ross, A. W. Armstrong, T.-Sergts. A. J. Reville, J. Ould, and Corporal J. B. Swanton. Many of our finest Anzac men had also fallen.

The 7th August brought us relief, when the Fourth Division took over the Second Division's sector at Pozieres. The Sixth Brigade had been in action for 13 days. To say that we were glad to hand over to fresh troops is expressing it very mildly. Men did not need to be told twice to take their departure from that front.

The 24th Battalion rested at Tara Hill, in the direction of Albert, on the night of the 7th. Here we suffered a heavy blow. The German guns were active that night, and a heavy shell burst in a disused gunpit temporarily occupied by our Headquarters staff. Major C. E. Manning (second in command), Captain W. Tatnall, M.C. (adjutant), Captain H. Plant (R.M.O.), and Lieut. J. B. N. Carvick, M.C. (assistant adjutant) were killed by this one burst, and the C.O. (Lieut.-Colonel Watson) was rescued, in a state of collapse, from under the heavy debris of the ruined shelter. This sad event, after the ordeal of Pozieres and the heavy casualties sustained there, had a depressing effect on all ranks, and the Battalion was not in the happiest of moods as it tramped away on the 8th to Warloy-Baillon to reorganise its broken ranks.

When General Birdwood heard of the loss of these four officers he wrote as follows to Lieut.-Colonel Watson:
—" I cannot tell you how extremely sorry I was to " hear about that disastrous shell. It is one of those " things of which nothing can be said. It is a great " blow, after the heavy losses at Pozieres. I well know " what excellent fellows Manning and Plant were, and how

"you will feel their loss." General Birdwood added that if our C.O. was unable to return to the field he hoped to be able to meet him some day to personally thank him for the good work the Battalion had done under his command.

Captain G. M. Nicholas was promoted major, and took command of the Battalion, with Lieut. I. A. Macindoe as adjutant. The company commanders were:—" A " Coy., Captain G. S. McIlroy; " B " Coy., Lieut. R. H. Jones; " C " Coy., Captain T. C. E. Godfrey; " D " Coy., Captain W. M. Trew.

It was a relief to be moving away from such a place as Pozieres, but we had a suspicion that it would be only a brief respite. Already there were reports that the First Division was preparing to go back to the front.

We had a few days at Warloy, and when the troops had rested and looked fit 'for the journey we set out for Berteaucourt, which was to be our resting area for a week.

While at Warloy the Battalion, with other units, was lined up on the road outside the village and inspected by His Majesty King George, who was on a visit to the front.

Berteaucourt and the contiguous village of St. Ouen were not the worst places we encountered. The people were hospitable and optimistic, and the boys had many a good meal of meat, eggs, and chips at the houses which traded in these things.

On the 18th we started back to the front, and on the first night of the journey camped in an apple orchard at La Vicogne, with no shelter but the fruit trees, while rain fell in a soaking deluge. Toutencourt and Harponville were other resting places on the way, and on the 21st we arrived back at Albert, where we bivouacked for the night at the Brickfields. Fatigue parties were sent out on various duties on the following day, and in the afternoon orders were received to prepare for action. It was a hard day for many of the men. The fatigue parties, after toiling all day, arrived back just in time to move off to the line.

MOUQUET FARM.

Before the advent of the Australians into the Somme Push the German trench system continued from Pozieres away to the left in front of Thiepval and Beaumont Hamel. Thiepval had proved practically impregnable to repeated and gallant frontal attacks by British regiments. The capture of Pozieres and the ridge beyond meant that Thiepval, some two or three miles away, was really in the left rear of the Australian Corps, whose line on the ridge now ran close to Mouquet Farm. In days of peace a farm so named had once marked the site, but the spot was now a redoubtable stronghold in the German system, with deep subterranean shelters and tunnels running away to the rear. Outflanking efforts had also been made at Beaumont Hamel, on the left of Thiepval to us, but these not proving successful, it was decided to drive the Australian wedge still further into the enemy defences on the Pozieres side. Mouquet Farm was where the thin end of the wedge was driving, and this sector was consequently subjected to the enemy's heaviest concentration of artillery fire. At times a veritable deluge of shells rained on the front of this spot, and the trenches were in places utterly destroyed. The German barrage fire was particularly deadly.

It was here that the 24th Battalion was to resume activities.

Setting out from Albert late in the afternoon on 22nd August we reached Pozieres in broad daylight, and half-a-dozen enemy aeroplanes overhead reported our presence to the German gunners, who gave us one of the liveliest hours of our lives while we struggled through the communication trenches to our positions. Fallen trees, tangled telephone wires, and a variety of obstacles hindered our progress. In spite of the feeling we had that we must all be blown to fragments before we reached the line, we pushed on, and the relief was accomplished successfully, though the stretcher-bearers were busy with wounded, and the whole of the shell-churned field, particularly when darkness overtook us, was like a horrible deathtrap.

The 24th Battalion was to take over from the 9th and 12th Battalions. " C," " D," and " B " Coys. were placed forward, while the greater part of " A " Coy. was posted in support for a few hours in Fourth Avenue, a sap running off Kay's Trench, so well known to us in the Pozieres engagement. " C " Coy. suffered heavily while moving in. The guide was killed, and the officers pushed ahead with their platoons with uncertainty. The intense darkness and the heavy shell fire disorganised the parties, and at the hour appointed for the relief only about a dozen men out of " C " Coy.'s four platoons and one platoon of " A " Coy. (which had been attached) had reached the line. The rest of the men groped their way forward by degrees, and the night was well advanced before the relief was completed. Gas was prevalent over the whole field, and added to the difficulties of the situation, which were beyond description. Lieut. W. A. Coward, a Duntroon cadet, who had joined the Battalion in Flanders, was killed, and a number of our finest troops were among the casualties.

Early in the morning " A " Coy. moved forward and took over the left flank of the Battalion's sector from " C " Coy., which was sent round to the right.

Regiments of the Prussian Guard were at this time holding Mouquet Farm. In view of the evident strength of the enemy, preparations were at once made to meet an expected attack, which, however, did not eventuate. We were also warned to look out for gas. At this time the enemy H.Q. had strong faith in the effectiveness of poisonous gases emitted from canisters which were carried to his front line to be used when the wind was favourable. Occasionally his troops at Mouquet Farm were observed carrying these canisters on their backs, and were fired on by our machine gunners and snipers. A number were hit, and in several instances the canisters exploded, and gave off clouds of smoky vapour.

When the Battalion had established itself in the line, parties of "C" and "B" Coys, went out to make advanced posts and dig communications. Meanwhile the Boche bombarded our positions and reduced our fighting strength.

An old German shed in the quarry on the left of the

Battalion sector was used as " A " Coy.'s headquarters, and also as a temporary aid-post, where the bearers attended to the wounded and kept them sheltered till daylight, when they were evacuated with less danger, as Fritz usually slackened his barrage after daybreak.

This quarry was fortunately situated with the steep side nearest to the enemy, and the men of " A " Coy. perched up just under the lip were thus fairly safe from anything but a direct hit.

On 24th August we received orders to change over in broad daylight with the 21st Battalion, then on our right. It seemed a suicidal move, as it was difficult to find a portion of the line where a man could stand upright without exposing himself, but in war obedience to orders is the fundamental principle governing all operations. So we prepared to obey. Fortunately, an attack by the Scots on our left partly diverted the attention of the enemy, and the change over was carried out successfully, but not without loss. Among the killed was Sergeant A. B. Arnel, M.M., a soldier whom, like many other brave men who fell in those days, the unit could ill afford to lose.

The Huns effected a relief of their front line troops that night, and our guns penalised them severely during the operation.

At about 5 p.m. on the 25th the enemy put down a heavy barrage behind our line, cutting us off for the time being from all communication with the world excepting his strong forces in front, and it looked as if we were to experience very close contact with his mustering troops. Our line was defended by a mere handful compared with the strength of the enemy, and there were no troops close enough to come to our aid in time to save the position had we been overwhelmed. In that very precarious situation all waited grimly for the expected German charge, but for some reason the Boche did not attempt an assault. Later we came to the conclusion that the enemy had himself feared an attack by us that evening, and the object of his barrage had been to prevent such a development.

RED AND WHITE DIAMOND.

It rained during the night, and the trenches became boggy and slippery, and added to the general unpleasantness.

The Boche specialised in Minenwerfer bombs. These deadly big bombs were fired at a high angle across No-man's-land on to our trenches at night. Their direction could be followed by a faint fiery trail resembling that of a rocket, but they fell so swiftly and so vertically that there was little hope of getting out of their way.

Bombing parties were sent out to attack enemy strong posts in the vicinity of the Farm. These activities were intended as a diversion to facilitate an attack on the left. A party under Sergeant Robinson effected an entrance into the enemy's position from the south, and exhausted their ammunition on the Boche before they withdrew. Sergeant G. D. Pollington led a party which advanced from the northeast, but was met by fierce machine gun fire. A number of bombs were bestowed upon the Huns, who responded with "potato mashers."

At dawn on the 26th the 21st Battalion attacked and captured a portion of a trench occupied by the enemy on the left, and our "B" Coy. went forward to link up with this advance by digging in on a line conforming with the new position on their flank. The Boche shelled the new line all the morning, and the locality became so hot that one of our strong posts had to be evacuated. The 21st Battalion was also obliged to fall back a short distance, but dug in about 200 yards from the position from which they moved forward.

Lieut. J. A. Mahony and a party of the 24th Battalion, who were assisting in the work of consolidating the front at the time the advance was made, distinguished themselves by dropping their picks and shovels and joining in the fight. They attacked the Huns at an opportune stage of the operations, and put the enemy to flight. Lieut. Mahony was awarded the M.C. for this enterprise.

The Germans afterwards attempted a sneaking attack on our positions, but they became scattered in shell-holes in No-man's-land, where our men inflicted heavy losses on them with well-aimed rifle grenades.

Our line had the form of a salient, the most advanced point of which was directly opposite the enemy stronghold at the Farm, now nothing more than a heap of debris above ground, but a labyrinth of tunnels and capacious chambers underground, where a strong garrison held out by the aid of a nest of machine-guns.

"B" and "D" Coys. occupied the section facing the Farm, and Lieutenant A. A. Ball, now in charge of Battalion Lewis Gun section, was posted here with a crew of his excellent gunners.

In order to strengthen our front, extra strong-posts were established in front of our line, and these posts were linked up with the trench by digging connecting saps. A party under Lieut. C. A. A. Ellis established a post on the right of the Farm, and another post, under Lieut. R. O'Connor, was constructed near the quarry and close to the ruins of a house held by the enemy. These operations and also patrols and other duties kept the troops strenuously engaged every night.

The gallantry and resourcefulness of our men were typified by a patrol which one night advanced unusually close to the German line, and had one of the party (Lance-Corporal Harris) badly wounded. Falling back a short distance, the patrol coo-eed for stretcher-bearers, but as their calls were not heard Corporal (afterwards Lieutenant) McLachlan, M.M., returned to our line and procured a stretcher, returning to the wounded man and rescuing him from under the nose of the Boche. That intrepid party was led by Sergeant (afterwards Lieutenant) McCooey, D.C.M. Private J. T. Pengelly also distinguished himself by daring patrol work on this sector.

So many of our men were put out of action that by the 26th—our last day in the line there—the situation was causing our company commanders no little anxiety. What men were left were more or less exhausted, and if the strong enemy forces in the "Farm" had attacked that day our weak garrison must have been hard pressed, if not utterly overwhelmed. There were signs of German activity all day, and as a means of preventing an enemy assault our artillery put down a heavy barrage in the narrow space between the opposing lines. Our men suffered by that bombardment, but it kept the enemy in check.

When our Battalion was looking for relief, orders came for a bombing party of 24 men under Lieut. E. V. Smythe (afterwards temporary major, M.C. and bar) to attack Mouquet Farm immediately.

It was regarded by those in the front lines as a suicidal effort, but Lieut. Smythe, with characteristic valour and coolness, merely asked if the men were ready, and then set forth to carry out the order. It was found difficult to secure 24 men fit to undertake the task. The party was selected with a forlorn hope.

As our artillery was engaged shelling other localities a bombardment of the Farm by trench mortars was ordered to precede the attack. Only two mortars were left in action in the line, and the ammunition available was so limited that when it had been exhausted the German stronghold had hardly been affected. Representations were therefore made by the acting C.O. (Major G. M. Nicholas, D.S.O.) to headquarters that the task was impossible without the assistance of heavy artillery, and the projected assault was cancelled.

The audacity of the proposed adventure earned for Lieut. Smythe the title of "Mouquet Bill." It was fortunate that the operation was abandoned, for the strength of the German position at Mouquet Farm was later demonstrated when the whole of the resources of the Fourth Division had to be employed on this sector.

During these trying days in the line at Mouquet Farm we lost some of our best troops. In addition to the casualties already mentioned, the N.C.O.'s killed in action or fatally wounded included the following:—Sergeants A. S. Burvett, H. C. Tyrer, R. J. Robertson, T. Murphy, and J. C. Kerr.

The runners (despatch carriers) distinguished themselves by faithfulness in spite of peril and fatigue. Again and again they dashed over the shell-swept field with urgent messages for the commanders in the line, sometimes falling breathless into the trenches and holding up their despatches in triumph. Carrier pigeons were occasionally employed to convey reports from the line to divisional headquarters.

On the night of the 26th the enemy systematically obliterated portions of our trenches with Minenwerfer bombs, one of which killed 2nd-Lieut. R. Thomas and a dozen men. Lieut. Thomas had been promoted from the rank of lance-corporal a few days before the Battalion entered the line.

The Battalion was relieved on the night of 26th-27th August. It was daylight when the last parties filed through "Tom's Cut" and the "Avenues" which led to the La Boiselle-Albert road.

At Albert, where the remnants of the Battalion assembled on the morning of the 27th August, billets were provided for a brief rest, and on the following day we set out for Warloy, where our packs had been stored. Another day's march brought us to Herrissart, where we reached billets just in time to escape a heavy thunderstorm with torrential rain. Leaving Herrissart early on the 30th, we marched through heavy rain all the morning on our way to Bonneville, a distance of 14 miles. At midday the Battalion halted for lunch, but just when the men broke off the command decided to go on to Bonneville before the meal was taken. The troops had been on the road since 7 a.m., and, besides being wet, were exceedingly hungry. It is not a pleasant experience to be marching with full kit hour after hour without prospect of refreshment, and the worst feature of army life is that one never knows when the journey is likely to end. Distances which are given as three or five miles mysteriously extend to six and eight, eight to twelve, and twelve to twenty. With serious doubts about the distance to Bonneville, the boys fell in again and moved on, and an hour or two later the village was reached.

Here, on 31st August, General Birdwood presented ribbons to officers, N.C.O.'s, and men of the Brigade who had won decoration at Pozieres and Mouquet Farm. Major G. M. Nicholas had gained the D.S.O. for gallantry and initiative as a commander, Lieut. J. A. Mahony was awarded the M.C., Lieut. A. A. Ball, who had displayed marked coolness and gallantry as machine-gun sergeant, received the D.C.M., and a number of men, including several stretcher-bearers, were awarded the Military Medal.

General Birdwood, addressing the troops in that happy, homely way of his, informed us that Roumania had entered the war on the side of the Allies, and that the outlook was growing more favourable every day.

Several days were devoted to reorganising the companies. Promotions were in the air, as casualties had left a number of vacancies, particularly in the ranks of the N.C.O.'s.

Another move was made on 3rd September, when we marched to Gezaincourt, passing through Candas on the way. It was Sunday, and the sounds of church bells in the villages and booming guns at the front seemed to us a strange discord. In the billets that evening there were other discordant sounds. While some of the lads sang well-known hymns, others engaged in bombing attacks with green apples from the orchards.

On the 4th the Battalion paraded on the high ground above the village, and the acting C.O., Major G. M. Nicholas, D.S.O., had some very plain words to say to men whom he described as "shirkers"—men who were inclined to leave the fighting line on the least pretence, and hang around dressing stations seeking the sympathy of the medical officers. These remarks were provoked by the critical position in the line at Mouquet Farm, where a handful of each company held on against tremendous odds, yet after the Battalion was relieved the strength of the unit perceptibly increased. The 24th Battalion was not unique in that respect.

Leaving Gezaincourt at 5 p.m. on the 5th we marched to historical Doullens, where we entrained the same evening for Belgium.

BELGIUM.

The Battalion detrained at Proven, near Poperinghe, on the Ypres front, at 3 a.m. on 6th September, and after a route march in the rain we found ourselves in the area where the camps bore the name of Canadian cities, such as Winnipeg, Ottawa and Montreal. Our Battalion occupied the Winnipeg Camp. It was on this part of the front that the Canadians had made their fame, for Ypres was to the Canadians what Gallipoli was to the Australians. It was here that the Germans had made their first attacks with poison gases, and the locality was still a danger zone in this respect. Everywhere there were signs of the precautions to be observed continually. Every change of the wind was announced by sign boards and arrows, and gongs were provided at every camp for the purpose of giving the alarm when the approach of gas was expected.

The new box respirators made their appearance at this time, and the troops practised "gas mask drill" till they had all become expert in the use of the respirators.

With pleasant weather, light work on the front, and plenty of leisure time for sport, the days passed all too quickly. The autumn days would soon be gone and dreaded winter would follow with all its sting.

One of the advantages of the Winnipeg Camp was its large corrugated iron concert hall, erected by the Canadians for army amusements. Here the 24th Battalion boys had many a happy night. Many of the men will remember the entertainment which concluded with a "pathetic" little drama, entitled "A Night in Cairo," in which the actors, with the assistance of the transport section's mascot monkey and the use of blacking as face paint, attempted to portray some of the scenes of the Egyptian capital. The drama was entirely unrehearsed, and not one of the performers knew what he was going to do or say till he got on the stage. When the monkey attacked the actors the play was decidedly entertaining—for the audience, at least.

The padre (Chaplain-Captain Goidanich) had an inspiration, and resolved to have a cinema show in the hall for the troops. He called at Divisional Headquarters and asked for the loan of some films. When he had secured promises for the minor parts of the necessary equipment for a picture show, he added, "Well, now all we need are the cinema machine and the engine!" His resourcefulness was so appreciated that he got the whole plant. The next difficulty was to find an engineer and an operator. Privates Jack Shaw and Walter Luxford began experiments. The engine snorted violently for a minute, then stopped; started, and stopped again. And the days passed while the troops waited impatiently for the pictures. Perserverance won, and those two boys made good on that job, with the result that Shaw eventually became a master cinema man in the A.I.F., and Luxford was electrical engineer and lighting expert for the Anzac Coves, the most renowned of all A.I.F. concert parties. That spirit was typical of the men of the 24th Battalion.

At the Winnipeg Camp football was the popular recreation, and the Battalion was able to form a team, which for a long time defeated all comers. One memorable match was that in which our boys met the 21st Battalion team and gained a decisive victory. Matches between the officers and N.C.O.'s provided keen enjoyment for the troops, who relished the privilege when "barracking" of calling the officers' by their Christian names or nicknames. Even the Acting C.O. was not exempt from the popular practice. Off the football field he was "Major Nicholas," but when he was chasing the ball the lads exhorted him to greater feats by shouting "Go on, Nic!" The officers looking on became highly excited as they yelled, "Go on, offs.!" and the Diggers employed all their powers of humor in supporting both sides.

Several sports meetings were held in delightful weather. Soldiers who adopted the role of bookmakers laid the odds for all events, and it must be admitted that the element of speculation (to use a better word than "gambling") was pronounced among all ranks.

General Plumer (nick-named "Walrus" because of his

tusk-like white moustache), the veteran defender of the Ypres salient in the earlier and more critical days of the war, reviewed the Australians at this time. On another occasion we had the privilege of waiting in the rain to be inspected by a Russian General.

Major Nicholas having been appointed to the staff of the 2nd Division H.Q., acting Lieut-Colonel R. F. Fitzgerald, D.S.O., took over the Battalion for a few weeks, until Lieut.-Colonel Watson, C.B., V.D., resumed command on 12th October. Capt. Ellwood succeeded Lieut. Macindoe as adjutant.

In the large town of Poperinghe, where the men went often to enjoy themselves in the estaminets, to attend picture shows and English Army concerts, and to spend their pay on good meals at high prices, the German shells were slowly wrecking the buildings. Every week the shops became fewer, for the inhabitants were getting out through fear of the enemy's long range guns.

It was a long walk to Poperinghe. One of our sergeants borrowed a transport horse for the journey. After a good day in the town it was more than he could do to sit on that horse for the return to camp. So he gave the mount to a Belgian in the street, saying, "I don't want 'im, you can have 'im!" The Belgian was convinced that the Australian was a good hearted fellow, but three days later, when the transport section, after a weary search, found the horse, he changed his mind.

Meanwhile the men were doing various kinds of work on the front. Some were mining the German positions at Hill 60, some digging trenches and some toiling on roads, gun pits, and other jobs. For a while the unit was in the line at Zillebeke, outside Ypres, in the direction of Lille. Here, in dugouts along the old railway bank, the men voted on the conscription issue in Australia. The poll occasioned many heated debates, and these arguments, like the voting, indicated that the majority of the soldiers were opposed to conscription. Their attitude was that they did not desire conscripts in an army that so far had been raised by voluntary enlistment, while many adopted a most unselfish view, declaring that they would not vote to compel any man to come out to a life that was so perilous and hard.

Relieved from the line at midnight on 19th October, the Battalion passed back through Ypres and boarded a train for the Steenvoorde district, where we were billeted till the 22nd. While in this locality the village of Abeele was the rendezvous in the evenings.

BACK TO THE SOMME.

The Australian units in Belgium had been issued with maps of the Ypres front, and if the Somme offensive had been as successful as the high command had hoped, we would probably have found ourselves pushing the German line in the north, but it now came to our knowledge that we were going back to the Somme, and none of us relished the prospect, though nobody was much concerned about it.

The weather was getting less favorable as the days passed. It rained often and the temperature fell perceptibly. We had several stiff marches on the road to the railway, passing through Watten, and reaching St. Omer on the night of 24th-25th October. The railway journey ended at Longpre, and was followed by a march of about ten miles in search of the mean little village of Brucamps.

On the 27th a column of French motor-'buses came to our aid and took us through Flexicourt, Amiens and St. Sauveur to Buire. Here, on the Somme, winter appeared to have already set in. Mud held everything in its grip. Lucky for our peace of mind that we did not know at this stage what mud was to mean to us through the next six months. While at Buire the men explored the villages of Ribemont and Mericourt, the railhead at the latter place, and the whole of the surrounding country. Their observations were not for nought, for it was in these localities that we met the Boche in his sensational advance in the Spring of 1918.

November, 1916, was surely our worst month on active service. It was a period of indescribable agony.

Setting off from Buire on the 2nd, and taking with us by train from Mericourt a quantity of timber and a few tarpaulins, we arrived at Longueval. Our unit had been detailed for work on the extension of a railway in the vicinity of Delville Wood, about four miles in rear of the line, and the scene of a terrific struggle by the South Africans in the days of the Somme Push. There was no camp

EFFECTS OF SHELL FIRE.—A typical village scene on the Somme, 1916-1917.

or shelter of any kind here, and the men were marched on to a vacant piece of ground and informed that this was to be their "home." A dog might have died at the thought of trying to camp in such a spot. Mud and shell-holes were its conspicuous features. It was encompassed by the main roads, on which all the traffic of war ploughed through the slush; howitzer batteries on the edge of the wood kept up a continual din and drew enemy shells; the wood was reeking with the stench of the dead, and the whole aspect was one of turmoil and discomfort. The troops did not possess a blanket, and all that offered for shelter from rain and cold, as well as shells, were their waterproof sheets and greatcoats. Yet they settled down to make the best of the situation. The work on the railway was begun immediately, and after a day of strenuous labour, shovelling, picking, and carrying heavy timber or rails, they came back to make themselves a hole to sleep on the sodden ground. The mud had to be shovelled away to get a resting place, but to attempt the digging of a funk-hole meant the creation of a small dam, for water drained into every excavation that was made. Next day a few tents appeared, and then sand-bags were obtained and used in the construction of low walls, over which Esquimaux tarpaulin coverings were placed.

This went on while the enemy harassed the camp with sudden outbursts of shell-fire. A main road ran along the crest of the hill on the reverse slope of which our camp was situated, and a battery of heavy guns was in position along the road. These guns and the continuous strain of traffic made the road and the surrounding country a favourable target for the enemy artillery. Sometimes men returned from work on the railway to find their shelters wrecked and gaping shell-holes where their rough beds had been. Men were killed there, too, for the troops were not always away when the shells came. Sick parades were largely attended. Everybody had a cold, some developed bronchitis, while rheumatism was as common as iron rations.

Nor did the men always have the privilege of resting in their damp shelters after their day's work. Many a night they came in to find they were detailed for fatigue duty to the trenches, and they set out on the long tramp through darkness and miles of mud to the line before they had time to eat the scant rations which were available for their tea.

Aeroplanes were busy when the November fogs were not too dense for observation. Enemy planes dropped bombs on our parties while they worked and on the camp while men tried to rest. Tanks wallowed about in the mud, packhorses and mules laden with shells trailed across the fields, and the guns boomed and flashed all night.

HARDSHIPS AT FLERS.

One of the eventful periods of this awful month began on the 4th (two days after our arrival at the front), when the Battalion was ordered up to support the Seventh Brigade, which was making an attack on the German line near Flers.

In the afternoon we moved across to the left of Delville Wood to take up reserve positions, occupying Crest Trench while awaiting further orders. Owing to the limited accommodation in Crest Trench, "A" and "D" Coys. were sent back to the camp near Delville Wood, but they had barely arrived there when they were called out again, and went back to the vicinity of Crest Trench, where the men were scattered in shell holes among batteries of field guns. Intense darkness and rain added to the discomfort of a wretched night, while several casualties were sustained from enemy shellfire. Fatigue parties were sent out to carry jumping-off ladders (used to enable assaulting troops to jump quickly out of the boggy trenches), ammunition and rations to the Brigade in action. A ration party under Lieut. F. P. Selleck was out all night struggling with these supplies. In spite of the long journey and the deep mud, shell fire, and other handicaps, every bag of rations was delivered to the forward area, where the Seventh Brigade troops almost wept with joy at the sight of food and drink.

On the evening of the 5th, "A" and "C" Coys. went forward and occupied Cobham Trench at close supports, the other two companies remaining in Crest Trench.

Nearby in Goose Alley the M.O. of the 24th Battalion (Captain Fraser) and his staff worked through the whole night in the rain dressing the wounded 7th Brigade men as they were brought in from the line. Our own casualties that night included several of our regular stretcher-bearers.

The Battalion moved back to the camp near Delville Wood on the 7th, and next day resumed work on the railway.

Lieut.-Colonel Watson left on the 9th to take charge of the Second Division Military School, and on the following day Major G. M. Nicholas, D.S.O., again took command of the Battalion.

Units of the Fifth and Seventh Brigades and the Northumberland Fusiliers attacked the enemy again on the 14th November, and the 24th Battalion went up to help with the stunt. The most urgent work was the carrying of wounded from the firing line to the aid-posts and from the aid-posts to the Field Ambulance Stations. It was on this task that many of our men were employed for two days. Numbers of the wounded had to be rescued under heavy fire from No-man's-land and carried over the mud and slush a distance of three miles. The strain, even with six men to a stretcher, exhausted the strongest of the troops. It was difficult to distribute rations to these men, as they were scattered over the field, and many of them carried on without a bite for 24 hours. Officers and N.C.O.'s shouldered stretchers with their men, as heavy casualties called for the utmost energy from all ranks. The wounded from English units on the front often found themselves in the kindly hands of the Australians. An English officer who was being borne out on a stretcher remarked that at the front he could never distinguish Australian officers from their men. "It might interest you to know," replied one of the party, "that the Australians who are carrying you include a lieutenant and two sergeants, and the other three are corporals."

While leading portion of the Battalion to the front to support the offensive, our Acting C.O., Major G. M. Nicholas, D.S.O., was killed by a 5.9 shell in an old German trench named Turk Lane. Major Nicholas was a gallant soldier, and his death, added to the strain of the difficult operations on the front at that time, had a depressing effect on all ranks. Captain T. C. E. Godfrey then took command temporarily. The companies, however, were at this time divided and engaged at different points, and were acting under directions from the Fifth and Seventh Brigades.

On 15th November our "C" and "D" Companies moved into the front line trenches, and 120 yards of the first line was occupied by "C" Company, "B" Company also moved up, and after occupying positions at Factory Corner, took up duty in the front line, under the C.O. of the 21st Battalion. Snow began to fall as the companies moved into position.

The units of the Fifth and Seventh Brigades, which had been seriously reduced in numbers by casualties and the effects of the severe weather, were mere remnants of their former strength. Repeated attacks had been made on the German positions here, and although success had finally been achieved, there remained in the hands of the enemy an important portion of trench which our command had determined to capture. Consequently another attack was ordered. The remnant of the 25th Battalion and "C" and "D" Coys. of the 24th Battalion were allotted to the task. "C" Coy. was commanded by Lieut. H. Rigby, and "D" Coy. by Captain C. M. Williams.

At 4.45 a.m. orders were received that the assault was to be made at 5 a.m. The officer in charge of the 25th Battalion, who was O.C. attack, considered that his men were not equal to the task, as they were exhausted by strenuous fighting. The attack was therefore postponed.

The command then decided that the effort should be made in the evening. The time selected was 7 p.m. That hour had passed when the runner bearing the order for the attack reached the officer in charge. The belated arrival of the messenger was not to be wondered at. It was only by superhuman efforts that men moved at all over that quagmire. In some places a man would do well if he proceeded a few hundred yards in an hour, and he would be fortunate if he was not bogged so hopelessly as to require assistance before he could extricate himself.

The outcome of the delayed operations was that Brigadier-General Holmes, attended by his Brigade major, investigated the position. It was considered probable that the trench in question might not be occupied by the enemy, who had been falling back to more favourable positions. The Brigadier made a reconnaisance, and found that the trench was unoccupied. Our troops were then sent forward through connecting trenches to take possession, and the necessity of sending them over the top and exposing them to murderous enemy fire was obviated. These developments were, needless to say, a great relief to the units in the line.

While holding portion of the line at this time our men one night heard a call from No-man's-land for stretcher-bearers. The call appeared to come from a spot close to the German line. Suspicious of German treachery, our officers at first declined to allow our stretcher-bearers to venture out, but as the call, which resembled the cry of a man in pain, was repeated persistently, two of our bearers resolved to go forth, being unable to resist the appeals of the distressing voice. They climbed out of the trench, and fell riddled with bullets! They were dragged back by our men, but one of the gallant pair (Pte. W. C. Silver) died in the trench.

Sgt. George Cumming, M.M. (killed at Montbrehain in 1918), distinguished himself by patrol work on this front.

The companies continued duty on this sector, sometimes in the lines and sometimes on fatigue work, until the 21st November, when we were relieved.

The period of operations at Flers will remain as a dreadful nightmare in the minds of the men who were there. The whole field was a vast bog, while rain, intense cold, and dense fogs continued day after day. Men strained themselves to the point of exhaustion as they floundered through the mire, sinking deep in the slush, embalmed from head to foot with mud, and often unable to extricate themselves from the grip of the morass. Their weapons were at times clogged and useless, their clothes soaked and grimy, and their hearts threatening to sink in despair as their bodies sank in the puddled earth. Fatigue duty entailed a strain from which flesh and blood might well have recoiled, for to drag heavy burdens over the long distances from the dumps to the trenches under such conditions was a task almost too great for any beasts of burden. Yet even where strong horses and mules gave up, men struggled on at the call of duty and for the sake of comrades who were depending upon their labours. Death was a welcome deliverer from the physical and mental agonies of these cruel days, while wounds added pain and suffering indescribable, and made the afflictions of stricken men worse than the accredited tortures of hell.

It was with difficulty we got our men out of the worse parts of the trenches. Wooden planks and pieces of wire had to be used to drag them out of the veritable "slough of despond" into which they sank. Some, unable to move, became alarmed by the thought that in the dark they might be left behind, and they cried out in their despair.

A North Lancashire Regiment, which relieved us at Flers, arrived in the line in small groups, thoroughly encased with mud. Many of their men had been bogged on the way. Their officers appeared confident that most of them would reach the trenches eventually. In handing over a company sector, one of our officers asked a Lancashire captain if he was not afraid of being attacked and driven out before the rest of his men arrived, as the Boche was very restless. The Lancashire man, a soldier of the regular army, who had been through Mons and many other hard battles, and looked upon the war as a life-long job, replied with an unconcerned air: "Oh, well, if they take it from us to-night, we'll take it from them in the morning. They always bounce off the North Lancs!"

On 22nd November the Brigade entrained at Montauban and went back to Dernancourt, and we had visions of a rest; but on the 24th, when the other Battalions prepared to move further away from the front, the 24th Battalion received orders to go back to the battle area and carry on with road work. Major W. M. Trew was acting C.O. at this

BOGGED IN THE MUD.—Transport difficulties during the winter.

time. The return journey to the front was to be made on foot, and we moved off, with long faces, on the 25th in heavy rain. Part of the unit went into "Sydney Camp," and "D" Coy. went further on to "Adelaide Camp." For the next week rain and fog made the mucky field the most miserable place in the world. The main roads to the front around Bernafaye were in a shocking state, and while the heavy traffic ploughed and splashed through mud and water, our men toiled to improve the tracks. Deep gutters and pits had to be dug at the sides of the roads to drain off the slush, timber put down where bridges would not have been out of place, and metal put in where it was not likely to sink out of sight.

The men waded through deep mud every time they went out from the camps or returned. The huts were approached by raised corduroy roads, and elevated duckboards led up to the doors of the huts. The roads had the appearance of small piers running out on to a sea of mud, and the huts might have been taken for bathing boxes on a beach where the water was too dirty for bathing. It was a compliment to some of these camps to name them after Australian cities, but we hoped it was never inferred that there was anything characteristic of Australia in these dreary places. "Sydney" Camp, "Melbourne" Camp, and "Adelaide" Camp were bleak rows of wood and iron structures, where shells and aeroplane bombs and machine guns kept men's nerves unsteady and frequently set their hearts palpitating, where the wind whistled through the shrapnel holes in the corrugated iron and eddied up through the wide cracks in the boarded floors, where the rain played tunes on the roofs, where snow piled itself up at the doors, where soldiers lived when out of the trenches, and where they lay down to sleep at night, but shivered more than slumbered.

Occasionally a small issue of coal would arrive, but as these events were decidedly rare the hunt for firewood became the most engaging task of the day. When every movable piece of timber had been consumed and fuel was as scarce as sunshine, the troops pulled off the pine lining boards of the huts and enjoyed the bright glow of the blazing fire they made—for a few moments only. Every half hour a board was sacrificed in some of the huts on a particularly bitter night. It was done reluctantly, but under a policy of suicidal necessity, for every board taken from the lining left the occupants of the hut more exposed to the wind and cold. This method of obtaining fuel was known as "Once round the hut."

A soldier, however, lives a moment at a time. If he had a favourite text from Scripture it would probably be, "Take no thought for the morrow."

Even in these camps, life was as uncertain as the spot where the next shell would land, and men thought it sensible to have a fire when they needed it, for who knew how soon they might be removed from the comforts of earthly fires?

The effect of German shells was not always to the disadvantage of the men. When the explosives destroyed a hut without affecting the personnel of the unit, the achievement was regarded as a kindly act on the part of the enemy, as it provided firewood for a dozen other huts for the day.

On 10th December the Battalion shifted to Pommiers Redoubt Camp, near Mametz, which was an improvement in respect to living conditions, but involved more perils from enemy shells. When Fritz strafed the camp the boys adjourned to the old trenches in the locality, and came back when the bombardment ceased.

In this camp one evening a party of men had a wonderful escape from death. "Ike" Wilson, who in camp always carried on as a barber, and half a dozen of his hut mates were seated round a brazier trying to keep themselves warm. A shell came through the iron roof, cut through the boarded floor, and burst in the soft ground under the hut. The whole structure, with its occupants, rose with a cloud of smoke and fell in a tangled heap. Men from other huts rushed to the rescue, and found heads protruding from the wreckage. "Ike" was saying, "Poor old Kelly, he's under there" (pointing to the ruins). "They're all under there," he declared. But Kelly and the others had by this time scrambled out and bolted, not knowing that "Ike" was left behind. They all escaped with bruises and shock. Fifteen minutes later Kelly, who was a stretcher-bearer, calmly presented himself at the A.M.C. hut and asked for a dose of cough mixture for his cold!

A batch of 200 reinforcements for the Battalion arrived at this time, but the weather, with fogs, rain, snow, and intense cold, was so severe that some of them were immediately returned to the base, as the M.O. considered them physically unfit to endure the life. The reinforcements regretted that they had not chosen a more favourable season for their initiation, but they at least had the consolation of the assurance that however long the war dragged on it could not get worse; the limits of misery, hardship, monotony and agony had already been reached.

The one ray of light, the one gleam of hope, that came to men at the front in those days was "Blighty" leave, while to further relieve the strain and monotony of life at the front a few men every day were granted leave to Amiens, and those who enjoyed this privilege made the most of it.

A move back to Adelaide Camp was made on the 23rd, and some of the transport vehicles got bogged on the way.

Fatigue duty, including the carrying of rations and other material to the line, kept us busy over Christmas.

A DISMAL CHRISTMAS.

"A Merry Christmas?" Where had that phrase originated? Certainly not on a Somme battlefield. The utmost good fortune the troops could hope for was to be out of the trenches on Christmas Day, to have a letter from home bearing appropriate greetings (which meant that such words as "happy" and "merry" were wisely omitted), a Christmas parcel from home with cake and a few other luxuries, sufficient inactivity to contemplate what Christmas meant under peace conditions, and to dwell on the happy memories of the past.

The men were optimistic and cheerful enough to make the best of the situation. Parties went out to scout for wine, ale, and such edibles as were procurable, and the cooks gave their hearty co-operation in the preparations for the "festival."

This fierce war, with an enemy who had no honour and whose promises or assurances nobody could put faith in, put the mere thought of even a partial cessation of hostilities on Christmas Day out of mind. "Peace on earth and goodwill toward men" was not part of the Prussian creed. Bloodshed, pain, hunger, privation, mental and physical strain on the battlefield, and tears and sorrow at home were what Germany had premeditated and created.

But the Allies were not asking for mercy. With the natural spirit of peace in their hearts, they were ever ready to fight, and for six months they had hammered the foe back from his strongest grip of the territory he had invaded. On this Christmas Day our thousands of guns despatched to the German lines special and extra greetings in the form of deadly shells. Away back from Albert the big 12in. and 15in. guns sent their earth-shaking tokens roaring overhead like the noise of a distant storm, the 8in. and 9.2in howitzers gave smaller presents, but not a lesser quantity, and the field guns distributed their gifts as if high explosives were the cheapest articles in Santa-Claus's catalogue.

In the trenches the infantry watched the enemy's lines with unrelaxed vigilance, while in the camps behind our lines the troops off duty drank to the health of the folks at home, feasted on the contents of parcels forwarded by the Red Cross and the Comforts Fund, sang Christmas carols, and listened to the noise of worn-out gramophones, accordeons and mouth-organs, only stopping the celebration momentarily when a German shell burst close or whistled threateningly overhead. Whenever an explosion was near enough to shake the huts, the boys would exclaim, "The same to you, old sport," as if Fritz had in that deadly missive said, "A Merry Christmas to whoever gets this."

"Furphies" ran riot at this time. One of these stories was that there was to be a big Christmas spread in No-man's-land, to be attended by the German and British troops. All arms were to be left in the trenches! Another specimen of these imaginations was that three divisions of Germans were to surrender at a certain point at 11 a.m.—evidently in time for Christmas dinner in the Allied lines.

Death, familiar to the armies at the front, did not leave us on Christmas Day. The troops in the trenches, the men who waded to the line with rations, the gunners who fed the batteries, the drivers who struggled with teams and motors, engineers who made or repaired roads and railways, and airmen who skimmed through the clouds and mists, all said farewell that day to mates who left the world of strife for more peaceful spheres.

A fatigue party from our Battalion had gone out to the trenches on Christmas Eve carrying to the boys in the line their Christmas gifts from loving relatives and friends at home. They came back without several of our brightest soldiers. One lad, whose songs and funny stories were better to his company than doctors' prescriptions, and who had gone out to his last duty singing "There's a Long, Long Trail," had crossed the Great Divide in the first hour of Christmas morning. In his pockets he carried letters just received from his home in Australia, including one from his mother, which we saw him read over and over as he sat in the hut on the previous afternoon. The letter ran:—

"My Dearest Son,—Although we can hardly hope that you will have a merry Christmas, we trust you will have some comfort on Christmas Day. Be assured that we will be thinking of you, and although we cannot have you with us, we feel sure that God will preserve you and will answer our prayers for your welfare."

Was the faith of that mother and her family of no avail? Were their prayers unheeded? If earthly welfare were all, it might be so. But a mother who prays has a wider vision.

A lad (one of the reinforcements) who accompanied this particular party to the line on that dismal night was so distressed, especially by the sight of wounded men sprawled in the mud, that he came back in tears. He was completely overcome next morning, and paraded sick. Crying bitterly, he declared to the doctor that "a man should get the V.C. for such an experience," "Yes, I agree with you," said the sympathetic M.O.; "but the boys have been doing that kind of duty, and often much worse, for a long time, and they've got to keep on doing it."

The other Battalions of the Brigade, which had been resting for a month, now returned to the front, and the 24th Battalion at once linked up with them to resume operations in the line.

Men of the sister Battalions named the 24th "The Roadmakers." That was a title of which we were not ashamed, for our men had earned this distinction while the other units were away from the front.

1917.
IN THE GRIP OF WINTER.

On New Year's Day, 1917, three companies of the Battalion were at Adelaide Camp, Montauban, and "A" Coy. at B Camp, Bernafay. At least, these were their billetting places. Many of the men spent the day on the construction of a light railway over the boggy ground. Others were making deep dug-outs at Miller's Sap.

On 3rd January "C" and "D" Companies went forward and occupied Needle Trench, supporting the 22nd Battalion, and on the 4th the other two companies were carrying duckboards to the front line trenches.

The 24th Battalion took over the front line from the 22nd Battalion on the 5th, occupying Summer, Fall and Zenith trenches. Men lost their big trench boots in the bogs, and greatcoats became so heavy through clinging mud that they were a burden. Patrol work in No-man's-land was a heartbreaking duty, and the wounded were evacuated with the greatest difficulty. After three days in the line the Battalion was relieved. We remained a night in supports at Needle Trench, and on the following day went back to camp. The troops were in a sad plight. In some cases the trench-feet complaint was so acute that the feet were badly discoloured and so swollen that boots could only be removed by being cut off. Men groaned with the pain and the burning sensation that afflicted their extremities.

The trench-feet complaint was the result of the combined effects of intense cold, stagnation of the blood, and the absorption into the skin, through the medium of mud, of germs with which the whole battlefield, with its insanitary conditions, was infested. The worst cases were removed on stretchers, while those who could put their feet to the ground, even with much pain, were obliged to walk out, hobbling along the duckboard tracks and roads like a procession of lame ducks, with their feet wrapped in strips of blankets and looking like big puddings attached to their legs, which in many cases were quite stiff with cold and tortured with rheumatic pains. More fortunate men carried the afflicted ones on their backs or helped them to hobble along at a slow pace, which could not be quickened even when the enemy shelled the procession, which he never failed to do when he observed it.

The trench-feet complaint became so serious that special and elaborate measures had to be adopted to combat it. The French army was in the same plight as the British. Medical conferences were held, and the form of treatment decided upon was regular washing of the feet, an ample supply of dry socks, and the application of an antiseptic and soothing powder. Foot troughs were constructed, coppers procured, hot water provided, and in every camp one of the most important operations of the day was the foot-washing parade. This treatment was also carried out in the trenches as far as possible, but unless the front was particularly quiet the care of the feet had to give place to the more pressing duties of warfare. Trench boots (also known as gum boots), which reached up to a man's knees, were no protection from the mud and water when a man sank to his waist in the mire. Often men were dragged out minus their big boots.

The rum issue was never more appreciated than it was in those days.

It was not to be wondered at that men dreaded the thought of going into the trenches under such painful conditions. One evening when the Battalion was ordered to move into the line, a man turned to his mates and said, "I'm not going in; I'm finished." A rifle shot rang out, and the man dropped on the ground. He had shot himself through the chest.

All men are not equally brave. Some funked it on the way to the trenches. It would be unjust to say that these men (who, thank God, were few in number) were cowards, for the agonies men were called upon to endure were never meant for flesh and blood.

The hardships of that period drove the "leadswingers" to

adopt every conceivable ruse to avoid the trenches. They were regular attendants at the sick parades, and shammed every ailment prevailing among the troops. Rheumatism was the popular complaint. One man was so crippled by this disability that he could not raise his leg when the doctor requested him to do so. His name was put on the list of sick to be evacuated to hospital. He limped away, but, thinking he was not observed, forgot his rheumatism, and was seen hopping with agility over the ropes of a tent. It was a fatal slip. Instead of going to hospital he found himself on a fatigue party leaving for the trenches with heavy duckboards.

Another man who had got past the medical officer and was being conducted, with others, to the Field Ambulance, became concerned as to how he would convince the medical officer at the hospital that he was, as the sick report indicated, suffering from diarrhoea. He decided that he had better change his complaint, and he asked the corporal to alter the sick report so that he would appear to be suffering the torments of rheumatism. The corporal had the report altered, but not in the way the man desired. The "patient" found himself back with his Battalion in a few hours, and a midnight jaunt to the front line prescribed for the cure of his pains.

At another sick parade a man asked to be excused from duty because he was subject to fits. The dialogue between the M.O. and the soldier was as follows:—

M.O.: How often do you have fits?
Soldier: About every ten days.
M.O.: When did you have the last?
Soldier: Yesterday.
M.O.: Well, you will have time to do another turn in the line before you have the next.

Exit soldier.

Our medical officer, Captain John Hardie, was a busy man during these trying days. The M.O., whose duty imposed upon him an obligation to keep at the front every man who was able to carry on, had an unenviable task. If medical officers had been able to act according to their feelings, few men would have been left on the field in these days, when the troops were suffering so severely under the trying conditions prevailing everywhere.

Fatigue duty continued day and night till the 14th January, when the Brigade was relieved, and we moved back to Ribemont, where we spent the rest of the month resting and training. A heavy fall of snow, and then intense cold, left the country covered in a thick mantle of white. On the swamps, where ice was six inches thick, the lads skated in their heavy boots and bruised themselves badly in their sport.

The beginning of February took us back to the front. Several days were spent at Scot's Redoubt Camp, near Contalmaison. Here, on the 2nd, Capt S. G. Savige was appointed adjutant.

Another turn in the front line, near the Butte de Warlencourt, followed on the 5th, when we relieved the 17th Battalion and had another period of activity in the muddy trenches.

Relieved by the 21st Battalion on the 8th, we returned to Pioneer Camp, leaving "C" Coy. at Middlewood Camp—a few tin shelters in the snow, where one might have suspected an Arctic explorer had housed his dogs.

A move to C Camp, Fricourt, was made on the 13th, and on the 17th we took over the front line near Le Sars from the 17th Battalion.

During all these days of wearying toil and hardship the casualties steadily mounted up.

It was a long trail from the camps around Fricourt to the line, and the men became familiar with the winding duckboard tracks past Martinpuich and in the vicinity of the line near the familiar Butte de Warlencourt. It was on this sector, surely, that the troops named themselves "The Duckboard Harriers," for these interminable tracks offered sufficient scope for a cross-country championship. The first trip over these tracks was a perilous journey in the dark, but the trail became so familiar to the men that the treacherous places were well remembered. Reinforcements arriving at the front from England at this time used to remark

WAR IN WINTER—Troops going to the trenches in January, 1917.

"PEA SOUP OR COCOA?"—One of many similar cheering institutions. The "Soup Kitchens" were open day and night.

on the difference between the theory of war as they were taught it in the training camps and their experiences in the field "In Blighty," one said, "we were trained to march with our heads up. Here a fellow has to keep his nose on his knees to trace the duckboards and to look out for holes!"

One of the most popular and useful institutions on the front at this time was the soup kitchen—a dug-out or shanty about midway between the line and the camps, where hot pea soup, coffee, or cocoa was always in readiness for the troops as they trudged back from the trenches. It was a kind of friendly halfway house, the sight of which lifted the lads at once out of the trench atmosphere and sent them on with the warm drink reviving their energy, singing and whistling, towards their destination.

The Battalion band was never more appreciated than it was at this period. As the troops came out from the line in groups they were met by the band at the soup kitchen and marched off to the camp to the strains of bright music. On some nights the band made four or five trips with different parties. After they had led one group of tired men to the camp they would go back several miles for another, and the performance was repeated until the last party had been brought in.

A camp where a Battalion "cleaned up" after a turn in the trenches was a scene of drying, scraping and brushing. Clothes and equipment had to be dried and relieved of the mud with which everything was coated. A fine day facilitated this work, but rain drove the troops to the necessity of lighting fires in fire-buckets in the huts. The fire was welcome enough, but in the absence of fuel it was rather a problem, which was only solved after a prolonged experiment with wet wood and a demonstration of the disagreeable properties of smoke and the ineffectiveness of bad language.

The long files of men trailing over the snow to and from the trenches was one of the impressive pictures of the war. The unchanging glare of the snow afflicted men with snow blindness. Fires were kept burning at the water points to prevent the pipes freezing. The roads, with the frozen snow tramped into a kind of glass pavement, were the scenes of many accidents, in spite of the precaution drivers took to cover the hoofs of horses and mules with pieces of blanket. Men wore sand-bags over their boots and walked with the greatest care. Yet men and beasts slipped, skidded and sprawled as if they were all helplessly intoxicated.

When water was required for purposes of ablution, the men sometimes went out to the shell holes with a bag and a pick and brought in blocks of ice, which were melted by the fires.

In the trenches, men off "post" sat on the sandbags or boxes with their feet in the water, dozed off to sleep, and wakened to find their feet set in ice.

The cold was so intense that a wet garment hung out to dry would be frozen stiff in a few minutes, and a bucket of water poured on the ground would be ice before it had time to find its level.

All through the long wet nights parties of our men patrolled No-man's-land and scented the movements of the Boche. Opposing patrols met and fought, and Fritz must have begun to feel the truth of that old saying, "There's no rest for the wicked."

While the snow lasted, the patrols were obliged to wear white overalls and to paint their steel helmets the same colour, as a man in ordinary dress on the snow was as easily observed at night, particularly in the bright moonlight then prevailing, as he would be in daylight. So men stole about like ghosts, but they were more real than spirits and much more dangerous. (The troops will probably not object to the admission that the white overalls worn by them were women's night dresses, purchased at a shop in Amiens.)

Casualties in the Battalion had been comparatively light for a month or two, but on 22nd February we lost a brave soldier in Cpl. M. M. L. Dobbie, a Lewis-gunner, who was killed while on duty in the trenches.

The Advance to Bapaume.

On 24th February, 1917, the monotony of the situation gave place to excitement and a new outlook. The Boche showed signs of giving way.

While the infantry had dragged themselves in and out of the trenches for four bitter months, sometimes ready to welcome death as a relief from their mental and physical agonies; while the gunners had fed their batteries day and night and the iciness of everything they handled stung their fingers like the burn of a hot iron; while the transport men had contended with difficulties which nigh broke their hearts; while the airmen, petrified and bitten by cold, faced the dangers of the sky, they had all done better than they knew; their reward came sooner than they had expected. Patrols from the front line had discovered that the Boche, having apparently reached the limit of his endurance in that scene of utter misery, was quietly evacuating his positions and retiring to more favourable country in rear.

The first intimation to the units in supports and reserves was an order, unexpected but exceedingly welcome, to "Stand to," ready to advance at a moment's notice.

The whole front was thrilled with a new life. Men tumbled over one another in their hurry to get on their equipment and looked to their arms. Runners dashed to and fro with urgent despatches, telephones were rushed with work, officers and N.C.O.'s gave instructions, quartermasters distributed rations, and the troops fell in to await the word to move off.

Reports of activities came from all directions. The cavalry was said to be assembled for a dash at a favourable moment. Our Light Horse Regiment was ready to join in the drive.

At night the suspense was relieved. The first parties began to move. The advance had begun.

The 24th Battalion was at this time commanded by acting-Lieut.-Colonel Fitzgerald, D.S.O. Major Bateman, who had been second-in-command, had been transferred to the 23rd Battalion, and Captain J. E. Lloyd, who had come to us from the 21st Battalion, acted as his successor.

The 24th Battalion was "standing to" at "Acid Drop" Camp on the night of the 24th February. Shortly after midnight, "C" and "D" Coys., under Lieut. O'Connor and Capt. Maxfield, were ordered to move up, and the other two companies waited until the morning. "A" and "B" Coys., commanded by Capt. Lloyd and Capt. W. H. Ellwood, arrived at "Flers Switch" on the forenoon of the 25th, and that night the Battalion was ordered to take over a sector of the front line facing Warlencourt. "C" and "D" Coys. had been sent on fatigue duty at the front, and had not returned when "A" and "B" Coys. moved into the line. Fortunately a heavy mist enveloped the front next morning, and the adjutant (Capt. S. G. Savige) took the risk of sending "C" and "D" Coys. forward in daylight. By this time "A" and "B" Coys., having reached the line at about 3 a.m., had pushed forward and established a thin line of outposts in front of Warlencourt on a sunken road. When the four companies were in position, the Battalion prepared to advance. The enemy had been raided by the 22nd Battalion, and had evacuated part of his line.

The position was very confusing for a time, as the Hun was mysteriously and suspiciously quiet. After excellent reconnoitring under the direction of Capt. Lloyd and Capt. Ellwood, the situation became clearer, and it was decided to advance on Warlencourt. The companies pushed on with a good deal of bluff, and we marched through the ruined village of Warlencourt and around it as if we owned the place. By this time the fog was lifting, and orders were given to dig in.

The advance through Warlencourt had been accomplished with few casualties. Cpl. J. A. A. Bruce was killed on the 25th.

The weather, favouring the retreat of the enemy and also our advance, took a decided change. The sun shone often, and the mud began to disappear.

A patrol under Lieut. G. R. Barclay and Lieut. F. W.

Murphy carried out a brilliant reconnoisance in the direction of Loupart Wood, advancing along the enemy trench system for about 1600 yards and gaining valuable information concerning the enemy's whereabouts. The patrol had a brush with the Hun in the Grevillers trench system, where some bombing took place. The Germans, it was discovered, had withdrawn to the Grevillers line, a distance of about 1000 yards, and were posted in Loupart Wood.

On the 27th February we were relieved by the 28th Battalion, and returned to camp at Fricourt. Here Major W. E. James rejoined the Battalion and was appointed second-in-command.

We were called up again on 2nd March. After taking breath at Sussex Camp, near Bazentin, the Battalion moved forward again by way of Malt Trench and Misty Way to get at grips with Fritz opposite Avesnes les Bapaume, near Grevillers.

Parties led by Capt. J. E. Lloyd and Lieut. E. V. Smythe entered Grevillers in search of the enemy, but he appeared to have evaded the village.

Then a number of raiding parties, or fighting patrols, under Lieuts. Seabrook, Barclay, Pollington and Granter, successfully engaged the Boche at different places, and the Battalion was enabled to advance its line considerably, having passed through Grevillers and driven the Hun towards the railway, working in conjunction with the 21st Battalion on our left.

After the long period of trench warfare, without appreciable change in the situation, this advance, particularly during the night, was a new experience, and everybody felt the lack of confidence in respect to the operations. The only safe course was to keep close on the heels of the enemy, and in the dark this was at times an exceedingly difficult task, owing to our not being familiar with the country and the nature of the German defences.

During these operations we suffered a number of casualties. Major James was wounded and evacuated, and Capt. Lloyd succeeded him as second-in-command. Lieut. G. R. Barclay, who had rendered excellent service, was wounded, and the killed included Sgt. A. B. Mundell, Sgt. E. Harrison, T/Sgt. A. J. Clegg, Cpl. Walter Snadden, and Pte. L. Trezise, all very gallant soldiers. Lieut. E. V. Smythe temporarily succeeded Capt. Lloyd as commander of "A" Coy.

The Boche attacked our outposts at several points, but was repulsed, and he was gradually pushed back on Bapaume.

Our successful advance was largely due to the initiative of Capt. Lloyd, who was untiring in his efforts to keep in touch with the enemy at every point. The troops, too, were eager to push ahead. The advance had a wonderfully heartening effect on all ranks, and although the strain was severe, the men were keener than they had ever been before during the war.

Lieut. Baldock and his signallers distinguished themselves by maintaining communications under fire. Lieut. Baldock was awarded the M.C.

The Boche left many traps for our men. Many old watches, revolvers and other appealing souvenirs lying about were attached by cords to hidden explosives. A few of our fellows were caught, but they soon became wary of these Hun tricks.

The scenes which attended the advance inspired the troops with new life. Along the main Albert-Bapaume road there was a double procession of war traffic, on one side the columns moving up, on the other the waggons and teams going back for fresh loads. There were howitzers hauled by tractors, lighter guns drawn by horses, motor waggons carrying material for repairs to railways and roads and shells for the guns, infantry units going forward to take up the fighting in their turn, ambulance cars with wounded, batches of enemy prisoners under escort, limbers with rations, working parties with picks and shovels, and groups of men on all manner of duties, all keen on their work and flushed with a sense of victory.

The whole equipment of war had to be moved up on to the new fields. Ordnance stores, workshops, hospitals, camps, and every department of the field establishment had to go forward. But it was pleasant work, for the old scenes of desolation on the Somme had been left behind, and green fields met the eye wherever one turned. All the villages, however, were more or less in ruins.

Troops going back to the Somme and passing such places as Le Sars, Martinpuich, Contalmaison, and Pozieres stood and gazed at the old battlefields with a deep feeling of satisfaction. That ground which had been churned in the cauldron of shell fire for months, where everything was demolished, battered and blighted, was now quiet and peaceful. What remained of trees and plants were bursting into leaf, and the birds, which had hung around through all the days of strife, were already rebuilding their nests. How sweet was peace!

The 24th Battalion had been in action for four days and five nights, and the men were greatly fatigued. They were therefore withdrawn. They had played an important part in the capture of Bapaume, for when our men handed over, the Germans were already quitting the town. As we withdrew on the night of 16th March we could see the buildings bursting into flames, and on the morning of the 17th the Australians hunted the German rearguard out of the streets. Brigadier General Gellibrand congratulated the 21st and 24th Battalions on the success of their operations and the considerable advance made during their four days of hard fighting.

There has been a good deal of discussion as to which unit first entered Bapaume. This honour belongs to the 23rd Battalion, which took over from the 24th Battalion on the night of the 16th-17th March and entered the outskirts of the town, chasing Germans out of the streets. The Eighth Brigade entered the main part of Bapaume, and is therefore rightly credited with the honour of occupation. The 23rd Battalion's front did not take in the main part of the town, but that unit continued its advance, following the Boche as far as Vaulx.

The 24h Battalion moved back by way of Hexam Road to Eaucourt l'Abbaye and Flers Switch, where, with improving weather, the men were able to make themselves fairly comfortable.

Salvage work on the field over which the Boche had retired was undertaken, and about £50,000 worth of material was collected in a few days. For this work the Battalion received congratulations from Corps Headquarters.

About 16 days were spent in the camps at Mametz and Becourt. Route marches and energetic training, with impromptu concerts and other amusements, kept all ranks occupied. These pleasanter phases of war carried us well into April.

Major F. Parkes, who had been on duty in the training camps in England, joined the Battalion again here.

April had opened with winter still holding the country in its merciless grip. Snow blizzards, rain, and wind swept the fields, though it was time these things were abating.

Thoroughly rested and in good heart, the Battalion set off for the front again on 13th April, under the command of Capt. Lloyd, acting C.O.

The Germans had meanwhile been pushed back to the Hindenburg line, which ran by Cambrai and Bullecourt, and the British command was preparing for what it was hoped would be decisive battles in the spring. Our Fourth Division was busy at Bullecourt, and the Second Division was already marked for its turn.

At dusk on 14th April the Battalion arrived at Beugnatre, after a march of about 15 miles, and fixed up shelters for the night, but orders were received to move on immediately to the front. The troops, exceedingly fatigued, got their equipment together and fell in with misgivings which they did not attempt to disguise. It was at times such as this that the hard life of active service impressed itself most forcibly upon the men. The prospects of battle never daunted their spirits when bodily strength felt equal to the task, but to go into action after a day's march which had reduced them to exhaustion tested men as severely as the fiercest fighting.

"B" Coy. (Capt. Ellwood) and "D" Coy. (Capt Maxfield) were to move forward with the 22nd Battalion and garrison the line, while "A" Coy. (Capt. Smythe) and "C" Coy. (Capt. Godfrey) were to follow as far as Noreuil.

The country here was all new to us, as the Battalion had never been in this area, and in the night, without guides, the two rear companies found it difficult to keep their direction. Vaulx was reached at 11 p.m. The adjutant (Capt. Savige) rode ahead and found a road junction where several tracks branched out in different ways. It was only a misfortune of war that the wrong track was chosen. At about 2 a.m. the two companies found themselves close to the front and, for the time being, hopelessly lost. The adjutant and Lieut. Baldock reconnoitred and inquired from a gun battery the direction of Noreuil. Striking across the strange country, which appeared to be made up mainly of sunken roads, Noreuil Gully was eventually reached, and here the men, ready to drop with exhaustion, pitched for the remainder of the well-spent night. At daylight, when all were snoring blissfully in spite of the din of our artillery around them, the transport drivers arrived with the rations.

Then from the front came the noise of battle, and immediately afterwards a strong force of enemy troops was seen swarming over the country towards Noreuil. In an instant everybody was astir. The Germans had broken through at Lagnicourt. Units for miles back were soon "standing to."

The dash of the enemy was quickly stopped. In Noreuil Gully were posted the Sixth and Second Machine-gun Companies, and these men at once brought their guns into action. Units on the flanks smote the Huns with a withering fire, field guns fired point blank at the advancing force, cooks abandoned their pots and took up rifles, and clerks on the Brigade staff turned out to join in the fusillade. Even the Brigadier was firing with the aim of a keen rifleman. It was the best bit of shooting our men had had for many a day. The Germans melted away, and the defeated remnants retreated at the double.

When those Huns started they had no idea what a foolish thing it was to rush into a hot bed of Australians, and very few of them got back to impart the bitter knowledge to their comrades. As they fell back they got held up on their own wire entanglements, and were shot down like trapped rats. The enemy force was composed of about 4000 Prussian Guards, all dressed in new uniforms and looking as fresh as troops on review, and it was subsequently ascertained from prisoners that they had attacked with the object of capturing the high ground near Vaulx in order to give the German command time to properly organise their defence on the Hindenburg line, to which they had been hustled from Bapaume.

The Germans had got dangerously close to our cookers that morning, and one of the cookers came out of action with scars of battle. The cooks were proud of their participation in the fight, and the cooker afterwards bore a gold stripe on the flue as a mark of honour showing that it had been hit in action.

Noreuil Gully (which was also known as Death Valley) was under almost continuous enemy gun-fire, and our companies there suffered many casualties.

After two days the companies changed over, "A" and "C" Companies going into the line, and "B" and "D" returning to the Noreuil Gully.

During four days we suffered about sixty casualties in this valley of death, which was packed with our artillery and was consequently a marked target for the enemy's guns.

We went back on the 20th to Favrieul, where the Brigade began preparations for even more eventful days.

The weather now gave up its unpleasant ways, and the sun announced the arrival of Spring. The woods were bursting into leaf, and the whole of the country here, having escaped the devastating effects of battle, had a pleasing and restful view, though a few miles away guns and all the implements of war were carrying on their deadly work.

The Battalion Band, which had been reorganised at the beginning of this year, was now a strong combination, having benefited by the arrival of a number of first-class instrumentalists with the 15th reinforcements. These bandsmen had been members of the Royal Park Camp Band which toured Victoria during the recruiting campaign.

Anzac Day (25th April) was celebrated pleasantly in the camp in the Favrieul Wood.

A system of preserving a nucleus of the Battalion had now been established. A small percentage of officers, N.C.O.'s and men, including Lewis gunners, signallers, and other sections, was to be left in camp every time the Battalion went into action, and after every engagement the personnel of the nucleus was to be changed, so that a different group of men would enjoy a rest on the occasion of every battle. This system would assure the unit a composite fighting force. however small that force became, and would preserve experienced men to fill vacancies caused by casualties.

BULLECOURT.

On April 11th the Fourth Australian Division had captured a portion of the Hindenburg line, but after a heroic fight, without supports, and eventually running out of ammunition, had been forced to evacuate. The Second Division, in conjunction with British regiments on a wide front, was to resume the offensive.

Many lessons had been learnt, and realising that we had rather a hard nut to crack, another attack could not be contemplated without much preparation and practice.

The fields around Favrieul were clear and free from shell holes, and a tract of country similar in contour to that over which we had to attack was selected for the rehearsals. Trenches were outlined, wire entanglements and roads represented by wire and tapes, and the whole field was set on exactly the same lines or bearings as those existing on the battle front.

At first the attack was practised in daylight, but when the men became familiar with the ground, these stunts were rehearsed at night. The whole of the units in the Division would be marched to their rendezvous under cover of darkness with strict discipline. They would then be formed up on the tapes, and at dawn would advance under cover of an artillery "barrage" represented by mounted troops and signallers waving flags.

In camp the men were instructed by their platoon commanders, who received copies of all maps, aeroplane photographs and all available information, which were passed on to the men, so that in the event of heavy casualties amongst the officers and N.C.O.'s the men would be familiar with the operations and able to go on with the battle.

To keep the lads fit physical exercises, football, and other forms of recreation were compulsory to all. The band was sent to each company's quarters in turn to render a programme of the latest music, and everything that would cheer life was done, such as the establishment of a canteen

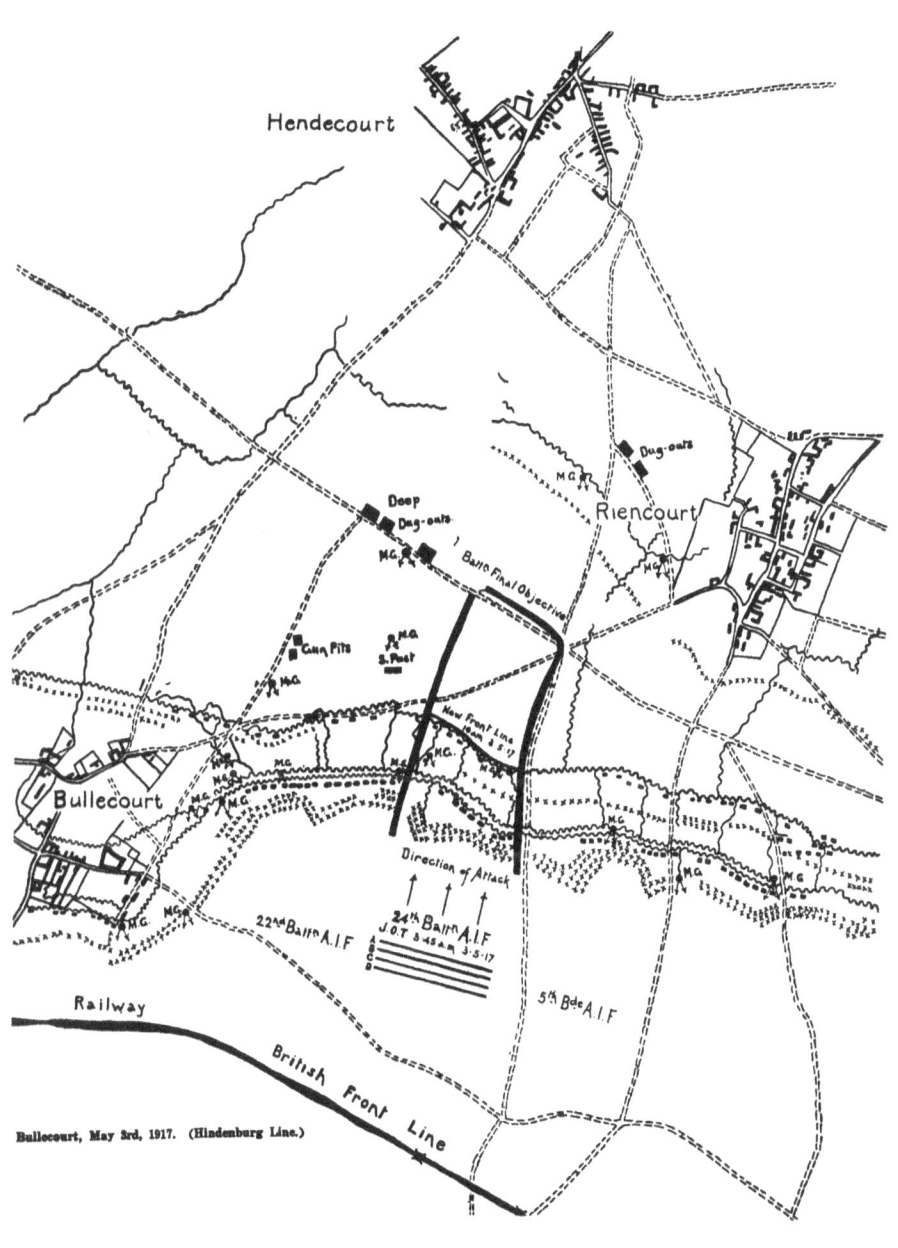

Bullecourt, May 3rd, 1917. (Hindenburg Line.)

and the spending of regimental funds to procure extra foodstuffs, a point always maintained in the Battalion, and which went a long way to make the 24th boys such a happy lot.

During this time many conferences of senior officers were held and every point of the battle was thrashed out; dumps were established in the front line, containing ammunition, bombs, wire, picks, shovels, and water. The troops holding the line were cutting the nearest belts of wire, and the heavy guns were tearing up the further stretches. Infantry patrols were sent out with long tubes of piping filled with explosives ("Bangalore torpedoes"), which were placed under the enemy wire and connected with an electric battery, which could be fired on the signal being given.

To form an idea of this battle-field, picture two perfectly made enemy trenches on the slope of a long rise, protected with four or five belts of wire, which in places was 30 yards in depth and breast high, and sighted to such perfection as to enable the German machine-gunners to fire along the fringe of the wire. To reach the first trench meant an advance of nearly 1000 yards over ground which afforded no shelter for advancing troops, beyond one or two sunken roads leading from our positions to the Hun lines.

At about 5 p.m. on 2nd May the Battalion fell in for final inspection, prior to moving off to the front.

Our line offered a striking contrast to that of the enemy. The Germans were posted in deep, well made trenches and protected dugouts behind a maze of wire. Our line was nothing but the shattered embankment of an old railway and was approached over the open. Still, we reckoned on ousting the Hun and benefiting by his months of labour in having a "home" prepared for us on our arrival

The Battalion was under the command of Capt. J. E. Lloyd with Capt. S. G. Savige as adjutant. The Company Commanders were:—"A" Coy., Capt. E. V. Smythe; "B" Coy., Capt. W. H. Ellwood; "C" Coy., Capt. T. C. E. Godfrey; "D" Coy., Capt. G. M. Maxfield. The Brigade was operating under the command of Brigadier-General Gellibrand.

Before leaving camp every man was issued with rations for 48 hours. Two sandbags were wrapped around the legs over the puttees and two thrust through each of the shoulder straps of the tunic. These bags were to be used for consolidating the positions after the assault. On arrival at the railway bank the troops collected extra ammunition and six Mills bombs each, while some carried picks, shovels, boxes of bombs, flares for signals, and expanding wire-netting for bridging uncut wire entanglements. The average load per man must have been not less than 100 lbs. It was considered advisable to carry into action as much ammunition as the men could manage in case difficulty was experienced in getting up supplies after the advance. So heavily laden were the men of the carrying parties that in some cases rifles had to be slung across the back.

The Battalion band played the troops to Vaulx, the nearest point to the line for bands, and many a gallant boy went to his death with the strains of "Australia Will Be There" ringing in his ears.

We were well ahead of schedule time, and took things easily on the march up through the forward position, halting behind the last ridge to have a final smoke.

We were due at the embankment at 9 p.m., and on our arrival the other Battalions were getting into position prior to moving out to the tapes.

In the darkness, pierced at intervals by the flashes of bursting shells and the glare of enemy flares, great difficulty was experienced in getting the four Battalions into their allotted positions in such a limited area, and when one seeks an example of discipline one's mind turns back to that first hour of Bullecourt when the men were sorted out under such adverse circumstances.

The Brigade frontage was approximately 680 yards, divided into two sections, the plan of attack being for the 24th Battalion on the right and the 22nd Battalion on the left to capture the first and second lines of the Hindenburg system, and advance and dig in along a line about 600 yards beyond those trenches. The 23rd Battalion on the right and the 21st Battalion on the left were to continue the advance by passing through the other two Battalions and digging in behind the village of Reincourt, along a road which overlooked the country beyond. The Fifth Australian Brigade was on the right immediately in front of Reincourt, and an English Division was on our left in front of the village of Bullecourt.

The Battalion frontage extended about 340 yards, the advance to our farthest objective being some 1600 yards from the railway embankment. The assault was to be made in four waves, "A" Coy. comprising the first wave, with "B," "C," and "D" Coys., in that order. The first wave was to capture the enemy front line, the second and third waves were to capture the second line, and the fourth wave was to continue and dig in about 400 yards further on.

As soon as darkness had fallen a white tape to mark the jumping-off position of the first wave was laid in No-man's-land, about 400 yards from the enemy wire entanglements. Markers were stationed at intervals along the tape to indicate the right flank of each platoon frontage. Each succeeding wave was to form up similarly about 30 yards in rear of the wave in front, while the 23rd Battalion was to remain at the embankment until the attack commenced, and then follow in our wake.

The artillery programme was arranged to give an intense barrage for three minutes on the first stretch of wire, a further three minutes on the second belt of entanglements, then ten minutes on the front line, gradually lifting back at varying distances and periods, according to schedule, and finally forming a screen in front of the troops while they consolidated the last objective of the attack. The first wave was required to keep as closely up to the barrage as possible, so that immediately it lifted from the front line the men could rush in before the enemy had time to organise. The waves in rear corresponded in their movements to the leading wave. All watches used by officers and N.C.O.'s engaged in the stunt were synchronised, so that the attack would be made according to time-table, and the possibility of our men getting into our own barrage would be avoided.

Shortly after midnight the 24th Battalion cautiously made their way out from the embankment to the tape in No-man's-land, and as they got into position the men lay down in the long grass and shell holes to await the moment of attack. Those who were first out had a long period of suspense in the chilly night air, and as enemy shelling and machine-gun fire were normal, their reflections were divided between thoughts of home and loved ones and what the next few hours would have in store for them. The minutes seemed to drag painfully. Occasionally a man would whisper to his officer, " How long to go now?" The information being given, the man would remark " Struth!" or something more emphatic, which conveyed a wealth of meaning. Further out in front of the first wave and close up to the German wire, half-a-dozen gallant scouts were scattered along our front to attack and turn back any hostile patrols which might come out, for if once our intention to attack had become known to the enemy he would have cut us to ribbons before we had time to start. Unfortunately, two of these scouts—Corporal Harry Pollard and Lance-Corporal Fitzpatrick—were killed after the attack commenced.

The whole of the Battalion was in position shortly after 3 a m. A little before 3.30 all the " Sentimental Blokes " in the unit were much impressed to hear a lark high up carolling joyously to the accompaniment of an occasional bursting shell or the rat-tat-tat of a machine gun. At 3.35 the Germans must have observed some suspicious movements in No-man's-land, for they suddenly became " jumpy," and fired a number of flares. A searchlight was also turned on from the high ground beyond their line. Zero, or the moment to advance, was still ten minutes ahead, and during that time the Hun dropped a heavy barrage right in front of the embankment. The Fifth Brigade on our right was not then in position, and the movements of those men must have been detected by the enemy, as his artillery fire increased in volume, and the machine guns barked viciously.

At 3.45 a.m. our artillery fire opened at barrage rate, and the lads rose from the protecting shellholes and, dazzled by the flashes of the innumerable shells bursting ahead, moved forward. The barrage was terrific, and while the spraying shrapnel burst over the enemy's lines the "heavies" pounded the enemy's wire, strongposts, and known machine-gun emplacements, though many of these wasps spat their deadly fire on our advancing troops.

The capture and cleaning-up of the first trench was "A" Coy.'s job. To obviate difficulties in crossing uncut wires, the leading wave carried long stretches of expanded wire-netting, which was to be thrown over the wire, forming a bridge over which the troops might pass. It was eventually found, however, that the artillery had done its work effectively.

The waves moved forward over the first few hundred yards in perfect order, but on reaching the remnants of the wire a certain degree of bunching occurred. This was soon straightened out, and as the barrage lifted off the enemy front line, "A" Coy. rushed forward over the last hundred yards to get at grips with the enemy. Some of the men of this Coy. were actually in the German trench before our own barrage had lifted. Their rush was so sudden and determined that little difficulty was experienced in capturing the first position, though some hand-to-hand fighting took place on the left flank.

"B" Coy. on the right and "C" Coy. on the left formed the second and third waves, and had the task of capturing the second trench. The second wave passed over "A" Coy.'s trench and moved up to the creeping barrage, while the third sought temporary shelter in the trench. Like "A" Coy., "B" and "C" Coys. were in the German's second line before our barrage had lifted, and were mixing things to a nicety when their pals in the third wave jumped in to assist them. The work to be done here consisted of cleaning up the positions, collecting prisoners, establishing small dumps with the bombs and ammunition carried forward in the attack, and reversing the trench in order to engage the enemy.

"D" Coy., forming the fourth wave, with the trench railway as their objective, moved up and took temporary shelter in the trench until our barrage had moved forward. At this time it was seen that the Fifth Brigade on the right had met with great difficulties, which forced their temporary retirement to the railway embankment. Nothing was so far known of the Battalion on our left. Nevertheless, when the barrage lifted once more, "D" Coy. moved forward according to schedule to their objective, which they captured, only to find themselves in the precarious position of being 1600 yards out without supports on either flank.

On the signal being fired denoting the capture of our final objective, the Battalion Headquarters moved forward from the embankment to the second German trench.

Captain G. Harriot rushed forward his carrying parties to supplement the stock of ammunition in the forward position, and throughout the day this zealous officer supervised this dangerous and important work.

The Germans soon recovered from the first effect of the bombardment, and being in the same trenches as ourselves, commenced bombing along them in order to drive us into a central pocket. Our men had been instructed to collect all the Hun bombs, and from the outset mix them with our own, so that should we run short of Mills bombs the fact would not be detected by the Boche.

Our position, especially during the first few hours of the battle, was extremely precarious. The troops of the Fifth Brigade, with some of the Seventh Brigade on our immediate right, made another brave attempt to capture their ground, being led by Captain Gilchrist, M.C., of the Sixth Field Company Engineers, and Lieut. Rentoul, M.C., O.C. Sixth Brigade Signal Section, but very few reached the first trench, the deadly machine-gun fire decimating their ranks. Both Gilchrist and Rentoul lost their lives in their gallant efforts in this forlorn hope, for which they had bravely volunteered.

The 23rd and 21st Battalions were cut to pieces by the enemy artillery fire while forming up on their tapes behind the 24th and 22nd Battalions, and became more or less disorganised, but rallied to the assistance of the 24th and 22nd Battalions in magnificent manner, the 23rd affording us much valuable assistance on their right flank by manning a sunken road, thus forming a defensive flank.

Our "D" Coy., on their forward position, were in dire straits, but were in touch with Battalion Headquarters for a little while by telephone. A platoon from "A" Coy. was sent forward to their assistance, but being almost surrounded, and fighting against such odds, were eventually forced to retire to the second German line. Of that gallant company, only Sergeant Whitear, Corporal J. M. Smith and 17 men out of a strength of four officers and 168 other ranks returned at 11 a.m. Captain Maxfield and Lieut. Rynhardt were killed. Lieut. Harris was dying, and urged his men to go back without him, as his case was hopeless, and Lieut. Christian had been badly hit on the tapes.

On seeing the Fifth Brigade had been held up by a withering fire, Captain Smythe immediately engaged the Germans in the trench on his right flank, and held them in check by establishing a block in the trench 200 yards beyond the sunken road, holding on until about 200 Fifth Brigade men took over this portion of the trench. About 30 22nd Battalion men under Captain Kennedy were in the trench on Capt. Smythe's left flank, and they established a strongpost there, and held the Boche at bay.

Captain Ellwood held the right flank of the second German line, and immediately commenced extending his front by bombing to the right. Lieut. Pickett rendered valuable service here. Though wounded, he continued in charge of the bombers, bombing with them for five hours. Captain Ellwood was also slightly wounded, but remained on duty.

Captain Godfrey, on the left, immediately cleared up his section, and bombed along to the junction of a sunken road with the trench, and there established a block. Some men of the 22nd Battalion could be heard bombing further along. Later this bombing died down, and these gallant 22nd men were overpowered, fighting to the finish, surrounded on all sides. Captain Godfrey did his utmost to help them out, but as the Germans were pushed back, so they squeezed in the 22nd boys with sheer weight of numbers, until the inevitable came. Lieut. F. P. Selleck led his men gallantly in this quarter.

Fortunately we managed to get forward machine guns and trench mortars, which saved the day. The Vickers guns were placed in the most commanding positions on the flank, and the Stokes mortars were emplaced behind the bombers and rifle grenadiers, shelling the trenches held by the Boche in advance of our own bombers.

At 9 a.m. "B" Coy. were having a hard time in repelling bombing attacks on their right flank. "A" Coy. hurried reinforcements to the threatened point, and the Boche was pushed back once more.

The prisoners captured during the early stages of the fight were employed as stretcher-bearers, and for the time being the ground was clear of wounded. As the morning wore on, our casualties were mounting up, and stretcher-bearer after stretcher-bearer was shot down, the enemy in many cases turning his machine guns on the bearers as they carried out the wounded. The patience and heroism of our wounded were beyond all praise. When a lad was hit he would crawl to some sheltered portion of the trench and there wait patiently. The fighting was so continuous and heavy that the wounded had to be left almost entirely to the stretcher-bearers, who had a strenuous and difficult task. As men passed along the trenches, a word of cheer would be spoken to a smashed boy, who always responded thus, "Keep going; don't let them get in. Don't worry about me; I'll stick it!" The pain men endured, especially as the day was warm, was excruciating.

A little before 10 a.m. a message was received from Major Trew, of the 23rd Battalion, who stated he was securing our right flank by holding the sunken road in force. This was a great relief, as it enabled us to concentrate our attentions more to our direct front.

The enemy continued his bombing tactics along our flanks, and during the day launched five counter-attacks at different parts of our line.

During the morning a conference of company commanders was held at Battalion Headquarters in order to review the situation and the advisability of holding on or retiring. The unanimous decision was to hold on until night, as to retire in broad daylight would be suicidal. We had seen the Fifth Brigade cut to ribbons earlier in the day. But if we held on until nightfall reinforcements might be sent, or if the worst came and we were surrounded, then we would have a better chance of hacking our way out with cold steel.

Early in the day all telephone lines connecting us with Brigade Headquarters had been destroyed, and the receiving portion of the trench wireless was injured during the advance. Thus we were completely isolated, but the Battalion held on with grim determination, and proved worthy, as it did on other occasions, of its old motto—" No Surrender!"

The following table shows our fighting strength at 3 p.m. out of a force of 586 who lined along the Battalion tapes at 3.30 that morning:—

"A" Coy.—2 officers, 20 other ranks.
"B" Coy.—2 officers, 43 other ranks.
"C" Coy.—4 officers, 50 other ranks.
"D" Coy.—Remnants included above.
(With 4 officers and 25 other ranks of other regiments.)
Vickers' machine gun 1
Lewis machine guns 8
(One recaptured from the enemy.)
Stokes mortars 3

Frontage approximately 600 yards.

It must also be taken into consideration that not only was the frontage 600 yards, but that we were also holding the rear trench of the same frontage. At 2 p.m. "A" Coy., 28th Battalion, Seventh Brigade, were in the forward positions, and were holding about 200 yards of trench to the right of the sunken road on our right flank. On their arrival we were able to withdraw our men and reorganise for subsequent action.

At 5.15 p.m. a message was received by hand from Brigade Headquarters stating that another attempt would be made to capture the final objective, that ground which gallant "D" Coy. tried to hold; but before this attack was launched it was imperative that the 24th Battalion should bomb along to the left and capture another 200 yards of trench.

A party of our officers in reserve was brought up to fill some of the gaps caused by casualties, and four of these were killed during the next 24 hours.

The attack on the trench was commenced at 7 p.m., the bombing parties being delayed by our own artillery fire, which was playing on the ground over which they had to work. The plan was that "C" Coy. would provide a party to work along the forward trench, while "A" Coy. worked along the rear trench simultaneously. Capt. Godfrey organised "C" Coy., while Captain Smythe worked "A" Coy. The operation was completed at about 9.30 p.m., the whole trench as required being in our possession.

At 10 p.m. the enemy again counter-attacked on the right flank, and at about 10.30 p.m. the troops on our right withdrew from their positions, which left us in an extremely dangerous predicament; and, unfortunately, we did not receive word of the move until it had been completed.

Mysterious orders to retire were being given from some quarter, but our men refused to leave until ordered to do so by their own officers.

The great danger was that a communication trench running from Reincourt on the high ground junctioned the main trench system in the area vacated, and if the enemy received intelligence of this fact, his troops would be poured in, and in all probability the sunken road would be captured and our position commanded and enfiladed by the enemy.

Captain Ellwood grasped the position, and, thanks to his quick action and keen judgment, the line was regarrisoned by his men under Lieut. A. Wilcox, assisted by Lieut. A. J. Walmsley, of the 21st Battalion. These officers and ten men held out until they were relieved.

About midnight our hearts were gladdened by the appearance of parties of the First Brigade, who were to relieve us. One cannot speak of the incidents of this battle without referring to the generous help afforded by the officers and men of this Brigade. Seeing that our men were in a completely exhausted state, not a moment was lost in effecting their relief. No petty questions were asked nor minor details examined, as is usual in all trench reliefs, but as each of our posts was relieved the men were sent back for a sleep.

The relief was completed, and at 3.20 a.m. on the 4th the last men wended their way out along the communication trench dug by the 2nd Pioneer Battalion. Every man who saw that trench of nearly 1000 yards, dug under incessant artillery and machine-gun fire, with the parapets covered with dead pioneers, sang the praises of those men, who, without the excitement of a charge, dug like friends to help those who were out in the thick of the battle.

On relief we went into the support positions along the railway embankment, and remained there throughout the day under heavy shell fire. At night we withdrew to Noreuil as reserve troops.

Heavy as our losses were, great was the victory, due not only to the organisation of Headquarters and the able leadership of the officers, but chiefly to the indomitable spirit of the men. That day every man went out to win, with no thought of surrender or retreat, and win they did.

When the troops were leaving the line they saw two lads who had blown their own brains out, being unable to endure the fearful torment of lacerated bodies during the frosty night. These were boys who had said, " Don't mind me, I'm all right; but give Fritz hell."

Throughout those two days of deadly combat, peril, and indescribable strain, the courage of all ranks was displayed to a degree which causes one to reflect on the terrible ordeal with unspeakable pride. The commanding officer of the Battalion (Captain Lloyd) and the adjutant (Captain Savige) never rested throughout the battle, but were constantly with the troops in the thick of the conflict, organising the defences at weak points and cleverly distributing their limited forces to defeat the furious and heavy counter-attacks of the enemy. Small groups of men held out again and again when it appeared they must be overwhelmed.

It was one of the Battalion's hardest fights, and if the battle had gone well with the units on our flanks it would have been one of our most successful assaults, for, despite the stout defences of the Hindenburg Line, the Battalion gained all its objectives in accordance with schedule time, and retained them until relieved, with the exception of the furthest, which had to be relinquished by reason of the non-success of the flanks.

The strength of the Hindenburg Line can be gauged from the fact that out of seven Divisions which attacked on the morning of 3rd May, the Second Australian Division was the only one which gained its objectives.

Casualties were extremely heavy. Officers of the 24th Battalion killed or fatally wounded were Captain Maxfield, M.C., Lieuts. J. Harris, "Val" Fethers, and Rynhardt. Officers wounded were Captain W. H. Ellwood, Lieuts. E. J. Pittard, C. A. A. Ellis, M.M., R. J. Pickett, I. A. Macindoe, N. Christian, F. S. McCooey, D.C.M., J. L. Scales, M.M., and W. Graham. Lieut. C. B. Atkinson, a former 24th Battalion officer, was numbered among the dead. The fallen N.C.O.'s included men who had served with the Battalion on Gallipoli, and others who had proved themselves staunch and trustworthy in many operations. These were Coy. Sergt.-Major M. Cronin, Coy. Sergt.-Major A. W. Petch, Sergeants L. F. Dobson and P. H. Taylor, Corporals C. F. Harrison, F. C. Matthews, H. L. Pollard, R. W. Davidson, A. Ross, and Lance-Corporals A. J. Boak and Fitzpatrick.

Bombing was the outstanding feature of the battle. Our Mills bomb did deadly work, but the Hun, throwing his "potato-masher," with its convenient handle, got a longer range than most of our men managed with the Mills. To counteract this disadvantage our rifle grenades and mortars were used freely, enabling the bombers to concentrate their attention on the enemy at close quarters.

The Stokes mortars were used with disastrous results for the Boche. One of our transport drivers, with two horses and a limber, galloped into the thick of the fight with a battery of these trench guns in the middle of the afternoon. The Germans followed him all the way with their shells, but he got away in spite of their frantic efforts to stop him. The mortars he delivered were rushed to the defence of a hard-pressed part of the line, and they scattered strong forces of German infantry moving along the trenches. Every bomb lifted a batch of Huns into the air. The Stokes gunners suffered heavily, and in several instances a gun was left with a single member of the crew. At one post a gunner and a stretcher-bearer worked the mortar while a few infantrymen carried on with rifle fire.

Over the ridges and plains behind our front A.M.C. stretcher-bearers and Ambulance waggons carried on the strenuous work of removing the wounded. The Huns, in their vicious anger, fired on the bearers and Red Cross waggons with machine-guns and rifles, and cut down dozens of men engaged in this humane duty.

It was ideal weather for aircraft. So numerous were the planes that one might have imagined a hive of bees was hovering overhead. The planes of both sides skimmed over the heads of the infantry again and again, firing their machine guns at their respective enemies with remarkable daring, and dropping messages of encouragement and advice to the troops. Some of these gallant airmen paid dearly for their bravery. But they were days of desperate deeds, and men forgot their personal safety in their enthusiasm for the cause they served.

The enemy troops who opposed us were Wurtembergers, who ranked as high as the Prussian Guard in fighting qualities.

Noreuil Gully was no haven of refuge on the night of the 4th. Guns boomed and flashed with unceasing fury, and enemy shells crashed around the frail shelters where the troops rested along the sunken road. But the men, overcome by fatigue, slept soundly, unconscious of the din and danger which encompassed them.

Next day the Brigade moved back to the green fields at Vaulx, where, out of the four Battalions, or the remnants of them, one composite fighting unit was formed to stand by in case of emergency, each Battalion providing one full company.

It was no small relief when, at midnight, the Brigade received orders to move to Favreuil.

A WELL-EARNED REST.

The Division was now about to enjoy a prolonged rest from battle. Leaving Favreuil on the 8th of May we set out for Le Sars, part of the unit travelling by the light railway and part marching behind the band. A night was spent in tents near the main road, and next day the Battalion marched to Melbourne Camp at Mametz. Here Lieut.-Colonel Watson resumed command, and received an enthusiastic welcome. Lieut. F. P. Selleck was appointed assistant-adjutant.

Equipment was overhauled and some reorganising done, and on the 12th the Australians were inspected by the Army Commander, General Sir Hubert Gough.

A week at this camp was filled in with drill, sports and salvage work, and on the 17th we started for our favourite village of Warloy. At least, if this village was not popularly known to most of the boys then, it was destined to be, for we arrived there in the spring, and spent a month among hospitable people in the pleasant weather of May and June. The troops became intimate friends with the inhabitants, whose homes were enlivened by groups of jovial Diggers, and whose domestic life was for the time being very intimately associated with the personalities and manners of the men from overseas. Civilians and soldiers knew one another by name, and the householders came to look for the regular visits of their Australian friends.

The French village girl is not the dainty piece of femininity one beholds in Paris. Only a small percentage of the young women in the country possess that degree of charm which attacks the hearts of men. So in Warloy the few belles had many admirers, and the competition between the men "in the running" was the subject of much jest and good-natured banter. To venture through the street with mademoiselle from the estaminet and encounter the boys who spent many of their evenings at her saloon was to earn the greatest raillery of the day.

There was one French phrase which every soldier learned and made use of. That was, "Voulez-vous promener avec moi, m'selle?" And the answer was usually those significant, tantalising words, "Apres la guerre!" The French and Belgian girls became so used to saying "Apres la guerre" that when at last the war ended they forgot to alter the phrase. The use of the words had become a habit. The girls promised the soldiers all kinds of favours "Apres la guerre." Perhaps the apparently interminable duration of the war gave them a sense of security. Some promises, such as that sealed with a ring, were made seriously, and were eventually fulfilled, but as a rule "Apres la guerre" was equivalent to another phrase, which mademoiselle was fond of expressing in English, "Nothing doing."

The Battalion band, now an excellent musical combination, made the village streets resound with its martial airs when the unit was on the march, and when the band rendered a programme of bright music on a Sunday afternoon or in the calm of a pleasant evening, it helped the people to forget the trials of the war.

The sunny days were fully occupied with training for further combats with the enemy, but the troops went about this duty with light hearts, as if they were serving an apprenticeship to a peaceful trade.

Major W. E. James, who had been wounded in March, returned at this stage, and resumed duty as second-in-command.

The days passed all too quickly. Concerts and sports, leave to Amiens, and many pleasant diversions, including general merrymaking on pay days, made life in Warloy a pleasant phase of our campaigning. The social side of army life was highly developed by the Battalion in this village. It was always the policy of the command to allow the troops to enjoy themselves in the highest degree compatible with discipline when they were in a rest area, and everyone made the most of his oportunities.

During the month of June a Brigade football competition was held, and was won by the 24th Battalion, whose team held a long record of unbroken triumphs. In addition matches were played against the Light Horse and Field Ambulance units, who were well beaten. Company sports were also conducted, and a competition for a cup was won by "A" Coy.

Only one cloud fell upon the peaceful scene. This was an accident during a rehearsal with trench mortar guns outside the village. A premature burst of a bomb resulted in eight deaths and a batch of wounded. The whole village mourned for the dead, and when the bodies were buried with full military honours, the women, weeping bitterly, added their prayers publicly to the funeral ceremony, and followed to the cemetery with flowers for the graves of the fallen soldiers. It was the most impressive ceremony Warloy had ever witnessed.

The Warloy cemetery holds the remains of many of the 24th men who fell in battle at Pozieres and other places in that district. The graves are all marked by crosses bearing the sign of the red and white diamond, and wherever that badge is seen by the people of Warloy it is to them a sign which awakens cherished memories and invokes their profound respect. When the war ended, the people of Warloy had not ceased to pay their loving tributes to the memory of our dead.

When the victims of the Warloy accident were carried down to the road, a party of German prisoners working there looked on with a total absence of sympathy. One big Hun even laughed with satisfaction at sight of the mutilated Australians. His brutal grimaces, however, were interrupted by the butt of a rifle, which one of our fellows brought down sharply on his square head. When the rest of the Germans observed how Australians dealt with Hun insolence they became suddenly attentive to their work on the road, and the man with the rifle had no occasion to tap any more skulls that day.

Unfortunately, such salutary correction of Prussian offensiveness was not approved officially, and a man who assailed a German prisoner was liable to punishment.

At Warloy General Birdwood decorated officers and other ranks who had gained distinction at Bullecourt. The Military Cross had been awarded to Captains Lloyd, Ellwood, and Godfrey, and Lieuts. Pickett and Pittard. Sergeant Whitear received the D.C.M. A number of Military Medals were also awarded. These are recorded on another page.

On 15th June the Battalion marched out of Warloy and entrained at Varennes, en route for Le Transloy, between Bapaume and the front, where the Division was stationed in reserve. A tent encampment near the ruins of a large sugar factory proved a pleasant habitation for summer days. The country was overgrown with tall grass and wild flowers, with whole fields of beautiful poppies reflecting their bright hues on a peaceful, though war-smitten, landscape, for every village in the district had been laid in ruins.

Lieut.-Colonel Watson's stay with us was not prolonged. On 15th July he left to take up an important command in England. Brigadier-General Gellibrand was also called to a command in England.

Prior to their departure the Brigadier and Lieut.-Colonel Watson were entertained at dinner by the officers of the 24th Battalion at Le Transloy. An entertainment was also organised for the troops at the sugar factory. Lieut.-Colonel Watson took the opportunity of addressing the men, but he was visibly affected at the thought of his separation from the unit he had commanded on Gallipoli. A demonstration made by the troops indicated how great was their regard for their Anzac commander, and he left the Battalion with the good wishes and esteem of all ranks. In England Lieut.-Colonel Watson was promoted to colonel, and, as acting brigadier, commanded the 17th Brigade, and afterwards the Overseas Training Brigade. Finally he was appointed C.O. of the Sutton Veny Depots. Brigadier-General Gellibrand had won the sincere regard of the Sixth Brigade, which he had commanded from the time he was first associated with it on Gallipoli. He had proved himself a capable commander and a soldier with the kindliest consideration for his officers and men. He was succeeded by Brigadier-General Paton.

Major W. E. James, who soon rose to the rank of Lieut.-Colonel, took charge of the 24th Battalion, and commanded the unit until the end of the war.

During the period spent at Le Transloy the Battalion was actively engaged in training and rehearsing battle tactics. Battalion, Brigade, and Divisional stunts were practised with the closest attention to the latest phases of the war. Night advances and daybreak attacks took place over the fields and around the villages of Beaulencourt and Villers au Flos.

The sunny summer days were now as pleasant as the winter days had been severe. The long twilight of morning and evening, and the mild temperature, even at midday, made camp life a congenial experience. The troops displayed a keen interest in exploring the country from which the enemy had been expelled. Entertainments and sports had their places in the programme of activities.

24th BATTALION MEMORIAL ON POZIERES RIDGE.—Lt.-Col. James addressing the troops.

BACK TO FLANDERS.

Arrangements were now being made for a move back to Flanders. We left Le Transloy on 24th July, and marched, via Lieny-Thilloy, Le Sars and Pozieres, to Aveluy, near Albert, going into a camp known as the Midland Huts, which, like many other habitations encountered in the field, required a thorough cleaning before occupation.

The camp, however, had one advantage which rendered it a favourable rendezvous for summer days. This was the abundance of water in the Ancre Valley, where the troops enjoyed the pleasures of bathing with a relish hardly surpassed at any seaside resort. Rafts and barrels were cast upon the water to add to the sport of the bathers, who crowded the bathing places in such numbers that at times one barely had room for the full exercise of his arms and legs, for the men of many units gathered to refresh themselves at the close of the day's parades.

Many of the boys will remember the strategy of the R.M.O., Major John Muirhead, in his quest for men afflicted with scabies, how he and his staff inspected the bathers as they undressed on the banks and filed past, took the names of victims, and had them packed off to isolation. The M.O., at least, prosecuted his scrutiny with an unrelaxing sense of duty, but where the inspection was left to his A.M.C. representatives many a suspect retained his liberty for the trouble of winking an eye or whispering a word in an attentive ear.

While at this camp the unit marched back to Pozieres to attend the dedication of the Battalion Memorial erected on the ridge of that battlefield. Pozieres and Mouquet Farm are marked by the graves of many men of the 24th Battalion, and the memorial was the visible expression of the unit's affectionate remembrance of the gallant soldiers who fell there in the summer and autumn of 1916. The memorial, which stands at the cross roads adjacent to the site of

Mouquet Farm, consists of a large oak cross mounted on a cement base, with an inscription in honour of the dead. The old battlefield had been overgrown with long grass and wild flowers in the year that had intervened, but the trenches and positions occupied by the Battalion were still clearly defined, and as the men assembled for the ceremony many tender memories were revived. Addresses were delivered by the C.O. (Lieut.-Colonel James), Chaplain-Captain Cleverdon (23rd Battalion), and Chaplain-Captain T. G. Campbell (24th Battalion). It was a gratifying thing to be able thus to honour our fallen comrades, and the troops left the scene assured that the name of the Battalion would live with honour on that historic field.

Orders soon came for the journey northwards, and on 28th July we entrained at Aveluy and travelled by rail to Arques.

There was no prospect of going into action again for some weeks; the Battalion settled down in billets in the peaceful village of Wardrecques to make the best of the well-earned and prolonged respite.

That there were strenuous days ahead everybody was assured, for the elaborate preparations proceeding on the Flanders front indicated an impending battle of great magnitude.

Soldiers do well not to concern themselves unnecessarily about the possibilities of the future, for life in an army at war is made up of uncertainties. The developments of a day may upset the best plans for the next, and the soldier is certain only of the present. So the troops made the most of their quiet days, and though strenuous training never ceased, the men resolved, as they were obliged to do on many other occasions, to let the future take its course.

Wardrecques was a village with which we already had some acquaintance. It proved a fairly comfortable "home," not because the billets were better than the usual order of barns and sheds, but because the weather was still exceedingly pleasant.

The canal which runs through Arques afforded good bathing facilities, while the interesting old town of St. Omer, a few kilometres away, was a convenient shopping centre, and a popular rendezvous for all the troops in the district.

The gathering to be seen in the St. Omer gardens when one of the military bands played in the rotunda on a Sunday afternoon was as interesting as any assemblage in Hyde Park, and much more cosmopolitan. All Allied armies were represented. There was the French officer in his brilliant uniform of light blue, with gold and silver facings, the English officer with his polished buttons and Kiwied leather, the Zouaves in their native dress, the Highlander in his kilts, the Tommy in his khaki, the Belgian with his tasselled cap, the Dominion men (Canadians, Newfoundlanders, New Zealanders and Australians) in their distinctive dress, Hindus with turbans, the Portuguese in their grey, and the Americans with the latest thing in army fashions. There were Japanese officers in the field for experience, coloured troops from the West Indies, French Algerians, and Chinese labourers. There were nurses and W.A.A.C.'s in uniform, soldiers in hospital blue, and civilians in silk hats and fashionable frocks. The world was there, or at least its representatives.

These gatherings took place under the menace of the enemy's bombs, for air raids kept the inhabitants in constant dread. While the band played melodies of peace, the bang of an anti-aircraft gun would set the people racing for shelter and leave the soldiers to display their contempt for enemy raids.

Many reunions of Australians long separated took place in the surrounding villages. These villages were closely situated, and favourable to friendly associations between the troops of the different Brigades and Divisions, though at times these friendly associations developed into disagreements and fights, which, however, cemented the good spirit of comradeship in the long run.

An army is a big concern, and while men in a Brigade see one another often enough, two Divisions might not come into direct contact once in several months. Consequently brothers, cousins, nephews, and uncles went looking for their kith and kin at favourable opportunities, and lads who were pals at home sought each other with equal eagerness. The troops, after drilling during the day, would walk miles in the evening to meet a relative or mate. It relieved the loneliness of life in a strange land, for in spite of all their sprees, their frequent visits to the estaminet, and the exploring of towns and villages, the troops lived mainly to themselves. Their bosom friends were the boys of their home town, and their confidences and troubles they poured into the ears of one another in their rough billets with as much satisfaction as women ever experience at an afternoon tête-a-tête in a comfortable drawing-room. It was a delight to be able to have a visiting pal to tea, even if there was nothing but bully-beef or bread and jam to offer him.

Vegetables were plentiful in the fields, and the rations improved as a consequence, being supplemented by the expenditure of regimental funds, and in many instances by the unauthorised exploits of the men in the dark of the night, when they might have been seen struggling home with capacious sacks crammed with potatoes, carrots, turnips, cabbages, and other wholesome products of the soil.

The Battalion band, which was now in a flourishing condition, attracted much attention in the village, where musical programmes were rendered on the square for the joint benefit of the troops and the civilians.

Route marches were frequent, but, without packs, a march was preferred by the men to tiresome drill at the "Bull-ring," a training site where they spent much of their time. The syllabus of training included a daily route march of not less than seven miles.

When the 24th Battalion, with its band at the head of the column, swung through the village on the march, there was always a flutter of excitement on the part of the people, who flocked into the streets to see the troops.

The Battalion invaded St. Omer one day on a route march. In the narrow streets of the old town, with its cobble stones and closely packed buildings, the men felt the thrill of the strange linking up of history past and present. The occasion of Australian soldiers marching, with rifles at the "slope," through that old town, where marks of the French

Revolution still existed, and which everywhere reflected its antiquity and told a story of the distant past, was a picture full of significance.

Divisional sports, with championship boxing matches, and other competitions for all sections of the army, aquatic carnivals, and entertainments, kept the troops fit and in excellent spirits. The carnivals had the nature of a huge picnic. Cookers were taken to the rendezvous, and the midday meal partaken of on the banks of the canal.

Liberal prize money was awarded to the winners, and novice bookmakers laid the odds for punters. " Four to one; five to a loaf," was the favourite cry of one 24th Battalion " bookie," who took delight in throwing off at the army bread ration. At these gatherings humorous characters were sustained in costume by lads with a comic vein. Female costumes were numerous. Australian bush types, English Johnnies, French gentry, were all portrayed. For the female characters the boys borrowed from the French demoiselles their complete outfits, and the figures cut by the Diggers in the frocks and lingerie of the village girls amused the civilians as much as they entertained the troops.

Although the days were pleasant, the nights were full of the horrors of air raids. Gotha machines purred overhead, bombs crashed on the towns and villages, and anti-aircraft guns spread shrapnel broadcast.

The sporting instinct of the troops was demonstrated one day when the Battalion was taking part in a practice attack over the fields. The manoeuvre was required to be done as noiselessly as possible. General Plumer, the Army Commander, who was watching the operations, had the privilege of seeing our fellows change their direction en masse in pursuit of a rabbit, and yelling excitedly as they raced after the bunny. The general remarked that it was " a splendid attack, but was accompanied by a little too much noise." A counter-attack was made by a Frenchwoman, who resented the invasion of her bean field. This development was met with smiles and more or less consoling remarks on the part of the troops, who hinted that she might apply to the army for compensation, a practice which, they knew, the people of that district resorted to on the least pretext of damage or loss through the operations or depredations of the soldiers. Our lads probably had in mind an occasion on which a farmer sent in a bill for 30 francs for the loss of a pedigreed rabbit. Whether the soldiers had stolen the rabbit was never proved, but the lads remarked at the time that if it had been devoured, the pilferers would have enjoyed their meal a good deal more had they known that particular bit of meat was so valuable and aristocratic.

Towards the end of August the Australian Divisions were inspected by General Birdwood preparatory to a review by Sir (afterwards Lord) Douglas Haig, Commander-in-Chief of the British armies. One Battalion from each Brigade was chosen to march past the saluting base at the review, and the 24th Battalion had the honour of representing the Sixth Brigade on the march. The review, which was held on the plains near Arques, was one of the most spectacular demonstrations held by the Australian forces. The 24th Battalion turned out in its best style. The men wore the sleeves of their tunics rolled up to their elbows and the first button of the collar undone. This style of dress was considered most appropriate for the warm day. It was a decided innovation for a review, and when the Battalion marched past the saluting base, the Commander-in-Chief was observed to sit higher in his saddle and open his eyes wider. The brown arms of the troops, swinging in perfect rhythm as they marched to the excellent music of the band, made the "hit" of the day. When the Battalion had passed Sir Douglas Haig remarked to one of his staff, "If any man had told me that troops turned out for review with their sleeves rolled up, I—well, I don't know what I would have said. But that is one of the finest sights I have ever seen on a parade."

While we were at Wardrecques our adjutant (Captain S. G. Savige) was transferred to Brigade Headquarters as staff-major trainee, and Lieut. Selleck was appointed adjutant.

During the prolonged period of rest, the arrival of several

drafts of reinforcements and the return of men from hospital had built the Battalion up to full strength, and at the end of August the unit, which had trained energetically since it left the front at Bullecourt, was in a state of the highest efficiency.

When September opened we were making ominous preparations for battle. Orders were received to move into Belgium, and we set off, on the 12th, for the Ypres sector.

Before we took our departure from Wardrecques, the Mairie, on behalf of the residents, presented to the C.O. an official letter expressing the people's esteem for the Australian troops, and also their gratification at the high standard of discipline displayed by the members of the Battalion, with whom the inhabitants had established most cordial friendships.

The first day's march took us to Steenvoorde, where we billeted in the farms close to the border, and on the following day we pushed on towards the front, passing through Abeele and Reninghelst. Progress on the roads was slow and jerky owing to the heavy motor and horse traffic going in all directions. Our destination for the present was Devonshire Camp, where we were to make our final preparations for action.

Battles on the Ypres Front.

Ypres was already one of the most notorious places on the Western front. It had been the storm centre of Flanders for three years; it had been saturated with German gas, whose thousands of victims filled the military cemeteries behind the lines, while the town, famous for the early destruction of its Cloth Hall and the Cathedral, had been more completely demolished than any place of its size on the whole front. And the offensive which was now impending was destined to be one of the fiercest and most strenuous of the war. If careful and complete preparation could assure success, this effort deserved to be a brilliant victory.

The troops who were to take part in the operations had been rested and trained that they might be in good fettle for their work. Models of the fields of action—perfect reproductions in miniature of the country to be won from the enemy—were constructed by the engineers and studied by the infantry regiments so that the troops knew every feature of the ground. Guns were packed into the field till we wondered where the artillery commanders would place the next battery. Shells were piled up as if it were expected the war would never end.

The roads were packed with every variety of army traffic, from the caterpillar tractors, with parts of 15in. guns, to despatch carriers on motors cycles. Motor lorries in long columns hung on to each other in desperation lest artillery teams should push in and break the chain. G.S. waggons bumped along with two wheels on the edge of the road and the other two in the gutter, pack horses were buffeted between the wheeled traffic, ration limbers squeezed in wherever there was an opening, while officers on horseback attempted to hustle when they might as well have tried to fly. After every lorry, gun, waggon, limber, motor car, horse and mule that could be jammed in had joined the

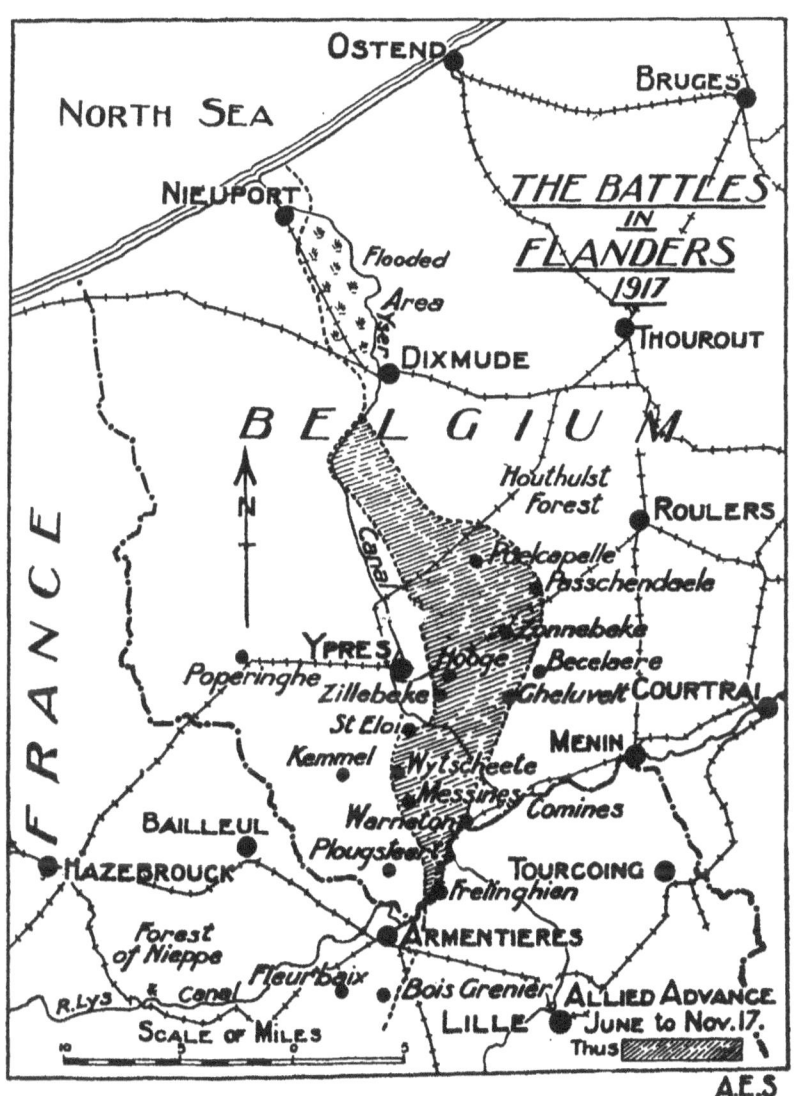

processions going or coming, the rest of the road space was left to the infantry!

Camps spread out in every direction—rows of wooden huts where soldiers rested when off parade and where rats ran riot over everything, camouflaged tents and the remains of partly demolished houses—anywhere that men could crawl for shelter. Behind the belts of timber, horse lines bred millions of flies and kept the drivers busy cleaning up, parks for lorries and waggons took up much of the space, and dumps for ammunition, fodder, rations, engineers' material, and everything used in war had their allotted spaces. Y.M.C.A., Church Army, and Salvation Army huts were there in the general congestion, also water points where water carts waited in queues for their turn at the tanks, and Field Ambulance stations where sick men paraded for treatment.

Above all this, in the wider sphere of the sky, the drone of aeroplanes never ceased. Battleplanes went out in flocks like migrating birds, heading straight over the enemy's lines and through his shrapnel with steady resolve and unchanging formation. Scouts climbed, dived and tilted like swallows, and the winged machines of war gathered and manoeuvred in such numbers that they were difficult to count. Enemy machines came over to fight and to observe our activities, and to be chased away or brought down like game shot on the wing, and our war birds went over to the country of the enemy to be accorded similar attention. From the busy earth beneath, anti-aircraft guns sent deadly shrapnel shells whistling into the dizzy heights, and clear skies were blurred by thousands of little clouds where the explosives burst. Squadrons of enemy bombing planes raided our positions in spite of all efforts to keep them off. The town of Poperinghe suffered severely. Thrilling combats took place in the air, and our Lewis gunners joined in the exciting work of harassing the hostile machines. German Gothas, carrying bombs up to 500 lbs., purred over the camp every night, and men turned out in their shirts to watch the effects of the gun fire on the German airmen.

Phosphorus bullets, which were used to assist the

machine-gunners in directing their fire at night, made a "striking" picture, even when they did not hit their object. From all directions chains of little fireballs went soaring into the sky, all converging on the enemy's planes, which, at an altitude of thousands of feet, were not easy targets, even when they shone white in the rays of the searchlights.

There was no adequate shelter from these deadly explosives, but the women in the houses, with the characteristic resourcefulness of females, buried their heads under the blankets and hoped for the best, while the soldiers often remained in the open, realising they were as safe there as in a frail hut. The crashing bombs demolished buildings, scattered dumps, killed men and horses, and kept everybody, including the few civilians who remained there, restless and fearful, and the only consolation we had was the knowledge that the enemy on his side was suffering infinitely more than ourselves.

The camouflaged artillery, with the noses of the guns poking up from the earth, carried on day and night, never permitting a cessation of the booming, screeching noises, but only distinguishing the quieter hours by pandemonium fury at frequent intervals. Batteries strafed batteries, horse lines were thrown into confusion when the shells came their way, infantry camps were regularly molested, dumps were special objectives, roads were sprinkled with explosives that spread the traffic about in particles, villages received their daily portion of "iron rations," and field hospitals were not immune from the "uplifting" influence of shells. For this reason the Australian C.C.S. at Dickebusch had to be moved further from the front. In one night the Second Division had 36 horses and mules put out of action. The mortality among the beasts everywhere was very high.

These were the conditions that prevailed from five to ten miles behind the battle line.

In the trenches, where the opposing infantry forces faced each other, war's routine—sniping, patrolling, bombing, outpost and strong-post activities, digging, observing, repairing the destruction of bombardments, and the evacuation of wounded—went on unceasingly.

The enemy must have known he was going to be attacked on no mean scale, but the day and the hour of the event he could only surmise, for that information was withheld from our own forces till the time arrived for them to take up their positions. We all knew now that the Australians were destined to take part in a grand offensive against the German positions on the ridges beyond Ypres.

On Sunday, 16th September, the British guns began a vigorous bombardment of the enemy's positions. The din was so continuous that at church parade in our camp the padre could scarcely make himself heard. His text, "Be strong and of good courage," was well chosen.

The opening of the battle was fixed for the dawn of 20th September, when the British forces were to attack on a front of eight miles between the Ypres-Comines Canal and the Ypres-Staden railway. The final objective was the high Passchendaele Ridge. The Australian sector embraced the formidable German strongholds at Westhoek Ridge, Glencourse Wood, Nonne Boschen, Veldhoek, Polygone Wood, Zonnebeke, the Broodseinde Ridge, and other positions strongly fortified with concrete block-houses known as " pill-boxes." It was not intended to attempt the capture of all these positions in one assault, but by a succession of attacks, in which every unit of the Australian divisions would have its turn—and probably several turns—in the general offensive.

Our Battalion was not attacking on the opening day, but was to assist in the important and strenuous task of keeping the assaulting troops supplied with ammunition and all other necessary material, improving the communications, and any duty that might present itself as the battle progressed.

The Battalion moved off from Devonshire Camp on the afternoon of the 19th, marching in sections to the wooded country in the vicinity of Belgian Chateau, where the evening meal was taken and a short rest and final smoke availed of while we awaited the cover of darkness. At dusk, when we were about to push on, rain set in steadily, and soon the roads and tracks were converted into a succession of waterholes, through which the troops splashed their way in the dark, the inky blackness of which was relieved only by the flashes of gunfire.

A few hours were spent in dugouts on the banks of the canal outside Ypres, and in the early morning we pushed on to "China Wall," where we arrived at 3.40 a.m. "B" Coy. and "C" Coy. moved on by way of the Birr Cross Roads to Bellewarde Ridge, "A" and "D" Coys. following shortly afterwards to the same locality.

The battle opened with great fury at dawn, and every unit on the front found abundance of work on the busy field. "B" and "C" Coys. were detailed for the work of laying a buried cable from Bellewarde Ridge to Albert Redoubt. "A" and "B" Coys. were posted at Bellewarde Ridge.

At 1 p.m. a party of 2 officers and 100 other ranks of the 24th Battalion was despatched to carry forward engineers' material for constructive work, while another party of 1 officer and 50 other ranks carried Stokes mortars to the front line. All other available men carried small arms ammunition to the troops in action. As the day advanced the numbers of casualties called for additional stretcher-bearers. Two officers and 112 of our men were set apart to assist in this work, the wounded being carried from the front at Westhoek Ridge back to the Menin Road. Meanwhile "B" and "C" Coys. worked at high pressure on the laying of the communication cable, which engaged them until 6 p.m. on the 21st, and for which work they were highly commended by the command. The other two companies had taken advantage of every opportunity to improve the trench system and construct bomb pits at Bellewarde Ridge.

Everything had gone well with the advance, and the assaulting troops were holding their gains, but the field was now littered with the bodies of the dead (mostly Germans), so we supplied a burying party to inter the remains of the fallen.

At the conclusion of their labours on the cable, "B" and "C" Coys. took up positions at Bellewarde, "C" Coy. going

BELLEWARDE RIDGE.—*The Battalion in reserve on 21st Sept., 1917.*

into trenches on the Ridge, and "B" Coy. moving to the rear of Aetang de Bellewarde.

The work of carrying supplies to the forward positions, the loading and unloading of pack-horses, and other duties were carried on by the Battalion till the evening of the 23rd, during which time two dumps had been established well forward under Brigade arrangements. The carrying parties often faced heavy enemy shell-fire, and sometimes were exposed to the Hun barrage. Our losses were 14 killed (including Corporals G. Castle, W. Parkes, and R. Sproull); and 3 officers and 73 other ranks wounded.

On the night of 23rd September the Battalion withdrew and returned to Devonshire Camp.

The offensive was resumed on the 26th September, and we "stood to" at the camp ready to move up if called upon.

ATTACK ON BROODSEINDE RIDGE.

Then came our turn as assaulting troops. Our objectives were the German positions on the Broodseinde Ridge. In accordance with the system adopted at Bullecourt, a nucleus of the Battalion was detached and sent into camp as reserves. This party moved to Caestre.

The following extracts from orders issued to the attacking units give interesting particulars of the operations:—

"The first Anzac Corps, simultaneously with corps on the flanks, will continue its advance.

"On the Second Australian Divisional front the Sixth Infantry Brigade will attack on the right, the Seventh Brigade on the left, and the Second Brigade on the right of the Sixth.

"The 22nd Battalion will carry and consolidate the red line. The blue line will be captured by the 24th Battalion on the right and the 21st Battalion on the left, after passing through the 22nd Battalion.

"The Battalion will attack in four waves on a four-company frontage, each company on a platoon frontage of 70 yards, 'A' Coy. on the right, 'B,' 'C,' and 'D' Coys. in order. The first wave will be of two lines, 15 yards between lines, remaining waves in lines of sections in file, 20 yards between waves. The third wave (platoon) of each company will be moppers-up.

"Special precautions are necessary to prevent loss of direction.

"At zero a barrage will be put down 150 yards in front of our present front line. At plus three minutes it moves 200 yards, at the rate of 100 yards every four minutes; thence to the protective barrage (200 yards beyond the red line) it moves 100 yards every six minutes. At plus 130 minutes it moves 100 yards every eight minutes, finally resting 200 yards behind the blue line. One smoke round per gun will be fired when the barrage reaches each of the protective lines. There will be other creeping barrages in depth.

"A machine-gun barrage will conform to the artillery barrage.

"Troops attacking first objective (red line) will have a red diamond painted on the back of their steel helmets, and those attacking the second objective (blue line) a blue diamond.

"Each man of the first three platoons of each company will carry 220 rounds S.A.A., 2 bombs, 4 sandbags, 2 days' rations, 1 iron ration, 2 full water bottles. Moppers-up will carry 2 additional bombs. Men of the three rear platoons will carry one tool (proportion 5 shovels to 1 pick). Rifle section will carry 10 extra bandoliers S.A.A. per man, Lewis gun section 2 extra magazines per man, rifle grenadier section 2 boxes grenades per man."

It will thus be seen how heavily laden the troops went into battle. With web-equipment, rifle, and all the articles mentioned above, a man was no "featherweight," and physical strength was essential to rapid advance over the rough country in the face of enemy fire.

From the jumping-off positions in front of the point known as Tokio, the troops had first to pass over the boggy ground along which ran the Zonnebeke Creek, and then up the rising ground past De Knoet Farm and across the

GERMAN PILL BOXES AND DUGOUTS.—Captured from the enemy on the Ypres front, Sept.-Oct., 1917.

Broodseinde-Becelaere Road, over the crest of the Broodseinde Ridge, and to the line of the objective on the forward slope. With that commanding Ridge in our hands, the way would be clear for a further effort against the final objective of the battle—the great Passchendaele Ridge.

The frontage of the Sixth Brigade's attack was about 600 yards. The 22nd Battalion was to operate over this frontage for the capture of the first objective (marked "red line"), a distance of about 800 yards, and for the assault on the second objective (marked "blue line") the 21st and 24th Battalions were to divide the frontage evenly, each covering a width of about 300 yards. The enemy held the rising ground by a system of trenches and many commanding points fortified with "pill-boxes" bristling with machine-guns, and from the crest of the ridge had a highly favourable view of the movements of the attacking forces. The Hun had all the natural advantages of defence. On our side we put our trust in the destructiveness of a deadly artillery barrage and the elan of the assaulting troops.

The 24th Battalion was commanded by Lieut-Colonel W. E. James, with Lieut. F. P. Selleck adjutant, and the company commanders were:—"A" Coy., Captain J. E. Lloyd, M.C.; "B" Coy., Captain W. H. Ellwood, M.C.; "C" Coy., Captain T. C. E. Godfrey, M.C.; "D" Coy., Captain G. Harriott.

Preparations for the attack completed, the Battalion moved off at 7 a.m. on 3rd October and marched to Gordon Area, outside the ramparts of Ypres, where the rest of the day was spent. By midnight we were on our way to the battle line, the assembling position being on the road to Tokio. Owing to heavy enemy artillery fire, the assembling position had to be changed, but the companies arrived at the line in good order and on time. At 4 a.m. on 4th October "A" Coy. led the way to the jumping-off positions, followed by "B", "C" and "D" Companies in that order.

Tapes had been laid to indicate the jumping-off lines by the engineers and Captain S. G. Savige, of the Brigade staff. The 24th Battalion took special precautions to avoid loss of direction by the companies. Tapes were laid back to

guide each company to its position on the J.O.T., while
scouts and guides were posted at all vital points to prevent
disorder. This work was thoughtfully arranged by the
adjutant (Lieut. F. P. Selleck), and was carried out under
the direction of our intelligence officer (Lieut. J. F. Gear),
who was ably assisted by Sgt. P. J. Molloy. The prompt
action of Lieut. Gear prevented one company taking a
wrong direction when the advance began.

While awaiting the hour of attack, the troops made use
of shell holes and old trench systems, which afforded some
shelter from enemy fire. Zero time was 6 a.m. (4th
October).

At 5.30, when everything appeared to be going well, the
Boche put down a heavy barrage, which made the situation
extremely painful for our waiting men, who hung on impatiently for the moment of action. Casualties quickly
mounted up as the enemy pounded our positions with high
explosives, including minenwerfers and shells up to 8in.
This was the heaviest shell fire the Battalion had encountered on a jumping-off line. Forty of our troops were
killed, including two officers (Lieut. F. W. J. Murphy and
2nd-Lieut. John Worrall), and the Battalion strength was
reduced by fully 30 per cent. before the assault commenced.
The 21st Battalion also suffered heavily.

The strain of lying inactive under that fire, with an important task and the probability of a desperate struggle
before them, tested the morale of the troops more than the
fiercest fighting could have done, yet they kept their nerve
and waited resolutely for the moment of action. Light
showers of rain were falling, but the men were almost
unconscious of the weather conditions.

At last, after what seemed an eternity our guns burst
forth like a clap of thunder. The enemy positions appeared as if they must be blotted out. The smoke of explosives enveloped the whole field, and objects could be only
faintly observed in the haze.

Then came the order to advance. The 22nd Battalion
led off, followed by the 21st and 24th Battalions. As the
Zonnebeke Lake was on the jumping-off line on the left,

the front for the three Battalions at the start was only about 300 yards, but when the lake had been passed the units on the left had to change direction to cover the ground allotted to the Brigade. The boggy ground at Zonnebeke handicapped the troops at first, but as they ascended the slope they found firmer footing.

Soon we discovered the reason of the enemy's artillery activity. A strong force of German troops with fixed bayonets was about to make an attack with the object of recapturing Zonnebeke, which they had lost in our last assault. These enemy forces met battle earlier than they had anticipated. Our troops, with a desperation born of their impatience, charged into the surprised Germans with so much vigor that all who were not put out of action were soon rounded up as prisoners. The three Battalions shared in the work of mopping-up these Huns. The bayonets of our attacking waves had an awe-inspiring effect upon the Germans, many of whom shammed to be wounded or dead. Several of these Huns rose up after our men had gone on and fired on our troops from the rear. Their death was real enough after they were caught in that act of treachery.

The attack was continued up the Ridge with equal success.

Docile Trench and De Knoet Farm were captured without much opposition, and the 22nd Battalion gained the first objective by 6.50 a.m.

On the right flank of the 24th Battalion's sector our men encountered determined opposition in Romulus Wood, but the enemy was overpowered after severe hand-to-hand fighting. The Seventh Battalion ably assisted us here. Machine-gun positions were mopped up and a vigorous assault made on a group of pill-boxes. The machine guns of these enemy posts were soon silenced, and many prisoners were captured in the stout fortifications.

At about 7.30 a.m. the 21st and 24th Battalions moved up close to our protective barrage. Captain Lloyd did excellent work here organising the men for the attack on the second objective over the crest of the Ridge. At 8.10 the barrage moved forward, and the troops followed it closely to the " blue line." Fleeing Huns made good sport for keen snipers.

Just before our men reached the Broodseinde-Becelaere Road they captured two German 77 m.m. guns. The gunners fought bravely until they were put out of action. On the road we took possession of three enemy food waggons containing cans of hot soup, quantities of black bread, margarine and other food-stuffs. An anti-tank gun also fell into our hands. After passing the road heavy fire from enemy snipers was encountered, and as the troops passed over the crest of the ridge they were subjected to artillery and machine gun fire.

On reaching the line of the objective, we immediately dug in and prepared for possible counter-attacks.

Throughout the advance the companies operated with excellent direction. and the troops were in great heart in spite of the nerve-racking ordeal endured before the attack was launched.. All enemy posts, including many concrete pill-boxes, where heavy fighting at close quarters took place, were thoroughly mopped up.

This was the first occasion on which the Sixth Brigade had operated against the pill-box system of defence, but the initiative and gallantry of all ranks proved equal to the task of dealing with these fortifications. The pill-boxes afforded excellent protection for the enemy machine-gunners until our troops assaulted these strong posts, but when it came to fighting at close quarters the boxes, like the deep dugouts used by the Germans on other fields, appeared to have affected the morale of their men, as they created a false sense of security. In desperation the Huns huddled together in these shelters, and their fortresses were then nothing more than traps in which they were well caught.

By 9.30 a.m. all our objectives had been gained and the flanks linked up with other units. While the troops were digging in, the Boche kept up his fire on the ridge, but the work proceeded briskly, and by night a continuous trench had been excavated along the new front. Lieut. A. A. Ball, D.C.M., as liason officer, rendered good service in linking up the flanks.

Flushed with the success of battle, and capable of further conquests, our men had halted on that slope very reluctantly.

BROODSEINDE OPERATIONS.—24th Battalion in the trenches.

Before them was the valley between the Broodseinde Ridge and the higher ridge of Passchendaele on the left front, and in the distance they could see the German infantry falling back. That was the most favourable moment the British ever had of capturing that last ridge on the Flanders plains. But under the system of limited objectives adopted by the higher command, the order was to "dig in," and during the day, as the men built up their defences on that line, they watched the enemy returning as they had seen him departing, and they knew that, with rain soaking the marshy country, the next attempt to advance would be fraught with further heavy losses and desperate fighting. The British regiments which fought their way to Passchendaele later realised the truth of these fears.

Looking back from the Broodseinde Ridge one wondered how in the earlier fighting around Ypres the British units had been able to effect reliefs and to deliver rations and other material to the troops in the line while the enemy held such commanding positions. From the Broodseinde Ridge the whole field was under observation, and as we gazed back over the country we could see plainly the movements of our own units on various duties. Guns, transport, and men were all exposed to the splendid observation from this position. It was a prize worth having, and our men realised the importance of the victory they had gained. Having gained such a prize, they set themselves to hold it.

Hundreds of German prisoners struggled back through our lines in abject misery. The look of terror on their faces showed how awful their experiences had been under our artillery fire. Many of them were wounded, and these hobbled along eager to get away from the field. One German officer, almost running in his hurry, remarked, "Let me go; I'll get out all right! Damn the war!"

Dark-skinned British troops from the West Indies, who were employed supplying the batteries with shells, almost danced with delight at the sight of the terrified Germans. They evidently felt it was a good thing to belong to the British Empire that day, for the old Lion was in a fighting mood, and his heavy paws and sharp teeth were mauling and grinding his enemies with a vengeance.

Carrying parties from other units, which had been engaged conveying ammunition to the line (as our Battalion had done in the earlier attacks), had suffered heavy casualties, and supplies were consequently much below requirements. Requests had accordingly to be made for additional quantities, and also for water.

The night was uneventful, but at dawn on the following day enemy aeroplanes were abroad, flying low over our lines, and registering our positions for the guidance of their artillery. This was done by dropping flares directly above our troops.

During the afternoon considerable activity was observed on the part of the enemy infantry, suggesting preparations for a counter-attack. Stokes mortars were brought to play on the Hun, and he must have been persuaded to think before he took any risks, as the afternoon was comparatively quiet.

An officers' patrol went forward at 4.30 p.m. and encountered a post of about 20 Germans, but owing to heavy sniping from other quarters the patrol was obliged to return.

The advance, though highly successful, was not accomplished without losses. Some of our finest troops had been killed in the advance, and many more were wounded. Our casualties had resulted mainly from the deadly shooting of enemy snipers. The dead included Captain T. C. E. Godfrey, M.C., Captain G. Harriott and Lieut. A. Wilcox. Captain J. E. Lloyd, M.C., was three times slightly wounded, but remained on duty until the captured positons had been consolidated. The 24th Battalion went into action on the morning of the 4th with 20 officers and 500 other ranks, and our casualties for two days were 10 officers and 254 other ranks. The enemy snipers took a heavy toll of our N.C.O.'s. It was evident that the Germans purposely strove to rob our troops of their leaders, and the manner in which they picked off the officers and N.C.O.'s bears testimony to the gallantry with which these men exposed themselves in the attack.

Captain Godfrey had embarked from Australia with the
original Battalion as a lieutenant, and had served with the
unit continuously. As an officer his ability, tact, and winning personality made him popular with all ranks. His
fellow-officers, the N.C.O.'s, and his men spoke of him affectionately as "Tommy" Godfrey—a name which was respectfuly honoured during his long service with the Battalion, and which will always be affectionately remembered
by his comrades in arms. Captain Godfrey's death was
one of the greatest personal losses the Battalion ever suffered. When it was known that he had been killed, strong
men's eyes moistened at the knowledge of their loss, and
everybody, from the C.O. to the men in the ranks, was
deeply affected. The Battalion had lost one of the men
who had been strong links in its bond of comradeship. He
was a brave soldier, a faithful leader, and an unselfish commander. His personal devotion to his men, in battle or in
camp, made him a man beloved by his troops, who would
have risked their lives at any time to save him. In his
death he crowned with glory his long and faithful service
to his country, his regiment, and his men.

Captain Harriott, a man of perfect physique, amiable disposition, and a lovable companion, had also seen long service
with the Battalion. As transport officer he had discharged
his duties with ability, and was beloved by every man of
that section. As a company commander he gave promise
of equal success.

The N.C.O.'s killed included Sergeants A. M. Henry, H.
C. Dickens, L. R. Rainson, M. Jones, V. C. Cleghorn, J. G.
Hewitt, P. H. Lingford, and Cpl. S. Walsh. Sergeant
Henry (an original member of the Battalion) was one of
our most promising young men, and had he been spared he
would soon have been promoted to commissioned rank.

The heavy casualties imposed a strenuous task upon the
stretcher-bearers, who carried on unceasingly with their
customary gallantry. Large parties of infantry were detailed from other units to assist in the work. Our M.O.,
Major John Muirhead, attended the wounded with skill and
devotion.

Throughout these operations our transport section played an important part in the general work which led to success. The 24th Battalion transport men could always be relied upon to get supplies forward, however hazardous and difficult the enemy made their task. One notable instance of their gallantry and their ability as drivers was the occasion on which the Sixth Brigade transport was ordered to move an ammunition dump from Bellewarde forward to Anzac House. This dump consisted of shells for the field guns (18 pounders), which had pushed ahead to cover the advance. The shells had to be loaded on pack-horses and mules. The night the job was to be undertaken the four transport sections of the Brigade sent their parties forward, but the enemy chose the time of their arrival for a vicious bombardment of all our lines of communication. The track past Bellewarde appeared to be impassable, so heavy was the barrage at this point. It required nerve to drive or lead horses or mules laden with explosives through that intense fire. Driver "Ted" O'Neill, with characteristic bravery, asked, "Who'll follow me?" Every man of the 24th party immediately answered, "I will." Then they headed through the crashing shells, handling their mounts like true horsemen, and setting about the dangerous work with fine soldierly coolness and pluck. They were rewarded for their bravery, for in spite of the heavy fire they accomplished their task without serious injury. There were no better horsemen or braver soldiers in the A.I.F. than the drivers in our transport section. Shell fire or the most difficult tracks never turned them back from duty, and though they often experienced the thrill of "a ride for life," their first consideration was always to get the supplies of ammunition and rations to the troops, who, they knew, depended on their faithfulness.

The Battalion Headquarters, which at first were established at Tokio, were afterwards moved forward to a position near the Broodseinde-Becelaere road, where our troops had captured a German intelligence officer and staff with a complete telefunken outfit. A large and powerful periscope was also found. With this instrument a man, without exposing himself, could scan the country for miles. At another post our signallers discovered a number of German carrier pigeons. Our signalling officer despatched two of these birds with greetings to the Hun Command. One message was "Deutschland Uber Alles! Ha! Ha!" The other read, "Hock the Kaiser—I don't think!" Lieut. Ball sent a more impudent message, and had the audacity to ask for a reply. The other birds provided pigeon pie for our signallers and runners, who were prepared to admit that however distasteful Prussian "kultur" might be, the flavour of German pigeons was highly satisfactory.

Quantities of wine and cordials were found by our troops after the objectives had been taken and they had time to explore their new possessions. Cigars were also plentiful, and men who had cultivated the tobacco habit (and even some who hadn't) were puffing at cigars. The tobacco was of fair quality, but the satisfaction of having taken the cigars from the German army added a relish which gave them a peculiarly agreeable flavour.

We were due for relief on the night of the 5th. The 18th Battalion moved in to take over the line on our sector at 6.30, but half an hour later the enemy, becoming nervous and fearing another attack, sent up his S.O.S., which brought on a brisk artillery action. The change-over was not completed before midnight.

The 24th Battalion then moved back to Gordon area, where the rough shelters, constructed of sandbags and shell-pierced iron, afforded little rest for their tired limbs. Such as they were, however, we would willingly have accepted their poor accommodation had we been privileged to remain. But fatigue duty called many of the men away to strenuous toil before they had time to clean up their arms and equipment. And still greater trials awaited us.

Though fatigued by the strain of battle, hard work, and long journeys over the field, the Battalion was called up again two days after it had left the line, and we went forward by way of Menin Road, Zonnebeke B Track, Kit and Kat, Anzac House, and Tokio to supports at De Knoet Farm. Enemy gun-fire was encountered before we got

into our positions, and it continued for several hours
Twelve casualties were sustained, and two of our Lewis
guns destroyed.

"OVER THE TOP" AGAIN.

When the Battalion (or what was left of it) arrived at
De Knoet Farm on the evening of 8th October we received
orders to prepare for another assault on the enemy on the
following morning! That order was a severe trial for
flesh and blood. The troops were already so exhausted that
they dragged their legs as men without energy. Physically,
they might have been regarded as beaten. Weaker men
might have quailed before the test of another assault, but
these stout-hearted fellows prepared to go on.

The object of this attack was to carry the line forward
to a position about 200 yards beyond Daisy Wood. The
right flank of the 24th Battalion's objective was on the
Zonnebeke-Moorslede road, with the left flank skirting Daisy
Wood.

In view of the reduced strength of the Brigade, it was
foreseen that at the conclusion of the attack the numbers of
men in action would not be sufficient to dig a continuous
trench for the new line, and it was decided to consolidate
by establishing a number of mutually-supporting strong-
posts along the front.

Rain had set in persistently now, and the fields had been
converted into marshes and bogs, rendering operations a
strain for the freshest troops. To tired men, the ordeal
was infinitely worse.

Owing to our small numbers and the loss of two company commanders in the previous attack, it was decided to
merge the four companies into three, commanded by Capt.
E. V. Smythe, M.C., Capt. R. H. Jones, and Capt. C. M.
Williams.

The 21st Battalion was to operate on our left, and the
22nd Battalion on our right, with the 23rd Battalion supporting. These and other units on the flanks were in a
similar plight to our own.

The medical officers of several Battalions were of the opinion that the troops were not physically fit to go into the line, and the Battalion, Brigade and Divisional commanders made representations to the higher command that they doubted the advisability of putting men in such a condition into an attack, as it was considered the men were too exhausted to undertake the task with a reasonable prospect of success under the conditions prevailing now that unfavourable weather had set in. The higher command, however, decided that the attack must be made. So the troops prepared to do their best.

Urgent orders had been despatched for what reinforcements were available from the nucleus camp, and a party of 60 arrived, after a forced march from Ypres, just in time to move off to the attack, and without the usual preparations for battle. To Capt. Williams, who led these trooops to the line, is due much of the credit for the success achieved by the Battalion on the following day, as the unit was so reduced that without this party our numbers would have been too small to hope for favourable results. Although reinforcements for other units failed to reach the line that night, Capt. Williams and his men battled forward with determination, and it was one of the sad features of the fight that this gallant officer and many of his brave troops were soon numbered with the dead.

The total Brigade strength in action was only about 600, and the distance to the objective at the furthest point was 1600 yards.

The units were in position on the J.O.T. by 4.15 a.m. (9th October).

In order to allow the artillery barrage to do its work on Daisy Wood and the known enemy strong-posts near our front line, the jumping-off tapes were laid about 200 yards in rear of that line, which was completely evacuated thirty minutes before zero.

Our heavy guns commenced a bombardment of the enemy positions at 5.19 a.m., and the field guns came into action immediately afterwards, but the barrage was weak compared with the energy and accuracy of the artillery on previous days, and the enemy was little disturbed. Consequently, as our tired men rose up to advance across the boggy ground, snipers and machine-guns cut many of them down before they had a chance to get at grips with the enemy.

The 24th Battalion attack went well until our men reached Daisy Wood, where heavy machine-gun and rifle fire were encountered. Casualties had reduced the units until the attackers became divided into small groups operating largely on their own initiative. The company on the right had three of its officers killed, including their commander, Capt. Williams, and a dozen men. Capt. Smythe was then the only senior officer left. "C" Coy., in the centre, merged with "A" Coy. on the left, and after determined efforts a footing was established. Two platoons of "C" Coy. dug in forty yards in rear of a hedge and held on in spite of strong opposition. Capt. Smythe, with the remnants of "A" and "B" Coys. and two platoons of "C" Coy., persisted in the attack on Daisy Wood. At 7.30 a.m. a party from the 28th Battalion arrived and filled a gap between the 23rd and 24th Battalions. The position was painfully obscure during the forenoon. By 2 p.m. Capt. Smythe and his gallant force had cleared Diasy Wood, and then held the southern and eastern edges of it, but they were unable, owing to insufficient numbers, to consolidate the whole of the ground over which they had operated.

Several enemy posts in the vicinity still held out. Lieut. J. L. Scales, M.M., led a party against these enemy strongholds, and by sheer bravery overpowered a machine-gun crew and captured the gun. This gallant exploit (for which Lieut. Scales was awarded the D.S.O.) enabled us to link up with the 19th Battalion, making our position much more secure.

Lieut. R. J. Pickett, M.C., attacked another machine-gun post single-handed, but was killed in his brave adventure.

Sgt. Arthur Prime, M.M., who commanded the twelve men left in "D" Coy., had established a post early in the attack on the wood, and this party defied all the enemy's efforts to dislodge them. Later Sgt. Prime organised a party and led his men bravely against the strong Hun position. He was subsequently wounded and evacuated.

A DUCKBOARD TRAIL.—Troops in fighting order going to the firing line on the Ypres front, October, 1917

Eventually the northern end of Daisy Wood was captured, and a number of Germans added to the list of prisoners.

The attack was only partially successful, but what was achieved, in the face of wholly unfavourable circumstances, reflected the highest credit on all ranks. The initiative and resourcefulness of the men won success where failure might have been expected. It was one of the most difficult tasks a small force ever faced. Robbed of their officers by enemy fire and thrown largely upon their own resources, the "Diggers" that day accomplished an advance, in the face of overwhelming odds, which stands to their credit as one of their most gallant achievements. With normal fighting strength there is little doubt the Brigade would have gained the whole of its objectives in spite of all other disadvantages. The factors which prevented complete success were thinness of the barrage, reduced physical strength of the troops, insufficient numbers for the attack, and the bad condition of the ground.

Throughout the night of the 9th our small forces were in a critical situation owing to the absence of a continuous line of defence. Some of the parties at times were isolated by the counter activities of the enemy, and were threatened with annihilation. The strain was tremendous for some hours, but in the early morning more hopeful reports began to come in from the line, and the brave lads held on till they were relieved by the 49th Battalion on the night of the 9th and 10th, when they moved back to the support line. The country was so perplexing in the night, and the task of keeping direction so difficult, that wide tapes were laid to guide the men back over the ridge.

The stretcher-bearers who operated on the field during those trying days had a task which called for the greatest feats of endurance and courage. The tracks over the ridges and valleys were churned into muddy holes, in many instances large enough to engulf a whole squad, while at certain points the bearers had to wade through water up to their hips, carrying the stretchers on their shoulders and straining to preserve the wounded from precipitation into the mire.

The work of our signallers was highly meritorious. Sgt. C. J. Mitchell, who supervised the laying of telephone wires, stuck to his task bravely. For most of the time on the 9th the 24th Battalion lines were the only telephonic connections by which messages could be communicated from the Brigade front to Headquarters.

Capt. Smythe's gallant leadership, his supervision of the scattered forces during the period of consolidation, and his characteristic tenacity in holding on to ground that had been won gained him well-earned distinction.

The 24th Battalion had gone into action with 12 officers and 220 other ranks, and the casualties were 9 officers and 104 other ranks. Of nine officers with the companies four were killed and four wounded. One company was led out of the line by a lance-corporal. The officers killed were Capt. C. M. Williams, Lieut. R. J. Pickett, M.C., Lieut. B. F. Nicholas, M.C., and 2/Lieut. N. C. Nation. Five officers were wounded, including Major John Muirhead (R.M.O.). The N.C.O.s killed included Temporary Coy. Sgt.-Major N. H. Sheppard, Sgt. D. S. Cumper, T/Sgt. A. R. N. Hallas, Corporals J. D. Rowlands, W. I. Norman, C. L. H. Hey, L. R. Mace, S. M. Hill, and L/Cpl. E. East.

Capt. Williams was an officer who had distinguished himself and won promotion by gallantry and devotion to duty. He was a strong man in every sense of the word, and an inspiration to the men whom he commanded. Lieut. Nicholas (a brother of Major G. M. Nicholas, D.S.O., who was killed at Flers in 1916), Lieut. Pickett and Lieut. Nation were three of the bravest officers the Battalion had in its ranks. These heavy losses, following so closely upon the casualties sustained in the Broodseinde attack a few days earlier, impressed the unit with a deep sense of its loss. Three captains had been killed in five days. The death of many brave N.C.O.s and men made the burden heavier for us all. Broodseinde and Daisy Wood were battlegrounds which the Battalion had cause to remember with tender feelings, but they also remain in our memory as fields hallowed by unsurpassed valour and great sacrifice crowned with success. The labours of the gallant dead were not in vain.

The Brigade casualties on the 8th-9th October were 24 officers and 392 other ranks.

The line established by the Sixth Brigade at Daisy Wood on 9th October was the farthest point on that sector reached by the British armies that year. The advance on Passchendaele was continued in another quarter.

A record of these operations would be incomplete without an acknowledgment of the cheerful manner in which the 49th Battalion took over the front from our men. We had no regular line to offer them, but a chain of posts established under the most wretched conditions imaginable. Notwithstanding these disadvantages the front was taken over in a most optimistic spirit, and with a desire to relieve our exhausted troops with the utmost despatch.

On the 10th a composite Battalion for emergency purposes was formed out of the four units of the Brigade. Several of our officers in reserve were called up. The medical officer was obliged to evacuate a number of men owing to their low physical condition, and the Battalion mustered 7 officers and 80 other ranks as its fighting strength! That evening, however, the Brigade was relieved from action, and we trudged back wearily over the muddy field to Ypres, a distance of seven or eight miles, to shelters outside the ramparts.

Who of the men left to make that journey will forget the straggling groups of the Brigade dragging themselves through the deep mud from the line to Zonnebeke and wading through the creek, the trail along the slippery duckboards and through the slush of the shell-battered Menin Road, and the inexpressible relief experienced at the sight of cookers when the rendezvous was reached in the early morning? The only bit of cheer on that long trail was a drink of hot cocoa provided by the Comforts Fund kitchen at the Lille Gates on the eastern ramparts of Ypres.

We left Ypres on the 11th, travelling by train to Abeele, and going into billets near Steenvoorde.

The broken ranks of the Battalion, with so many familiar faces and loyal comrades gone, impressed us with feelings of loneliness and sadness, but the struggles of battles, in which there had been many deeds of comradely devotion, and in which the men had stood shoulder to shoulder facing danger and death, drew those of us who were left closer together in the bonds of friendship. Pozières and Bullecourt had been similar experiences. The passing out of so many bosom pals was to men in arms like the breaking of a big family circle. Yet there was always the call to "carry on," and we did that the more readily for the sake of those who had fallen.

The work of reorganising was proceeded with immediately. Owing to the large number of casualties among the officers and N.C.O.s, promotions were numerous, and it was declared that the American flag (the Stars and Stripes) was being cut up and distributed once more. In the operations from 4th to 10th October the Battalion had nine officers killed. The nucleus which had been kept in reserve to fill many of the gaps caused by the casualties was now availed of.

Decorations awarded to members of the Battalion for gallantry in the operations extending from 4th to 10th October included the following:—D.S.O.: Lieut.-Colonel W. E. James and Lieut. J. L. Scales, M.M. Bars to M.C.: Capt. J. E. Lloyd, M.C., Capt. E. V. Smyth, M.C. M.C.: Capt. F. G. Savige. D.C.M.: Sgt. C. J, Mitchell (who was also awarded the Belgian Croix de Guerre). Military Medals awarded are recorded on another page.

The successful operations of the Battalion during September and October proved the ability of Lieut.-Colonel James as a commander, and his services were recognised and appreciated by the higher command. In all our subsequent engagements the Battalion had the fullest confidence in its commander, who was a keen soldier, yet sympathetic, with a fine understanding of the strength and weaknesses of men.

The organising ability of the adjutant (Capt. F. P. Selleck) proved invaluable to every section of the unit. His untiring energy, his coolness in the face of the most perplexing developments, and his optimistic and cheerful spirit were qualifications which all ranks recognised and appreciated.

During a brief period of rest training and sports occupied the attention of the men. The football team was still a strong combination, and fresh victories were added to the list of victorious matches against other units. One of the best games played on the field was the occasion on which the 24th Battalion met the 6th Field Ambulance team The exhibition of football was equal to Melbourne League standard. Generals, colonels, and other officers of high ranks attended as spectators, and the barracking reached the highest pitch of excitement. The 24th team proved just too good for the Ambulance boys, who put up an excellent fight. Another notable match was a victory over the 21st Battalion by 26 goals to 2 goals.

Our days of respite were not many, for on 27th October we set our faces towards the battlefield once more, and that day reached Ottawa Camp, shifting on the following days to Dickebusch. Several days were spent here, and on 2nd November we pushed on to Gordon Area, where we remained as reserves till the 7th. Major H. J. Smith was acting C.O. of the Battalion at this time.

Our orders on the 7th were to relieve the 19th Battalion on the left of the Divisional sector in the front line, the disposition of companies being as follows:—"A" Coy. (Capt. E. V. Smythe, M.C.), on the left, with five posts, and one platoon in close supports; "D" Coy. (Capt. F. W. Frawley), on the right, with 7 posts; "B" and "C" Coys. in support to the forward positions. On the left we linked up with the First Division, and on the right with the 22nd Battalion.

Patrol work was carried on energetically in order to watch the movements and operations of the enemy, as it was still very probable that he would make an effort to regain his lost positions. The companies in supports carried out much useful work, repairing communication trenches and duckboard tracks and generally improving the position behind the firing line.

The weather, which had been showery and wet, now assumed decidedly wintry conditions. Heavy rain set in and continued till the positions were in many places badly flooded, and the troops were obliged to turn their energies to draining funk-holes in the trenches and turning the water off from the firing posts, which threatened to assume the appearance of small reservoirs.

The whole field was soon held in the unrelaxing grip of winter, and it was evident that the advance could be continued only with extreme difficulty. It was almost impossible to move the guns, and even pack-horse traffic was only practicable on corduroy tracks. The Australian Divisions had figured prominently in the operations for over seven weeks, each Division having participated in several strenuous battles. The Battalions were reduced in strength, and the troops were tired and longing for relief.

It was, therefore, a welcome sight on the night of 11th November when a Yorkshire Regiment arrived at the front and took over our part of the line.

GERMAN PRISONERS.—Australian soldiers busy collecting souvenirs.

MOMENTS IN FLANDERS.

Moving back to Gordon Area that night, and resting a few hours, the Battalion set off next morning with the object of leaving that strenuous battlefield well behind. The column marched by way of Kruisstraat, Dickebusch and Reninghelst, buffeted by a congestion of waggon and artillery traffic on the roads, and embalmed with mud and slush.

At midday we were still marching, and though we knew not our destination, we were thankful that the direction was satisfactory and that we were on the way. Late in the afternoon we arrived at our old billeting area between Abeele and Steenvoorde.

It was a tiring journey, and the strain of the long march was not brightened by the sight of more fortunate units riding in motor waggons. That circumstance was considered sufficient justification for the boys to abuse (without malice) the army administration which failed to secure corresponding comfort for every Battalion, even though we recognised the order was a large one; while the troops who rode past in the 'buses only laughed and informed us that we were "stiff." We were, in every sense of the word, for not only were we unfortunate (which is the accepted meaning of the word "stiff"), but our legs felt like wooden pegs, and our muscles threatened to go on strike at any moment.

Rest is a wonderful cure for that "fed-up" feeling which assails men at war. A peaceful snore in the barns worked wonders, and the following morning the boys were ready to clean up equipment once more and improve their personal appearance, which would never bear the test of critical inspection after several days in action in muddy trenches. The process of regeneration was so complete by the second day that the lads were permitted to indulge in a game of football, and the following days were occupied by training in the forenoon and sports after lunch.

The surrounding villages afforded some merriment in the

evenings, when the men resorted to the eating houses and estaminets to spend their hard-earned pay and to forget the hardships of war.

The farms in that district were not ideal habitations, so we shed no tears when we learned that we were to move to more comfortable billets in the camping area at Locre, at the foot of the famous Kemmel Hill. To this locality we migrated on 18th November, marching in column of route via Reninghelst and Westoutre. We invaded Locre with all the pomp of a regiment on review, marching with martial step to the music of the band, and satisfied that the people who turned out to watch our entry into the village must have gained the impression that the Australians were highly respectable and well-disciplined soldiers.

Our Battalion was allotted to the Birr Barracks, which we hailed with delight, for no camp we had ever encountered offered so much comfort for winter days. Cosy wooden huts with brick chimneys, a huge coal dump at our doors, and shops, army canteens and places of entertainment in the vicinity were luxuries which caused the boys to hope that they might remain there for the duration. The day the lads marched in there they recorded their unanimous conviction that the outlook in respect to the war was highly favourable to the Allies. In other words, they declared, "We're winning at last!"

The position of the coal dump was the strategic advantage which gave them the most satisfaction. The weather was cold in November, and a fire in the hut was the first consideration. Of course, the purpose of the dump was not to supply the troops with unlimited coal, which was "rationed" to all units like every other commodity. Armed sentries guarded the coal day and night, but while they talked to innocent-looking Diggers who inquired the way to Dranoutre, Bailleul, or some other locality, bags of it were carried off. Men came from all directions to the same source of supply, and every week the tally showed the stacks tons short of the quantities which ought to have been there. Even officers were tempted to go out in search of coal when their batmen proved too slow to defeat the watchfulness of the sentries. One night an Australian colonel, who set out to show his batman what could be accomplished by resourcefulness, narrowly escaped capture by the guard. He saved himself by falling prone in a gutter in the dark and lying there until the sentry moved away. Then the colonel sneaked off with his well-filled bag. If the "Tommy" sentries were conscientious men they must have had serious qualms regarding their faithfulness when they beheld the extravagant consumption of coal which blazing chimney tops betrayed every night. But those fires in the huts made all the difference to the troops. They were a serious handicap to the trade of the estaminets, for when troops had a glowing fire to sit by and tell their stories over, the majority of them had little time for vin blanc, while the favourite concoction of coffee and rum was more or less forgotten.

A syllabus of military training was prepared, and sports were conducted systematically as recreation and physical training. Cups were awarded to the most successful units, and prize money was paid to individual winners. The sports programmes provided scope for every form of athletics, from weight-putting to cross-country runs for harriers.

It was natural, however, that football should hold pride of place as the "national sport." Competitions were followed with the keenest interest by the soldier "sports." Every unit had its team, and the esprit de corps which animated every section of the army was reflected in these competitions. Battalions carried their colours to the field of contest, marched to conquest to the music of their bands, and strove to retain their reputation by every form of demonstration.

At Locre the 24th Battalion suffered its first defeat at football, the victorious unit being the 23rd Battalion. The match, which was played on a muddy field, was tremendously exciting, and the 24th Battalion was leading when everybody was waiting for the final bell. At that moment the 23rd team scored a goal, and won by three points. Up till that day the 24th Battalion had won 51 matches against different teams.

The readiness and completeness with which the troops forgot their guns and turned to sport showed how small a place war had in their natures. A victory at football was a greater event in their personal vision than the rout of an enemy's army, while a defeat of their team on the field between the goal sticks cast over them a greater gloom than the biggest success Prussian arms ever achieved against the Allies. The field of sport had a levelling influence in the army, and was one of the brightest phases of military life. Officers, N.C.O.s and men stripped together and went out to compete as men just as nature made them. There was no rank in the football team, no preference for stars or stripes when they faced the starter for the 100 yards sprint or the 5-mile event.

By this time our men had become well acquainted with the towns and villages of Flanders, and they knew where to go to make the best of a day's leave or to spend a pleasant evening.

The most attractive of the girls in the district were known to many of the lads by name, and in the camps the soldiers spoke of Marie, Lucille, or Jeanne as close acquaintances, and the young women knew the names of the lads with an equal degree of friendly intimacy. Bill, Jack, Tom, Harry, and such familiar names were in the circle, of course, but the titles which the girls favoured most were the nicknames used by the men to designate their pals, such as "Darkie," "Snowy," " Skinny," " Long'un," " Titch," and other equally distinguished titles.

Army concert parties were booming at this time. The need for relieving the monotony of life at the front had not always been sufficiently recognised. But to hope for the end of the war seemed vain, so men set themselves to make the best of the hard life in the army.

Every Division now had its concert party, almost every Brigade had its entertainers, while even the Battalions were beginning to organise troupes, which were to be set apart to do nothing more than keep up the spirits of the war-weary-men—a task which was difficult enough and important enough to justify all the efforts that were bent to it. The Anzac Coves, the original and oldest of the Australian theatre companies, was even launching into pantomime, and if the war had gone on for a few years longer, something in the form of grand opera might have been needed to meet the taste of the critical audiences that the army shows were developing.

To overcome the disadvantage of having no female artists in these companies, good-looking youths were selected to impersonate the lady characters. The "camouflage" was so successful that in many cases the civilians who patronised the performances or attended the shows as guests of the soldiers were often doubtful as to which was real—the deception or the "mademoiselle." "Clothes make the man" is the axiom of many a tailor, but the soldiers discovered through their experiments that clothes have as much or more to do with the make-up of women.

A word should be said here for the army cooks, whose department had been organised and superintended by experts in the endeavour to improve the treatment of army food. A school for training army cooks was, from the soldiers' point of view, one of the most important institutions in the war's varied enterprises. So artful did this branch of army industry become that army rissoles and puddings at times were greater mysteries than German sausage. The cookery department was another evidence of the general improvement in army organisation.

Experience covering a period of more than three years of warfare was bringing life in the field to a fine art, the perfecting of which was eventually interrupted by the collapse of our enemies and the consequent necessity for the disbandment of all our fine economic and social institutions under army management. The busy scenes in the field, the congestion of traffic, the establishment of industries at the front, the masses of men under arms, the enormous quantities of war material piled up everywhere, gave one the impression that the world had been transferred to the battlefield. We wondered what had been left behind.

And of all the implements and material put into use by the army, what were more useful than petrol tins and sandbags? What would the soldier have done without these serviceable articles? With sandbags he could build trenches, dug-outs, gun-pits, and shelters, carry rations and ammunition, use them for kitbags, leggings, and bunks, and employ them in a hundred ways. What would he have done for water, tea and soup in the trenches but for the utility of the petrol tin as a carrying vessel? What would he have done for a wash-basin in the field without it? If a soldier were asked to name the bare essentials for an army's equipment he would probably say. Rations, sandbags, petrol tins, rum, tobacco, and playing cards. And if he were asked what part of the army's equipment he would eliminate, he would surely answer, The soldier's pack!

During a month at Locre the Australian cinema at Dranoutre and the English Pierrot entertainment at the Locre theatre were well patronised by our men. To these places of amusement a company of the Battalion paraded about twice a week, the admission fees being paid out of regimental funds. The Y.M.C.A. also entertained the troops at cinema shows. The march to the Dranoutne cinema in the evening, when the boys swung along happily behind the band, and encumbered with nothing heavier than a cigarette or a pipe, was the kind of route march to which they did not object.

Thoroughly rested and reorganised, the Battalion was ready for action again in December, and on the 15th of that month we were ordered to the Ploegsteert sector, going first into camp at Kortepyp, near Neuve Eglise.

There was much work to be done in the improvement of the defences, as it was anticipated that the coming spring would see important developments on the whole of the Western front. Working parties were distributed to various tasks, and Christmas, 1917, found us a hard-working body of men.

Operations were not too strenuous, however, to permit a celebration of the Yuletide, so preparations were made for holding Christmas dinners in the Church Army hut at the

Kortepyp Camp. Each company was relieved as far as possible from duty on the occasion of their dinner, and for several nights different sections of the Battalion made merry while enemy shells whistled overhead. The dinners were marked by sumptuous feasting and a high degree of enjoyment by all ranks. The regimental funds were used to supplement the contributions of the men for the purchase of edibles and dainties which army quartermasters were not commissioned to provide, and to include liquid refreshments and "smokes." The company cooks excelled themselves in the preparation of tasty courses for the satisfaction of the hearty appetites which encompassed the festive boards. They were boards in reality, but the rough nature of the tables did not affect the flavour of the feast to men whose rough life in the field made this crude banquet hall a palace by comparison.

While the troops, with their officers and guests at the head table, wrought havoc with the roast beef, lamb, pork, vegetables, pudding, fruit, and jellies, and handled with the greatest care and affection the rum punch, whose delicious odour was as incense to the happy assemblage, the band, accommodated on the platform, rendered a programme of the latest music. The spirit of these dinners could not have been surpassed had they been held at the most fashionable hotel in Europe, and the speeches and toasts were more genuine than any speeches or toasts submitted at a festive board. The soldiers did not forget to drink health and happiness to the folks at home, nor to pay their reverential respect to fallen comrades, and when they had celebrated Christmas in a manner befitting war, they went out to duty, hoping to live to enjoy some future Christmas at home and in peace. Christmas gifts from the Australian Comforts Fund also helped to cheer the troops. Every man received a small box of dainties or useful articles, such as tobacco, biscuits, sweets, writing material and playing cards, while warm underclothing from the same source of supply was distributed, and plum puddings helped to make the Christmas festivities more real and homelike.

During these days the men were constructing wire entanglements behind the lines near Warneton, laying communication cables, loading and unloading shells on the light railway, carrying out salvage work, and performing a variety of duties, sometimes under cover of night, and also under fire. At times they were quartered in the Catacombs in the Ploegsteert Wood, and at other times they were accommodated in camp at Kortepyp.

Capt. S. G. Savige, M.C., who had been one of the most highly-esteemed officers of the 24th Battalion, and later was on the Headquarters staff of the Sixth Brigade, volunteered and was accepted for the British army's expedition in Mesopotamia.

[Capt. Savige was one of the brave band of 100 officers and 250 sergeants who, under General Dunsterville, made the desperate dash for Baku, one of the most dramatic adventures of the war. These heroes, drawn from all the British forces, disappeared for months from the world of their fellows, and among the deserts and mountain crags from the Caspian Sea to Persia opened communications, built roads, and endeavoured to organise the wild tribesmen into an efficient fighting force to thwart the Germans and make the capture of Baku a British victory. This gallant little band did its work so well that even the admiration of its enemies was stirred. On this daring expedition Capt. Savige won the D.S.O.]

1918.

WARNETON SECTOR.

The New Year, 1918, opened with the guns booming along the whole front and with the end of the war nowhere in sight.

On 12th January our Battalion took up duty in the firing line facing Warneton, a sector which proved eventful during the following days. A fall of snow was followed by heavy rain on the 15th, and the little river Douve quickly overflowed. The trenches collapsed, dug-outs filled with water, and everybody was in a bad plight. The flooded condition of the field caused one officer to record his fears that the line was in danger of being attacked by U boats, also his opinion that an issue of torpedoes would be useful to the troops.

Fighting ceased for the time being, and the troops devoted their attention to restoring the positions. The men suffered keenly from the wet and cold. Rheumatism and sickness put many of them out of action. A temporary Battalion hospital was established at Kortepyp by the R.M.O. (Capt. D. D. Coutts), and all possible attention was bestowed upon the sufferers. The worst cases were evacuated.

The company commanders at this time were:—"A" Coy., Lieut. C. A. A. Ellis, M.M.; "B" Coy., Lieut. G. D. Pollington, M.M.; "C" Coy., Capt. L. S. Marchant; "D" Coy., Capt. T. C. Seabrook.

Patrol duty, bombing and sniping were carried on at the front till the 17th, when the unit was relieved, and we returned to the Catacombs. Fatigue duty was resumed immediately, and kept us busy day and night till the 27th, when we moved out to Neuve Eglise.

We were now about to enjoy a few weeks well out of the range of the guns, and on 30th January we set out for the peaceful village of Lottinghem, about 25 kilometres from Bolougne and adjacent to the town of Desvres. The journey was made by train on a bleak night, and we were thankful for the hot cocoa supplied us by the Y.M.C.A. when we reached our destination at 2 a.m.

Five weeks at Lottinghem were spent pleasantly. Not even a hostile aeroplane interrupted the peace of that quiet village, for it was so snugly tucked away from the busier centres that had it not been for the unfailing direction of the railway line we would probably never have discovered it. Training, sports, entertainments, and a day's leave to the coast occasionally was not an irksome life for active service while the great war was in progress. This period of rest was granted to one Division at a time, and the Battalions were distributed over a wide area embracing many towns and villages, so that crowding and the congregation of troops in large numbers was avoided. The change was accordingly in marked contrast to the hustle and tiring activity at the front, and proved highly beneficial to the men. Leave ' buses ran to Boulogne and back every day, and the men were granted the privilege of this joy ride in turn, so that all had the opportunity in due course.

At Lottinghem the allotment of English leave was greatly increased, to the extreme delight of men who were awaiting their turn to cross the Channel and spend a fortnight in blissful liberty. As many as 22 men in one batch left to catch the leave boat at Calais or Boulogne and hide themselves in the peaceful scenes of the Old Country, where prospective brides were plentiful, and the people always kind and generous to the troops from overseas.

At this time Major H. J. Smith took his departure for Australia, and Major J. E. Lloyd, M.C., left the A.I.F. to join the staff of the Imperial army in India. Capt. D. D. Coutts (R.M.O.) was promoted Major. Major W. H. Ellwood, M.C., temporarily commanded the Battalion in the absence of the C.O.

At Lottinghem Coy.-Sgt.-Major G. M. Ingram, M.M., was promoted First-class Warrant-officer and appointed Regimental Sgt.-Major of the Battalion. The men who held the position of R.S.M. from time to time proved themselves capable and distinguished soldiers. The office was first held by Warrant-officer R. Cunningham, who became a captain in the 46th Battalion and gained the M.C. Warrant-officer J. Harris gained a commission, and was killed at Bullecourt, where he distinguished himself with "D" Coy. in a hard fight. Warrant-officer G. J. Bowden rose to the rank of captain and company commander, with an M.C. Warrant-officer G. M. Ingram, M.M., also received a commission before he won the V.C. at Montbrehain. Warrant-officer R. L. Williams, D.C.M., was another member of this distinguished succession. Warrant-officer L. W. Newman also held the position for a considerable period, during which time he assisted in maintaining a high standard of efficiency in the unit.

Our football team was still a strong combination, and a Brigade competition afforded opportunities for adding fresh honours to our good record. The match of the "season" was played against the 23rd Battalion, which had been the only unit to secure a victory against us. Our boys were anxious to redeem their name after the 23rd Battalion's victory by 3 points at Locre in November, and now they had the satisfaction of defeating that unit by 7 goals 14 behinds to 4 goals 7 behinds.

The Sixth Brigade held a horse show at Quesque on 1st March, when the 24th won the following prizes in keen competitions:—First for best turned-out pair of limber horses (second year in succession), first for best turned-out cooker (second year in succession), second for officer's hack, second for shoeing, second for driving. Our transport section was particularly proud of Driver George Russell's pair of chesnut horses, which always attracted attention at demonstrations of this kind.

The 6th March found us on our way back to the front. Rising on a frosty morning and breakfasting at 2.30, we were on the train bright and early. The work of entraining a Battalion, with all its paraphernalia, reminded us very much of a huge circus loading up. It was a slow and tedious performance, and on a cold morning, with ice and frost over everything, was not fruitful of much enjoyment.

We were back to Kortepyp by the evening of the 6th, and prepared at once for duty in the firing line, going into the Warneton sector on the following day, under the command of Major Ellwood, M.C.

The Battalion on this occasion travelled by the light railway from Connaught Siding to Hyde Park Corner, from which point "A" and "B" Coys. moved forward by Warneton track, and "C" and "D" Coys. by Messines Road and Douve Walk. The line was taken over from the 34th Battalion, the relief being completed by 10.30 p.m. "A" and "B" Coys. were posted in the front line at Wally Support, with "C" Coy. in close supports at Gray's Trench, and "D" Coy. in reserve at Avenue Farm. The Battalion held the left of the Brigade sector opposite the ruins of Warneton, with the River Douve on the left flank.

Hostile artillery was very active from 5.40 on the following morning till 1 p.m., particular attention being paid by the German guns to our front lines and the Warneton track. By way of reciprocating this hostility, our guns began a brisk bombardment of the enemy trenches at 9 p.m., and till 12 p.m. the Hun was strafed most liberally. Our artillery fire was too much for the enemy's nerves. Fearing an infantry attack, he fired his S.O.S. and brought on a general artillery engagement, his barrage being directed upon our firing line, supports and communication tracks. Fortunately most of his shells fell just wide of our positions, and though we sustained some casualties, we came through the eventful night more satisfactorily than might have been anticipated.

At 4.50 a.m. on the 9th, when the gunfire had subsided, a bugle was heard in the German line, followed by the firing of green flares. These performances were probably Fritz's signal to his troops to stand down. Outbursts of gunfire on both sides occurred during the day, and that night the Boche supported his artillery with minenwerfers, with which he pounded our line. Our trenches were badly damaged in places, and steps had to be taken immediately to repair the positions. We felt sure, however, that Fritz was heavily involved in the same urgent duty.

Patrol work was carried on consistently throughout these unpleasant nights, and our parties often came into conflict with Huns on the same errand. The initiative and pluck of our men usually gave Fritz second honours in the warlike greetings exchanged by these prowling and inquisitive soldiers.

Our artillery at this time evidently had the fighting spirit highly developed, as the gunners showed no inclination to give the Boche any rest. They eased off for a while only to break out with added fury, and the German batteries, obliged to keep pace as far as possible with the energy on our side, resorted to the use of his gas shells as well as high explosives. Our position in the line was accordingly decidedly unhealthy.

Along the whole front the enemy was subjected to shocks imparted by raiding parties, who kept the Boche in constant fear. These raids were accompanied by brisk bombardments. Whenever our guns broke out with unusual energy, the Hun immediately "stood to" to receive his uninvited visitors. To put him off his guard as much as possible, the guns indulged in frequent short, severe actions at times when no raid was contemplated, and the Germans must have been highly annoyed as well as puzzled.

The front had livened up beyond all comparison with the conditions prevailing a month earlier. Important developments were anticipated on both sides. It was noticed that the enemy had been busy constructing bridges over the Lys. Instead of the half-dozen crossings observed hitherto, there were now about 20 bridges over this stream, and this was regarded as a sure sign of German preparation for offensive operations.

Our command had plans to counteract any attack by the Boche here. In the event of a German assault, a strong counter-attack would have been launched with the object of pushing the enemy out of Warneton.

Our heavy artillery had been hammering away at the enemy's positions with good results. A concrete tower in Warneton, used by the Germans as an observation post, and which had for a long time withstood the fire of our lighter guns, had now disappeared.

In spite of the increased activity on the front, every effort was made to supply the troops in the line with hot meals. The company cooks established themselves within 800 yards of the front line, and were supplied with charcoal so that they might have the benefit of smokeless fires. A soup kitchen was also established near the R.A.P., close to the line, and here cocoa supplied by the Y.M.C.A. was kept hot for men who came under the doctor's eye, and also any others who felt the need of a stimulant. The Y.M.C.A. was also able to supply a few cigarettes per man occasionally.

A trolley line from Ploegsteert Wood to the trenches was a great convenience for fatigue parties who had to deliver rations and other supplies to the line. The men loaded the trolleys in the wood, and at night pushed them over the hill to the front. This track could not be used in daylight, as it was under enemy observation, and even at night it was often a dangerous path, being at times heavily shelled by the German guns. It was not light work pushing the trolleys up the hill, but on the return journey the boys were able to indulge in a "joy ride," sitting on the trolleys and allowing them to dash down the slope with all the momentum they could gather. A stick jammed against one of the wheels acted as a brake, but if this failed to reduce the speed at dangerous curves and a trolley was overturned, it only added excitement to the ride.

Rain on the 10th gave us an unrequisitioned supply of water in the trenches, involving a good deal of labour in draining our positions.

During the forenoon of the 13th three Huns were observed sneaking towards our wire. A few bullets stopped their stealthy advance, one being killed and the others driven to cover. In the afternoon Lieut. Graham and Cpl. Molloy (two of our most intrepid soldiers) went out to see what had become of the little adventure, and to get indentification of the German regiment opposing us. Cpl. Molloy observed a Hun in a shell-hole only about five yards off. Although the German was armed with a rifle and several bombs, Molloy dashed at him and knocked him over, desiring to capture him alive and produce him to our Intelligence staff in the hope of eliciting some valuable information. When Fritz was brought in he gave his name as Germeiner Karl Wangemann, and his regiment the 228 R.I.R., 49th Division.

At 6 p.m. Lieut. Graham and Pte. L. Waxman went out and located another Hun, who showed fight. Our men covered him with their revolvers, whereupon he got up and bolted, hotly pursued. He refused to halt. This was foolish on his part, for our men were good shots. He fell shot through the heart. He had an Iron Cross and another decoration, and was also in possession of two of our Mills bombs.

It was discovered, by the identification of shells, that the Germans were using British 4.5 guns against us here. On one occasion they employed these guns to shell Battalion Headquarters, probably being desirous of stressing the point that they had somewhere made a capture.

The Warneton sector at this time was noted for minenwerfer activity on the part of the Boche. These trench guns, firing a large high explosive bomb, wrought havoc with our positions when they fell into the trenches, and the terrific concussion was one of the most nerve-racking sensations of the war.

Our speciality was the use of gas projectors, of which we had an unlimited supply. As many as 800 gas cylinders were used in one attack on the Hun positions. These gas attacks, which made a spectacular glow on the field and in the sky at night, must have been extremely costly to the Boche, whose stretcher-bearers and ambulance waggons were always observed working "overtime" after one of these illuminating demonstrations. When a gas attack was in course of preparation, large supplies of the cylinders were carried to the trenches, and the troops in the line were always thankful when they were used up on the Hun, as their presence in the trenches constituted a danger under enemy shell-fire.

The 23rd Battalion relieved us on the 16th, and we moved back to the Catacombs.

The transport lines during the Battalion's operations at Warneton were at Antrim Lines, near Romarin.

After a day's rest and a clean up at the baths the Battalion was again divided into working parties for various forms of labour on the front. These duties included the refitting and fire-stepping of trenches in the support line, cleaning up River Lane, digging gun-pits at Stinking Farm, wiring behind the front line, and building up the parapet at Ugly Lane. The names given to these localities will indicate, without any description, their peculiar characteristics, as the terms employed are expressive of the conditions obtaining at these places.

These were busy days in this locality. Our command was anticipating a German push, and everywhere men were toiling day and night, working in shifts, putting up more wire, improving trenches and firing positions, laying cables for communications, getting up large supplies of shells and other ammunition, and making ready for the big days which everybody felt were coming very soon. In the front trenches the men were kept busy on the defences. At night all men not on post turned to with picks and shovels, and toiled through the hours of darkness to make the positions more secure. When out of the line parties of men, mostly those with some knowledge of brickwork, were employed constructing concrete posts for machine guns.

The large Ploegsteert Wood everywhere showed the scars made by the shells that had been thrown into it from time to time. Little cemeteries, where many soldiers slept peacefully, had their places here too, and around them on every side batteries of our heavy howitzers barked and spat at the enemy a few miles away. There were shanties barricaded with sandbags, where tea, cocoa, and biscuits were served to the troops as they passed in and out of the line. Regimental cooks kept their fires going day and night preparing food for the men, who sometimes had their breakfast at 3 a.m. and their evening meal at midnight.

But the feature of the Wood was the subterranean dwelling place known as the Catacombs—passages cut into the side of Catacomb Hill (otherwise known as Hill 70), where hundreds of men lived and slept when off duty, secure from shells and all the dangers of war. These commodious chambers resembled huge ant beds, for whole Battalions of men disappeared into the earth and came out in swarms, as if they were emerging from some other world underground. Bunks, made of wooden frames and wire netting, ranged in tiers and set close together in the long corridors, all fitted with electric light, constituted the furnishings, and the corridors were all named like thoroughfares in a town, for this underground "village" was so extensive that when searching for a mate one required to have his "address," which would be something after this nature: L/Cpl. Snorer, No. 3 Platoon, 24th Battalion, Block 13, Bunk No. 975, Henry Avenue.

The construction of these Catacombs had been commenced by the New Zealanders and completed by the Australian Tunnellers and the Royal Engineers, and the work equalled, if it did not surpass, any effort of the Germans at burrowing. The main entrances were named Christchurch Road, Melbourne Road and Plumer Road, while the intersecting corridors in the interior were mostly known as avenues. A large figure of a kangaroo over the Melbourne Road entrance indicated that the Australians had a big claim on this habitation.

When the sun shone—a rare event at that time of the year—all the soldier ants who were not asleep came out and sat in the open-air, for the atmosphere "indoors" was exceedingly thick.

Some of the soldiers named the Catacombs the Hotel Cecil. On fine days bands were sent up to the wood, and they played outside the "hotel." With a favourable wind Fritz could hear the music distinctly, and he sometimes sent over a salvo of shells to liven up the programme. When a shell screeched past or landed close to the band it was a big effort for the instrmentalists to keep their attention on the music and put in all the notes, for a shell is a splendid thing to take away one's breath. In the first year of the war, that scene, with guns flashing, shells bursting dangerously close, men sitting about in exposed positions, and a band playing under the nose of the enemy, would have been considered a picture indicative of a community of lunatics. But the men who lived there got no further back from the front for weeks at a stretch, and the bands were employed to brighten the hours of those very dreary days. It was just one of many evidences of the fact that the army had settled down to a weary task, whose prolonged duration was its worst feature, and men who were set apart to keep up the spirits of others were regarded as doing a work almost as important as the killing of enemy soldiers.

MUSTARD GAS.

While our "A" and "D" Coys. were occupying dug-outs at Prowse Point on the night of 20th-21st March they were subjected to a heavy bombardment with gas shells. From 1 a.m. till 5 a.m. the locality was drenched with mustard gas. It is estimated that 5000 shells of 77 m.m. and 10.5 c.m. were fired into an area of ten acres. As soon as the presence of the gas was detected the gas section gave the alarm and warned the occupants of the dug-outs. Respirators were put on and worn for several hours continuously. The gas, however, had pervaded the whole area before these precautions could be put into operation, as the men were asleep at the time, and the bursting of gas shells in the soft earth was not a sufficient disturbance to rouse the troops. This gas had a delayed action, and it was not until 30 or 40 hours after contact that its effects were fully felt. Then the eyes and nostrils became acutely irritated, and in many cases temporary blindness resulted.

Casualties were numerous, though only one death occurred. Seven officers and 212 other ranks were evacuated to the Casualty Clearing Station. The victims of the gas were in a sad plight. One could have imagined that the aid-post at the Catacombs was an asylum for the blind.

Men were led about or groped their way in partial blindness, with eyes bandaged and faces blistered. The R.M.O. (Major D. D. Coutts), with his A.M.C. staff and the regimental stretcher-bearers, worked zealously and untiringly to relieve the afflictions of the men, and more serious results might have followed but for the efforts of the medical staff.

It was necessary to evacuate the gas area, and later, when the fumes had passed off, the equipment which the troops had discarded in their plight was salvaged, being collected by the aid of sticks and hooks, for the collectors were not disposed to touch anything with their hands, having no particular liking for blisters and poison.

Fritz paid dearly for his use of gas on that occasion, for our guns fired gas shells on to his positions till his lines must have been reeking with fumes.

The German Drive.

On 21st March, 1918, the Germans launched their big attack on the Allied line in their last desperate attempt to reach Paris. It was several days before we gleaned much information concerning the Hun advance at Cambrai and St. Quentin, but the knowledge that the enemy had broken through on a wide front and was advancing every day made us restless and anxious. The expected crash had come, and we realised that for us as well as all other units momentous days were at hand. Everybody had an intuitive assurance that we would not remain long in Flanders now, but until orders were received for more important duties, we must carry on in our present location.

While the Battalion was on the Warneton sector a small party of our best entertainers was set apart as a pierrot troupe to provide amusement for the troops when they were out of the line. Stage scenery was painted, and costumes were obtained from the Y.M.C.A. Several highly successful performances were given to other units while waiting for an opportunity to show before our own men, but the German swoop put an end to our little enterprise. Every man was urgently needed to build up the unit's fighting strength.

REDUCED FIGHTING STRENGTH.

The Battalion was now seriously reduced in strength, and we were due for duty in the firing line on the Warneton sector on 24th April. The C.O. (Lieut.-Colonel James) was so confident of his men that he decided to carry on without asking for assistance. It was not possible on this occasion to leave a nucleus in reserve. Every available man was put into action. "A" and "D" Coys., which had gathered in a few men from other duties, and also had a few of their gassed men on duty again, were now only represented by remnants, so "B" and "C" Coys. took over the Battalion sector of the front, with "A" Coy. of the 23rd Battalion in support, while the "Remnants" took up positions at La Potterie Farm and Watchful Post. La Potterie Farm was surrounded by a moat, which had to be crossed by boats or rafts. One of our men was drowned at this spot.

The front was not particularly active until the night of the 26th, when our Stokes mortars bombarded the German lines in front of Warneton, and Fritz made a weak retaliation. He endeavoured to balance the scores on the following night by using his minenwerfers against us, but when he found this stirred up our artillery and brought further trouble upon himself he ceased fire. During the next few days, however, the Hun indulged in outbursts of shell and bomb fire on our front line, adding some gas to give his "iron rations" a little flavour.

The morning of 30th was more eventful. At 1 a.m. our artillery launched a gas attack on Warneton. Fritz made a spectacular display with his signals, using a variety of flares with much liberality, and giving us quite an entertaining exhibition. His guns returned our fire for a while, but a favourable wind appeared to carry our gas to his battery positions, for his energy quickly waned.

It was evident that the Boche was for the time concentrating his energy on his advance towards the Somme. At least the weak retaliation he made against the heavy fire of our artillery on our part of the front suggested that he had removed some of his guns, as he had adopted a ruse of firing a particular gun in many directions, contrary to his usual methods. This, however, may have been a piece cf deception on his part, with the object of leading the British command to the conclusion that he had weakened his line here, and by persuading us to do the same, or what we supposed he had done, open the way for another successful drive. (These speculations, of course, are prompted by the nature of the sensational developments which followed, as it will be remembered that this is just what happened.)

Meanwhile the German horde was pressing on towards

the Somme. The whole front was agitated, and the troops were in a state of apprehension. Rumours of an alarming character got abroad in consequence of the undisputed fact that the enemy was still pushing on. Two Australian Divisions (the Third and Fourth), which happened to be out of the line when the crash came, had been hurried away to the big battle, and the Fifth Division was to follow them at the earliest moment. The First and Second Divisions had to be left on the Flanders front till they could be relieved. The troops knew their turn would come, and they awaited orders impatiently.

It was not till 1st April that the 22nd Battalion, Wilts Regiment, which had been through the fiery ordeal of the German push, arrived to relieve us. The Wilts, though partially reorganised during their hurried transfer to the north, were still minus important parts of their equipment, and notwithstanding that our Battalion had orders to move out immediately and get on the road early the following morning, some of our Lewis gunners and guns had to be left in the line for some hours till the relieving troops established themselves and made good their shortages.

BOUND FOR THE SOMME.

The 24th Battalion left the line at Warneton at about 10 o'clock on the night of 1st April, and boarding the train on the light railway at Racine Dump under shell-fire, travelled to Romarin Siding, from which point the men were marched to billets at Neuve Eglise.

The Division was to move back to the permanent railway system and organise for battle on the Somme.

An early reveille on the 2nd, a hurried breakfast, and we were soon aboard a column of motor waggons bound for the rendezvous. The route was by way of Locre, Fletre and Caestre, and our destination the locality of Strazeele, where we were to go into billets and prepare to move at the shortest notice.

As we rattled away from the front we were struck by the deserted aspect of the field. In the reserve areas where thousands of troops had always hitherto been encountered not a single fighting unit remained, and the men could not help remarking: "What if Fritz came at this front now?" A few men on isolated duty here and there, a prison cage with a batch of defaulters, a workshop, or a small staff of soldiers at the baths, with no patrons for their usually crowded ablution huts, marked the deserted camps.

All were in great spirits in spite of the prospects of heavy fighting, and the one topic of conversation was the possible outcome of the big battle further south. Would the Boche be able to push the great assault to a victorious conclusion, or could he be held and the tide turned on his horde? With an intimate knowledge of the country from Amiens to the Hindenburg line at Bullecourt, everybody knew where the enemy could have been held or where a successful stand could yet be made. That Bapaume had fallen was a painful piece of intelligence, for our men remembered only too well what it had cost the Australians to win that town a year before.

The 'bus journey was completed early in the day, and there was time after getting to billets to accomplish much in the overhauling of equipment and arms, discarding unnecessary paraphernalia, and penning a few vague lines to the folks at home on the sudden and critical developments at the front.

On the following day the Battalion was ready for inspection by the C.O. Although everybody was anxious, there was no outward sign of excitement. The band played as usual, and the officers and N.C.O.s went about their duties with coolness and good humour.

The C.O. availed himself of the opportunity to express his appreciation of the cheerfulness with which the men, in spite of their greatly reduced numbers, had carried out their duties in the line during the last period of trench work at Warneton. With such a spirit of resolution, he felt sure the Battalion would acquit itself with credit, whatever the tasks of battle might be ahead.

The suspense was broken on the 4th, when orders were received to move that night. The Brigade was to entrain at Strazeele. Though the first parties were not to leave the billets until after midnight, few of the men tried to sleep. They were merrier that night than they had been for many days. They romped and wrestled on the straw in the barns, played cards by the light of candles, sang songs in chorus, told their funniest stories, laughed, and waited for the hour of departure.

By daybreak the last parties were on the road, marching in the rain to the railway siding, a distance of several miles. When the band ceased its music the boys took up the tune and whistled it, and the people who peered out of windows with anxious faces must have wished that they could have felt as little concern for fate in the immediate future as these light-hearted soldiers evidently did.

The troop trains were composed of the usual jolting trucks, but so long as there was anything which offered a ride the men were content. Soon we were on the way, and we travelled by way of Calais, Boulogne, and Abbeville. Never did the boys exhibit so much mirth on a tiring journey. Every stopping place was the scene of some new frolic, every town and village the object of a heartening demonstration, every smiling girl the recipient of hand-thrown kisses.

At Calais, where our train came to a standstill and gave promise of remaining for a while, the band got out to serenade a company of W.A.A.C.s, who waved their handkerchiefs and shouted their hearty greetings and good wishes, knowing full well whither the troops were bound. Just as the band struck up the train moved off, and instead of music the girls had the entertainment of watching the instrumentalists struggling to get on board, running along the line with their instruments held up to the out-stretched arms of their pals, and getting nearer the end of the train at every step. The bass drummer, being most awkwardly handicapped, was dragged into the last truck thoroughly exhausted.

It was a slow journey, and we did not detrain at Hangest-sur-Somme until 5.30 p.m. At that hour a march of 17 miles to Vaux-en-Amienois was before us. At 9 p.m. the column rested for an hour on the road, and the troops were served with hot tea from the cookers. Continuing in the dark, the Somme was crossed at Ailly, and we arrived, exceedingly fatigued, at our destination at 2 a.m. The company cooks, who had arrived earlier, had a hot stew ready for the troops. The C.O., knowing how severe the strain had been on the men, with their arms, equipment and packs, proposed to allow them to rest till the morning was well advanced. But rest was not a factor which counted much on the field into which we had now been thrown. The troops had scarcely got into their billets when orders arrived for action. The Battalion was to have reveille at 4.30 a.m., breakfast, packs stored, and on the way to the front in fighting order by 6 a.m.

It was a difficult task to rouse the tired men, but it had to be done, and the unit was on its way at the appointed hour. A march of four kilometres brought us to Bert-angles, where we embussed, and were then conveyed via Amiens, Querrieu and Pont Noyelles to a point on the Albert

Road. Then we marched again, and eventually arrived at Baizeux.

The rapidity with which orders were issued and changed for the disposition of troops on the front in those days of uncertainty and high tension is indicated by our experiences for the remainder of that day. At first we were to occupy billets at Baizeux, but at midday the unit was despatched to assist in the urgent work of putting up wire entanglements and digging trenches for the defence of Amiens. We reached Baizeux at 5 p.m., and fresh orders disposed the Battalion in the trenches in the vicinity. Later these orders were cancelled, and the unit was instructed to move up to support the line at Lavieville. Before this order was put into effect we were assigned to positions at Millencourt as close supports to the Twelfth Brigade, and here we spent the night. Rain set in at dusk, and we faced the discomfort of a cold, wet, dark night huddled against a hedge in a thoroughly wretched condition. Gun flashes and flares fitfully illuminated the field. (The Twelfth Brigade was commanded by Brigadier-General Gellibrand, formerly commander of the Sixth Brigade).

The three Australian Divisions which had preceded ours to the Somme had achieved wonderful successes against the strong forces of the enemy. The German hordes had been held up, but the situation was still exceedingly critical. Any hour might have witnessed another German assault. The defence of Amiens was still a comparatively thin line of troops, mostly Australians, and our units were scattered. Means of communication were few and difficult, and everywhere there was anxiety occasioned by the uncertainty of the position. Still, the men were optimistic, and were not disposed to worry over the enemy that night if fortune gave them an opportunity to rest. So they made the best use of their waterproof sheets, and lay down to sleep in the rain.

At dawn we moved into a gully, and here the men set themselves to "dig in." Millencourt, being close to the battle line, was crumbling to ruins under the fire of the German guns, and while it was no place to seek shelter, the men made incursions into the village and carried out timber for the erection of shelters in the safer region of the gully. They soon had the banks honeycombed with funk-holes, and when they covered the floors of these nooks with straw, they were fairly comfortable, even though their legs remained exposed when they lay down to sleep.

MILLENCOURT.

The village of Millencourt had been hurriedly evacuated by the residents owing to the sudden German advance, and the houses were found stocked with the general requirements of domestic life. Our men undertook, as a purely voluntary duty, to save from destruction as much of the people's property as they were able. A quantity of valuable furniture, hundreds of bags of oats, tons of potatoes, and other goods were salvaged while the Boche spasmodically shelled the doomed village. This property was handed over to the French Mission for distribution among the refugees, who had taken shelter in the towns and villages out of the range of the guns, and the thoughtfulness of the troops was greatly appreciated by the authorities and the unfortunate people who benefited by this labour of love.

Many of the boys salvaged cooking utensils, carted potatoes to their dug-outs, and fried "chips" until they exhausted the supply of fat.

Cellars in the village were eventually used as Headquarters, quartermaster's stores, aid-posts, and baths. For the purpose of ablution a number of wooden tubs were collected, fires and coppers put into use, and while Hun explosives burst overhead all ranks had a thorough clean up. In the absence of clean underclothing, the men in many instances made use of the lingerie which terrified females had left behind, and though lace-edged whatnots were not countenanced in army uniform, they were fresh and clean, and the lads were persuaded that the girls were not likely to regard the use of their garments as any personal offence, even though they might have blushed at the scene had they been present. Steel helmets gave place to silk hats, and frock coats were worn over the khaki tunics. So much civilian attire was put into use that the troops resembled a pantomime company. The novelty of "swanking" in black cloth and tall hats was a rare bit of relaxation, but the irregularity of dress became so pronounced that the command was obliged to issue an order prohibiting the wearing of civilian clothes.

wo men of a unit which had arrived on this front some days earlier had gone into action dressed as "the old man and the old woman." Impersonating a peasant woman enraged at the action of the Germans in destroying her house, one man had fought so well, in spite of the handicap of skirts, that he was awarded a decoration.

A notable exploit by a party of 24th Battalion men was the daring rescue of a valuable piano at Millencourt. Several of the bandsmen, doubtless actuated by musical sentiment, resolved that the instrument could not be left to suffer destruction while the girls who had spent many a pleasant hour in its sweet company wept over the fate of their home and all its treasures. Volunteers were called for, and while enemy shells crashed on the village, and men were being killed, they dashed through the debris-strewn streets to a deep cellar in which the signallers and runners had already placed the piano for safety. This had been a wise precaution, as the house in which the piano was found was already in ruins. The adventure was not to succeed without much difficulty... It had been hoped to place the instrument on one of the ration limbers which came up with supplies every evening, but that night the Hun bestowed upon us a vigorous bombardment with high explosives, and the transport boys brought the rations up at the gallop and departed in the same expeditious manner, being persuaded that it was no time to dally over a piano or even a thousand pianos. So the bandsmen took shelter with the signallers and runners underground, and resolved to spend the night between white sheets in beds which had been carried there from the houses. Fritz added gas shells to his bombardment during the night, and the village reeked with poisonous fumes.

During the night the piano was wrapped in thick layers of blankets and padded with civilian garments, ready for a rough passage on the following morning. After a breakfast of fried potatoes and coffee, the bandsmen set out to find a vehicle suitable for the transportation of the piano No horse was available, but the boys determined to supply "donkey power" themselves, so, hauling a heavy two-wheeled cart out of a yard, they backed it to the door of the cellar. With the help of the signallers and runners it was got aboard after much exertion, and as the bombardment had eased off, it was decided to make a load up by adding clothing and foodstuffs, which would be of service to the refugees. Duty called away all but two of the party, and the hefty pair started off with their heavy load. The journey to the edge of the village was a hard struggle, but here the road ran down hill past the gully occupied by the Battalion. Having no brake on the cart, the two men decided to "let her go" down the slope, taking the doubtful chance of being able to steer the vehicle round the curves when it gained momentum by its weight. The first bend was negotiated safely, but at the second turn the pace was too great, and the cart plunged into a gutter. Invoking aid, the boys, after an hour's labour, had the cart on the way again, and they reached the gully amid the cheers of the troops. Dragging the load a mile further, they awaited an artillery team moving back from the front, and hitched the cart behind a waggon. By short stages and with frequent delays they continued till late at night, and in the small hours of the morning unloaded their prize in the village of Montigny, where our transport lines had been established. For several days the troops in billets there gathered round the piano and sang all the songs they could call to mind, while a representative of the French Mission sought the owners to inform them of their good fortune. Some days later the piano, a handsome instrument, was handed over.

Was it worth while? The girls and their mother, with tears in their eyes, declared it was. And perhaps they were the best judges.

The clothes and food were eagerly and gratefully sought by aged women who had most need of them.

While the Battalion was at Millencourt we were also able to salvage iron and timber, and send this material forward for use in the construction of shelters for other troops.

Our turn for duty in the front came on the 11th April, when we moved in to relieve the 23rd Battalion, the change-over being complete by 10 p.m. "A" Coy. was placed in the out-posts, "C" and "D" Coys. in Pioneer Trench, and "B" Coy. in supports. The country here was familiar to us, but in the dark it was difficult to discover just where we were.

At dawn we found ourselves about 1500 yards west of Albert, with the famous "Hanging Virgin" looking down on the ruins of the old town, now in the hands of the enemy. Albert had been our Army Headquarters in the Somme offensive of 1916. It was with mixed feelings that we now viewed the historic field, particularly the ridge to the east, behind which lay Pozieres and the graves of many of our dead, now at the mercy of the enemy.

The front was not particularly active that day, and the men were able to improve the trenches and commence the construction of dug-outs. Light shelling was indulged in by the enemy on our area, and snipers were busy, but no casualties were suffered. A reconnoitring patrol went out, but no encounter took place with the Hun. Wire was put up to protect some of the forward posts.

At 12.45 a.m. on the 14th Lieut. J. T. Pocknell and 20 other ranks, with a Lewis gun, attempted to cut out an enemy post on the right of the Battalion sector astride the Albert-Amiens Road. The night was very dark, and the party crawled to within 50 yards of the objective. A heavy bomb fight was in progress 200 yards to the right, and the enemy was alert along the front. The enemy post was protected by three machine guns, which fired continually. Several attempts were made to enter the enemy's position, but the post was found to be too strongly defended by covering fire from other points, and the party withdrew. One of our men was badly wounded by machine-gun fire.

The enemy was too far away at this point of the front

for offensive action on our part. Our duty for the time was to garrison the line where our defences had been set up.

Although the Boche had been checked in his advance, it was anticipated that he would make another assault on a large scale as soon as he had reorganised his forces. Therefore every unit was urged to make the most of every hour by improving the defences. For miles behind our front thousands of men were toiling zealously day and night digging trenches and wiring a series of defence systems. The command was determined that, however strong the German army might be, if the Hun ever reached Amiens he would achieve that success only by fighting every yard of the way, and at tremendous cost. Even in the front line the units were working as well as watching. On our sector we were able to accomplish a good deal in the strengthening of the position. Pioneer Trench was deepened, an aid-post provided, additional wire put up, and the lines made more habitable for the troops.

Enemy artillery became more active on the 15th, and it was observed that the Hun was apparently practising S.O.S. fire.

That night we were relieved from the front line by the 23rd Battalion. While moving out two of our companies came under heavy shell-fire, and a number of men were wounded.

Going into our former positions at Millencourt, we carried on with the general work of strengthening the line, including the erection of wire entanglements in front of the Lavieville defences. The handling of barbed-wire was no pleasant job, particularly if carried out in the dark and attended by enemy fire.

We were due to return to the firing line on the evening of the 19th, but before we moved off a German bombardment caused us several casualties. The relief was effected on time, and that night our men erected 18 coils of "concertina" wire on the out-post line. Counter bombardments by the artillery made the following day more eventful, and our positions came in for a strafing by the enemy guns.

During this activity Signaller Cpl. V. Hughes, a popular and gallant soldier, was killed.

The nights were fully occupied with useful work, including the deepening of Pioneer Trench and the construction of firesteps.

At this time we noticed that the statue known as the "Hanging Virgin," which for several years remained suspended on the tower of the Albert Church, had disappeared, having fallen under the effects of the bombardment to which the town was again subjected. There had been a prophecy that the fall of this statue would foretell the end of the war. Most men were too sceptical to place much faith in the prophecy, but nobody had any objection to its fulfilment. Time proved that the prophet was not far out in his prediction.

A breeze from the north on the night of the 21st carried some gas on to our sector, but not sufficient to cause us any serious inconvenience, and the men were able to commence the work of digging trenches to link up the out-posts, though their labours were hampered by the fumes. Enemy shellfire put five of our men out of action.

The 23rd was a more trying day. The German guns shelled us frequently, and the vicinity of the Battalion Headquarters was heavily bombarded. Gas was also inflicted upon us, compelling the men at one stage to wear their respirators for half an hour. Cpl. W. M. Macdonald was killed on this day.

At about 7 p.m. a plane with Bristol (British) markings flew over our lines, descending to a low altitude and firing with a machine gun on the troops. Bullets lodged within a few feet of the C.O. Several of these bullets were dug up and were found to be enemy bullets. This was one of many proofs that the Hun used our aeroplanes against us when they fell into his hands.

Our patrols, which were continually on the lookout for enemy movements, discovered a large party of Germans at work on the night of the 24th, and our artillery, being advised of their whereabouts, soon upset their operations.

The linking up of the out-posts and the excavation of dug-outs for shelter proceeded till the night of 25th, when we were relieved and again went back to Millencourt.

Our transport section had done good work on this sector in delivering rations and other supplies every night. At some points the limbers had deposited their loads within half a mile of the line.

The transport lines were at Montigny. This village was the scene of an amusing incident. A batch of German prisoners, on their way to internment, were halted here for a night. The Germans had arrived in the afternoon, and had attracted a good deal of attention. Soldiers on duty here gathered where the Huns were placed under guard. The Germans were apparently glad that their fighting days were over, for several produced mouth organs and began to entertain and cheer their comrades. Then the whole company commenced to sing, having derived a feeling of contentment from a meal of bully-beef and biscuits. One asked for a violin, which a digger produced. The German proved a master of the fiddle, and delighted his mixed audience. Some of the Australians were anxious to hear the Huns sing "The Watch on the Rhine," and after much persuasion the prisoners, although fearing the hostility of the French residents, broke into this German melody. In a few minutes the elderly French residents besieged the prison quarters from all directions, and bombarded the Huns with bricks, sticks, and a variety of missiles. The music quickly subsided. On the village square, a hundred yards away, an Australian band played the Marseillaise as a counter melody.

The Germans could scarcely believe their eyes when they saw our troops with white bread and white sugar. They had seen neither for many a day, and they had been told that the Allies were reduced to similar straits. After that they were not so sure that Hindenburg was winning.

The 25th April, being the anniversary of Anzac Day, was celebrated in the back areas wherever duties permitted, though at the front there was no time for anything of this nature. Our Battalion band was selected to perform at an important celebration at the 3rd Australian General Hospital at Abbeville, where sports and evening entertainments were held.

The Battalion was now included in the Divisional reserves, but continued for several days in their old positions at Millencourt. After equipment and clothes had been cleaned, working parties were detailed to carry on various kinds of work, including the wiring of the defences at Lavieville.

On the evening of 29th the enemy began a systematic area shoot on the batteries near Millencourt, his purpose being to search the whole of the locality piece by piece, and so make sure of destroying our guns. This procedure eventually involved our camping site, and we were obliged to get out of the way for the time being. The boys were often put to the necessity of dodging shell-fire, and they were well trained in the methods of evading bombardments of specified areas when they were not "on post."

Spring was now brightening the country, though war had no sympathy with her tender mission, and bright flowers which began to bloom had no security against the blighting effects of shells or the withering breath of poisonous gases. The woods, now bursting into leaf, harboured birds, hares, and other game, and, in spite of forbidding orders, the men at times could not resist the temptation of "potting" something for the cooks.

About this time the Battalion received its 20th draft of reinforcements.

WARLOY AGAIN.

At the beginning of May preparations were made to move back for a short period of rest. Leaving the front on the 2nd, we set out for Pont Noyelles, on the little River Hallue. Passing through Henencourt, we arrived at Warloy, where we had the opportunity of meeting some of our friends among the residents of our former happy billeting area. It was a sad reunion. When we left Warloy in the summer of 1917 the little community, then well out of reach of enemy guns, was battling cheerfully and hopefully against the hardships of war. But now the German avalanche had gone close to mopping it up in a wild overwhelming rush. Most of the inhabitants had fled at the approach of the enemy, who had been held up at the threshhold of the village. Deadly explosives crashed among the houses occasionally, and only the people who were prepared to stay and face the worst had dared to remain. They rushed to greet the Battalion they knew so well, clasping the hands of the men and shaking them excitedly with great admiration.

Parties of our men who were able to halt for a while in the village were dragged by the people into the houses and compelled to drink till their capacity for coffee and vin blanc was in danger of being overtaxed. Then they moved on, carrying with them the good wishes of the inhabitants and passing out of view while the excited people waved their hands and smiled in spite of their heavy hearts.

After lunch at Contay the march was continued, and at Montigny the band and a number of details joined the column, which passed through Frechencourt and reached Pont Noyelles in the afternoon.

The country here offered a pleasing view, and was an acceptable change from the conditions at the front. The standing crops in the fields and the wooded country in the river valley, viewed from the higher ground, made a picturesque landscape, marred only by the ceaseless war traffic on the roads.

A week spent at Pont Noyelles was made as pleasant for the troops as circumstances would permit. The billets were fairly comfortable, and the river, with the trees clothed in their spring dress of fresh leaves, made the valley a cosy corner for a few days' rest. Efforts were made to improve the rations, and altogether the men lived well. Practice alarms had the Battalion "standing to" frequently, but nothing more serious than a few enemy shells from long range guns and nocturnal prowling and bombing in the vicinity by aeroplanes disturbed the contented men. The village had been almost completely deserted by its inhabitants, who had gone back to safer regions.

The 8th May, the third anniversary of the Sixth Brigade's departure from Australia, was celebrated in some form by all original members of the unit. The number of "old hands" had dwindled sadly during the three years of strenuous service, but the reputation of the Battalion was safe in the hands of the splendid men who had joined up from time to time as reinforcements. The officers held a dinner in honour of the day, attended by original men only. It was a pleasing thing to note that only four of the officers at this dinner had not been promoted from the ranks. That was a testimony to the good soldierly qualities of the N.C.O.s, who were always recognised as a highly efficient part of the unit's machinery. The wisdom of selecting officers who had served in the ranks, and who had the inestimable advantage of field experience, had long been recognised, and the success which the Battalion achieved in action from time to time was admittedly largely due to this policy.

While we were at Pont Noyelles our Regimental Quartermaster, Lieut. P. S Carne, M.S.M., was the victim of a serious accident. Anticipating orders to move forward again, the R.Q.M. rode to Franvillers to select a store in the new area, and on the road, among the heavy traffic, his horse took fright, throwing its rider on to the hard metal. Lieut. Carne sustained concussion of the brain, and after a long period in hospital died in England.

IN ACTION AT BUIRE.

On 9th May the Battalion marched to Buire and took over a sector on that part of the line, near the Albert-Amiens railway, the River Ancre forming our right boundary, and on our left being the site of the abandoned C.C.S. The officers in charge of the companies here were Capt. J. A. Malhony, M.C., Lieut. E. S. Baldock, M.C., Capt. G. J. Bowden, and Capt. A. A. Ball, D.C.M. The enemy unit opposing us was the 54th R.D.

The men soon settled down to trench routine again. The first night was quiet, and covering patrols had nothing of note to report.

Every opportunity was taken to strengthen the positions. For this purpose the wire entanglements in front of our out-posts were added to.

Patrols were active on the night of 11th-12th, when encounters took place with enemy parties in No-man's-land. Lieut. Edgerton's party claimed several enemy casualties.

A minenwerfer gun was located by our patrols, and our Stokes mortars quickly put it out of action.

At the suggestion of the O.C. "C" Coy., our posts were advanced on the night of the 12th.

The site of the old C.C.S. was productive of a quantity of useful material. Parties of our men on salvage expeditions in the night recovered a number of tents and a complete X-Rays outfit. This hospital had been abandoned at the time of the sudden German advance in March, as the enemy had gone dangerously close to capturing the ground on which it stood, and which was now only a few hundred yards from our front line. The removal of the tents, under the nose of the enemy, and also under machine-gun fire, was therefore no playful task.

The country here was still productive of many things pertaining to civil life. A goat which had refused to desert its old home was taken on strength by the commander of "B" Coy., who, to forestall his rivals, got up at 5 a.m. every morning to milk this solitary relic of the district's dairy herd. In spite of his early rising, he got little milk, for resourceful Diggers milked the goat at midnight.

Life in the line was brightened by an innovation in respect to the Battalion canteen. Supplies of canteen stores were conveyed to the company quartermaster's, who sold the goods to the men. Trade was brisk, as much as 400 francs worth of cigarettes, biscuits, tinned fruit, etc., being disposed of to one company.

The belief held by some men that crucifixes were providentially protected from the destructive weapons of war was not always borne out by facts, but a crucifix near Buire appeared to be thus mysteriously blessed. It was probably the only spot on the field which did not occasionally come under the fire of the German guns. Consequently our transport men chose the crucifix as the proper place to deposit the unit's rations every night, being persuaded that food for the troops was equally deserving of the favour of the unseen power which could deflect enemy shells.

Lieut. Edgerton at this time made a reconnaissance of the bank of the River Ancre, and gave valuable suggestions for the placing of new foot bridges, and parties from "A" Coy. were detailed for the work. Others expended a good deal of labour deepening Emu Trench.

Among the few casualties sustained at this time was the death of Sgt. C. A. Collins, who was killed on the 15th.

We were relieved by the 23rd Battalion on the night of the 15th. Covering patrols were provided by Headquarters scouts and "D" Coy. The change-over was accomplished without interruption, and we went into the support lines evacuated by the relieving Battalion at Merricourt l'Abbe. At this place, Battalion Headquarters were established in the cellar of the chateau. "C" and "B" Coys. were in Ballarat Line, and "A" and "D" Coys. in Tasmanian Line, on the west of the Ribemont-Buire Road.

By collecting tubs from the village and using the hot water service of the chateau, the troops were able to enjoy a refreshing bath.

A cellar containing large quantities of red wine was discovered in this village. Guards were mounted over the cellar, and the wine was issued daily in liberal quantities to the companies.

Preparations were commenced for an attack on Ville-sur-Ancre, and reconnaissances and patrols were carried out with the object of making the troops familiar with the field over which they were to operate.

VILLE-SUR-ANCRE.

The Sixth Brigade attacked and captured Ville-sur-Ancre on 19th May. The object of this operation was to improve our lines and deprive the enemy of a covered line of approach. The plan decided upon by Brigadier-General Paton for the capture of the village was to invest it on three sides, smother it with shell-fire, and afterwards mop up the reduced garrison. Our line would then be established on the east side of the village. The main part of the attack was entrusted to the 22nd Battalion, which was to operate on the southern side, and the 24th Battalion was to attack on the northern side. The 23rd Battalion was to mop up the village, being assisted by the 21st Battalion, which was also to throw in a company to hem in the enemy garrison on the south side and link up the 22nd and 24th Battalions on the line of the objective after the village had been passed.

On the 24th Battalion's sector the country offered a marked contrast to many of the battlefields on which the troops had previously been engaged in France and Belgium. Instead of the scenes of desolation, chaotic ruins, and trenches to which the men had become accustomed, the Ancre Valley, having hitherto escaped the devastating effects of war, had an appearance of rustic beauty, for although the battle line had settled here for the time, the scars of war were yet almost unnoticeable in the timber and tall grass along the little stream. The village was doomed, but the fields were covered with wild, prolific vegetation. Marshy ground offered difficulties for advancing troops, as certain places were impassable, but the tall reeds, while affording shelter for the enemy and his machine-guns, also provided an element of the "sporting chance" for our men. The conditions were a welcome change from trench warfare.

SCENE NEAR VILLE-SUR-ANCRE.—Showing one of the footbridges over which the Battalion advanced to the attack on 19th May, 1918.

In the course of preparations for the attack our patrols had become fairly familiar with the country and had made useful reconnaissances with the object of selecting suitable points for the construction of foot-bridges, on which our men would cross the river for the assault. For several nights Lieut. Edgerton and others had annoyed the Boche along the river by waiting patiently in the long grass for a favourable moment to bestow Mills bombs on mystified Huns.

The main part of the 24th Battalion's task fell to "A" Coy., under Capt. J. A. Mahony, M.C. This company was to cross the river, capture the ground between the stream and the village, and link up with the 21st Battalion on the line of the objective. "D" Coy. (Capt. A. A. Ball, D.C.M.) was to advance without crossing the stream, and carry the line forward on our left flank.

Following his policy of conserving the strength of the unit as much as possible, the C.O. (Lieut.-Colonel James, D.S.O.), decided to put only two companies into the attack, and hold the other two in support. Experience had shown that where a small force could accomplish a task it was unwise to subject a whole Battalion to enemy fire.

The crossing of the river on frail improvised bridges (constructed by the Sixth Field Coy. Engineers with the assistance of our men) involved a good deal of risk, as these crossings were under enemy shell-fire, and the troops could pass over only in single file.

On the night of the 18th "D" Coy. made an early move and pushed as far forward as possible before "zero," while "A" Coy. was ready to advance at the moment of action. Battalion Headquarters were established in Buire-sur-l'Ancre.

At 1.40 a.m. on the 19th the Engineers reported that the construction of one of the bridges had been delayed by enemy gun fire.

At 2 a.m. our barrage opened as one gun, and the attack was launched north and south of the village. The enemy immediately fired his S.O.S. and illuminated the locality with numerous parachute flares, which, floating over the village and adding their bright lights to the continuous quivering gun flashes and the fire of bursting shells, made the scene highly spectacular and exciting.

"D" Coy., starting off from a position in advance of Emu Trench, met with little opposition, and soon gained their objective. "A" Coy. encountered German machine-gun posts, and were involved in some sharp fighting, during which a number of men distinguished themselves. Reinforcements who had gone into action for the first time displayed excellent fighting qualities. Wherever they had the opportunity they used their bayonets with awe-inspiring effect on the enemy.

On account of one of the bridges not being in position, Lieut. G. E. B. Munro ("A" Coy.) was unable to cross the river with his platoon at the appointed place, and while endeavouring to find a crossing was fatally wounded. Sgt. Collery took charge of the platoon, which eventually came into action. The bridge was later found overturned by shellfire.

"D" Coy. fired success signals at 2.35 a.m., indicating that the objectives from Buffer Post to the river had been occupied. At 3.52 a.m. Capt. Mahony reported that he was digging in on the line of the objective, and was endeavouring to get into touch with the 21st Battalion beyond the village.

The attack had been a complete success.

Our platoons on the right, where the ground was particularly swampy, established posts as far forward as possible, approximately 200 yards south of the river.

From Lieut. Kopson's platoon Pte. R. Holloway was sent to ascertain the position of the platoon on their left flank. On the way he encountered an enemy machine-gun post. He attacked it single-handed, and put it out of action.

Lieut. Edgerton's platoon had a busy morning. The right party encountered a German machine-gun, which was promptly rushed and captured, one of the crew being killed by L/Cpl. Johnson, M.M., and another being bayonetted by Sgt. E. V. White. The rest of the crew fled. The left party of this platoon came into contact with a German post. Bombs were thrown, and the Huns replied with machine-gun fire, wounding three of our men. Finding an enemy machine-gun active on the left, and noting that Lieut. Munro's party had not then crossed the river, Lieut. Edgerton proceeded to make his left flank secure. An enemy machine-gun post was rushed by this officer and Pte. Blankenberg and captured.

When Sgt. Collery got forward with his platoon he established three posts to cover Lieut. Edgerton's flank. A party of the enemy advanced against one of these posts, but they soon became casualties to our Lewis guns and rifles. When our men had established themselves they found the enemy snipers in the village "potting" at them from the houses. Lieut. Edgerton resolved to interrupt the operations of the Germans in the nearest house. Peeping through a hole in the wall, he observed a party of about a dozen Huns firing through loopholes at parties of the 23rd Battalion advancing through the village. He attacked them with his revolver, firing through a window. The Germans dropped their rifles and huddled in the corners for shelter. One or two appeared to make an effort to crawl up the chimney. Sgt. Holloway arrived at this moment, and kept the Huns dancing while Lieut. Edgerton called upon them to surrender. A party of 23rd Battalion men who were completing the mopping up of the German garrison in the village came on the scene, and the Huns were marched off. The prisoners included an officer.

At about 5 a.m. a party of the 23rd Battalion was observed almost directly in front of Lieut. Kopson's platoon. As it was impossible to establish posts at the appointed position, this platoon posted itself in rear of Lieut. Edgerton's platoon.

When the mopping up was complete an effort was made to get into contact with the 21st Battalion. This was accomplished by Captain Mahony at about 10 a.m. at the west end of the village. The troops here were operating in the river valley, where posts were in some instances separated by an impassable morass.

The enemy began to shell our new positions when he realised that the village was in our hands, and his guns increased their activity as the morning advanced. With the exception of the Lewis gunners covering the front, our men were spread out behind the trees to avoid heavy casualties.

At 2.30 p.m., after consultation with the Brigade major, all the posts of our right company were withdrawn to a new line, as it was found that they were masking the fire of the 21st Battalion.

Eleven posts in all were established by the 24th Battalion and held till 11.45 p.m. on the 19th, when we were relieved by the 23rd Battalion.

Our carrying parties from "B" and "C" Coys. rendered excellent service in getting forward supplies of small arms ammunition and bombs to the posts.

The German shell fire was at times severe at points where hostile airmen had located our men, but our casualties were not heavy considering the success of the operation. Our wounded were exposed to hostile fire while they were being removed, and wounded German prisoners suffered further at the hands of their own forces.

Our signallers carried out their duties with promptitude and success. Telephone communication with the captured positions was established immediately the objectives were gained, and the telephone lines were maintained with a marked absence of interruptions.

The barrage put down by our guns was excellent up to the time the objectives were reached, and the shooting showed wonderful accuracy. The pace was a hundred yards in three minutes.

The 24th Battalion casualties were:—Killed, 6 other ranks; wounded, 3 officers, 22 other ranks. The casualties for the whole Brigade numbered 256 (mostly wounded).

The prisoners captured by the four Battalions numbered about 900.

The complete success of the operation was due to the fine offensive spirit of all ranks, and careful preparation and studied co-operation by all units.

The statements of enemy prisoners showed that the attack was expected, but rather in the form of a demonstration simultaneous with a big attack further north. Many of the German prisoners were partly dressed in English uniform, indicating that the Boche was short of clothing. This uniform had probably been captured from British army stores during the enemy's advance.

The whole of the Brigade units co-operated effectively throughout the operation. The work of the Sixth Machine Gun Coy., the Stokes Mortar sections, and the Brigade snipers was most praiseworthy, while the Sixth Field Coy. Engineers, in spite of enemy fire, proved themselves masters of the difficult work of bridge building.

The mutual support of all forces in action in the Ville-sur-Ancre attack was typical of the helpful co-operation of the various branches of the army at all times, and was a happy feature of all operations. The keenness with which the artillery units applied themselves to the task of giving the infantry the utmost possible assistance established a mutual admiration among the men. The same spirit of co-operation was manifested on the field behind the lines. The Sixth Field Coy. Engineers were always generous to us when their assistance was invoked, and they never refused our boys a sheet of iron or a piece of timber for the construction of a field shelter, while at times they rendered us liberal assistance in supplying material for dugouts and other purposes.

Many Germans at Ville-sur-Ancre fought bravely, and our troops respected them for their valour. An incident which followed this engagement showed that our boys admired a brave foe. A German soldier who had fought gamely until he was wounded was afterwards carried out on a stretcher. He already had won an Iron Cross. Later the men who had captured him found him at a dressing station without his Cross, greatly distressed. He indicated that the Cross had been taken from him. Our men went in pursuit of the decoration, threatened the souvenir-hunter with severe treatment, and, recovering the Cross, pinned it on the German's breast, to his unbounded delight. They also attached the following note:—" To whom it may concern. Leave this Iron Cross alone. This man fought bravely. (Signed) Dinkum Aussies."

In the early morning of 20th May the 24th Battalion moved back to the Divisional reserve area, and the men established themselves in rough shelters in Bomb Gully, near Bonnay. This gully owed its name to the fact that it lay on the track of the German airmen who passed over the lines every night to carry out bombing raids along the Somme as far as Amiens, and who often deposited portions of their destructive cargo on this particular spot.

Congratulations on the success of the Ville-sur-Ancre operation were here received from the Army Commander, General Sir Henry Rawlinson. Decorations awarded included two D.C.M.'s, the recipients being Sgt. E. V. White and Sgt. E. Holloway.

Fine warm weather marked the period spent in reserve. Work was plentiful, but the men had time for swimming and other recreation. Parties were allotted for work at the sawmills (where timber was cut for army use), and for laying a cable from Heilly to Buire. Demonstrations were given with captured German machine-guns with a view to enabling our men to turn these guns on the Hun in succeeding engagements.

A German airman was brought down at this place one afternoon. The Hun evidently became "rattled" by the fire of the Lewis guns, as he and his machine were found to be unharmed. "D" Coy. claimed Fritz and his machine as their prize, but so many other claims were put in by units in the vicinity that the credit was mutually divided. Our boys were the first to take possession of the airman and his machine, and they were not altogether pleased when a party of officers from some unit of the Imperial Army arrived and escorted the Boche off in style in a motor car. "If he had been a Digger," they observed with disgust, "the ———would have been obliged to walk!"

GENERAL BIRDWOOD LEAVES THE A.I.F.

General Sir William Birdwood was appointed to the command of the Fifth British Army, and Lieut.-General Sir John Monash took command of the Australian Corps.

On 28th May we sent our representatives with those of other units of the Brigade to Brigade Headquarters at Frechencourt to bid farewell to General Birdwood. It was a memorable gathering. While the Australian Corps appreciated the fact that we were to have one of our own brilliant officers at the head of our army, there was unanimous regret at the departure of the popular general who had commanded the A.I.F. from its infancy, and who had earned the esteem and confidence of our troops on Gallipoli. We all felt that the names Birdwood and Anzac must always remain in close association in the memory of Australians. General Birdwood was beloved of the A.I.F. because he proved himself a gentleman as well as a soldier.

RIBEMONT AND BUIRE.

The Battalion was back at Ribemont (supports) on 1st June. Here we were subjected to a heavy bombardment with gas shells, both "mustard" and "phosgene." In about three hours during the first night the Boche put over on our area about 3000 shells. In spite of all possible precautions we suffered 23 casualties, while many of the men who remained on duty were more or less affected. It was an aggravating experience, and but for the prompt measures adopted by Major Ellwood, M.C., who was acting C.O., our casualties must have been much heavier.

The weather at this time was warm and pleasant, and when the enemy was less active the troops sprawled about in the crops, enjoying a snooze and a sunbath simultaneously, or reading any stray piece of literature that chanced to be at hand. It was necessary to rest as much as possible in the day, for there was work to be done at night. The defences were now well established, but there was still room for much improvement, and nothing was being left to chance. Timber was salvaged from the ruins of Ribemont and taken forward to improve the lines, while work with pick and shovel was always a useful pastime.

Our turn for the front line came again on 8th June, when we relieved the 23rd Battalion at Buire. The feature of our duties here was patrolling No-man's-land and keeping a keen eye on the Hun, for the enemy had not yet given up his ambitions in respect to the capture of Amiens and Paris.

While patrolling the front on the night of the 8th-9th Sgt. P. J. Molloy, M.M., one of our bravest and most popular soldiers, was killed. Sgt. Molloy was leading a patrol through the crop when a party of Germans were encountered. Our boys at once attacked the Huns and drove them off, but the gallant sergeant fell in the engagement. One prisoner was brought in for identification.

For two days and nights the front was singularly quiet, and the men often remarked that the war on that sector appeared to have subsided completely. But it was only a lull before a storm. Our artillery and mortars broke out in deadly fury on the 11th, and the Boche, expecting an attack, replied vigorously. Consequently the infantry positions became decidedly warmer, and the uncertainty of life at the front was once more strongly impressed upon everybody.

Fritz was plainly nervous, displaying many signs of uneasiness.

Our scouts were exceedingly active, patrolling the front in a thorough and systematic manner. Pte. Munro, a company scout, growing tired of the German inactivity, crawled out through the crop in daylight on his own initiative. He came across two Huns sleeeping in the sun. Munro, with a well-aimed bomb, put the two men out of action, but others rushed to their aid. These our scout also bombed with remarkable coolness, and although he was wounded by the fire of the enemy, he exhausted his supply of grenades before he retired. He was strongly recommended for his brave exploit, and was awarded the M.M.

The 12th was another eventful day. Our artillery shelled the German trenches, and when the Huns attempted to change their positions and take cover they were fired upon by our Lewis guns.

Fritz responded with some gas shells and minenwerfers on our lines, but this only brought more trouble upon him. At about 2 p.m. our guns fired 200 gas projectors on to the enemy positions. These burst with a terrific roar, which pleased our men as much as it alarmed the Boche. The shell fire which was directed against our posts during the day was at times particularly heavy, but fortunately the explosives usually missed their marks, and the boys suffered more frights than serious injuries.

Another demonstration by our guns on the night of the 14th provoked the enemy to fire his S.O.S., which brought on a lively artillery action.

At 11.30 that night a party of 25 of our men under Lieut. J. T. Pocknell raided the enemy, securing six prisoners and a machine-gun. The raid, though successful, was marked by a sharp fight, and our losses included Cpl. C. S. McLiesh, M.M. and Bar, who was reported missing when the party returned. The enemy position attacked consisted of two machine-gun posts and an ordinary strong-post. The Huns abandoned two of their posts after resisting for a while, and our men then captured the third, where the gun and prisoners were secured. Cpl. McLiesh and two other men pursued the Germans who made off, and in their eagerness to overtake them chased them into an old mill. This proved to be a German stronghold, and our daring trio must have been captured, as they failed to return.

One of the German prisoners was sent along to our intelligence officer, whose characteristic humourous bent led him to interrogate Fritz with dramatic austerity and to warn him that any statement made to mislead the atrocious people known as Australians would provoke them to eat him! After trembling before the I.O. for some minutes, Fritz was relieved to hear that august person ask for cigarettes (a noted weakness with that authority), and when the Hun produced a box of 50 and saw the glow of satisfaction in the eyes of every Australian in the dug-out he breathed more freely, and after being treated to a feed was sent on his way to the rear, convinced that the cigarettes had saved him from being sacrificed at a cannibalistic feast!

One of the German prisoners stated that he had once been a waiter at a hotel in Sydney. Another appeared to be in a very sour temper, and he informed his captors that he had been granted leave to visit his wife, whom he had not seen for a year, and he was to start for his home on the following day. A Digger informed him that he was "dead stiff."

Aerial photography had now been brought to a fine art. On every part of the front the enemy positions were revealed by photographs taken from aeroplanes. These supplied valuable and absolutely reliable information, and were of great assistance to the infantry in their operations. The German airmen were equally busy photographing our positions.

The 58th Battalion relieved us on the night of the 15th, and we moved back to Bomb Gully, near Bonnay. While in the line at Buire, "A" Coy., which had been in reserve and did the carrying through the shell fire, had suffered more casualties than the companies on post.

IN RESERVE AT QUERRIEU.

Led by the band, the Battalion marched back to Querrieu, via La Houssaye and Pont Noyelles, on the 16th, and went into shelters in the Divisional reserve area, where we were to spend about ten days reorganising and resting preparatory to another tour in the line.

The Second Division, while in reserve, was disposed for the retention of the La Houssaye plateau and the defence of Amiens in the event of an enemy attack in force. The Division was kept in readiness to be thrown in at any part of the front in case of a break in the line and the necessity for a recovering counter-attack. The critical nature of the operations at this stage is indicated by an order issued to the front line troops, both French and British, to fight to the last and hold the enemy until the reserves were rushed up.

The senior officers of the Battalion made a reconnaissance of the front at Villers Bretonneux and Hangard Wood. In the event of a German attack the Battalion would probably have been thrown in on that sector.

The time spent near Querrieu was occupied with training and recreation, and as the summer weather was pleasant, the men made the most of these agreeable days.

Several notable events marked our sojourn here. The first was a dinner given by the officers in honour of the C.O., Lieut.-Colonel W. E. James, who had just received the D.S.O. award, in recognition of the Battalion's successful operations in the Ypres battles.

A special parade of the Brigade in the grounds of the Querrieu Chateau on a fine Sunday morning, when the Corps commander, Lieut.-General Sir John Monash, decorated a number of officers and other ranks, and the 24th Battalion band did the musical honours, was a ceremony which did the Sixth Brigade great credit.

Sports included an aquatic carnival on the River Hallue, when the competitors in the water had the novel experience of a new sensation. Fritz must have learned of the carnival in that secluded spot, for he landed a number of high explosive shells in the water. The swimmers and spectators had time to get out of the way before any casualties were suffered, but the fish were less fortunate. After the shelling ceased the soldiers gathered a number of dead fish floating on the water, and they had fried fish for tea.

At Querrieu the Battalion held one of its most successful sports meetings. The grounds were flagged and taped off in the most approved style for the athletic events, refreshment booths were erected, and the whole scene, with the band playing, officials busy, competitiors keen on every event, and an enthusiastic crowd of spectators, was typical of an up-to-date carnival. Bookmakers were noisy and reckless, and the tote had a profitable day, showing a surplus of 240 francs. The "Mule Cup" was the most entertaining event on the programme, because most of the "mounts" refused to keep on the course. The most successful riders were Driver McIlroy, Lieuts. Wells and Baxter. The 100 yards foot race, in which our best runners competed, was won by Pte. Len. Harris, with Major Ellwood 2nd. The 220 yards event was won by Cpl. (afterwards Sgt.) Clarence Wilson.

The 108th American Engineers were good enough to send their concert party and band from their neighbouring camp to entertain our boys in the evening, and the "Sammies" were delighted with the warmth of the reception accorded them.

Cricket, Divisional sports at Allonville, and other recreations proved highly entertaining and beneficial to mind and body.

Even here, however, we were not immune from enemy shell fire. From the high ground on which we were camped a commanding view could be obtained of Amiens, whose noble Cathedral was then a target for German guns, and the city was being destroyed by enemy artillery fire and air raids. Amiens, a city of 130,000 inhabitants, was now almost deserted. The extensive gardens on the river flats were taken over by the army, and large quantities of vegetables, abandoned by the gardeners, were distributed by the A.S.C. to the units in the field. The crops, also abandoned by the farmers, were garnered by the soldiers and purchased by the army for fodder.

The villages on the front suffered their share of destruction. Querrieu being one of our busiest centres, and situated on one of the main roads, was often strafed by enemy guns. While our service waggons were passing through this village one afternoon a shell fatally wounded one of our most popular men—Cpl. C. M. Paget, of our quartermaster's staff. "Monty," as he was affectionately known by every member of the Battalion, was our football umpire, a keen "sport" and a lovable comrade. On the football field he had few rivals in the army as an umpire, and his reputation as a sporting enthusiast was as clean as his record as a man, which was unimpeachable. His death was a heavy blow to the boys, and no man in the unit was more sadly missed by his many pals. The Battalion accorded Cpl. Paget a funeral with full military honours as a tribute to his memory.

VILLERS BRETONNEUX.

We were on our way back to the front on 28th June. The transport lines and details were moved to Lamotte Brebiere, on the Somme, and the fighting strength went on to Blangy-Tronville, on the other side of the river and nearer the front. Here the Battalion was in reserve to the line at Villers Bretonneux, and we had on our right a Zouave Regiment. The French and Australian troops quickly established a warm friendship. Some of our men occupied shelters which had been built by the French out of reeds and other material at hand, and which testified to the ingenuity of the Poilus in the construction of field habitations. Duty did not preclude frequent opportunities for swimming, which was a popular diversion in the warm weather.

The French had in action here a heavy long-range gun (cleverly hidden in the earth under the trees), with which they shelled the railway junction at Chaulnes, then in the enemy's hands.

One of our companies was posted in the trench system skirting le Bois de l'Abbe, another was bivouacked alongside the White Chateau, and two nearer the river. The companies exchanged positions frequently in order to allow the whole Battalion the opportunity of bathing in the stream and the billabongs on the river flats. The defences here were known as the Aubigny system, which was noted for enemy gas attacks.

Standing crops, which had come into ear since the farmers had abandoned the land at the time of the German advance, were being garnered by the army for fodder, and on the fields, which a few months earlier had been peaceful and under cultivation, there was now an elaborate system of defence, in which trenches and wire entanglements predominated.

The "Spanish influenza" was at this time rampant in the field, and every unit had a number of men stricken with the illness, which in many cases was acute and critical. The hospitals and Field Ambulances were full, and the units were obliged to improvise temporary hospitals of their own for the treatment of the patients. Our Battalion established a hospital at Lamottee, where our A.M.C. details, under the able supervision of our M.O., Major D. D. Coutts, had a house full of sick. Medical comforts were supplied by the Red Cross and Battalion funds, and every attention was bestowed upon the patients, who, in spite of the discomfort of lying on the floor, were wonderfully resigned to the hardships of the campaign at this critical period, and the excellent work of the medical service was greatly assisted by the optimistic and patient disposition of the boys.

It was at this time that the enemy was daily expected to renew his great offensive, and the fighting units were keenly concerned over their reduced strength in consequence of the epidemic. Every day large batches of sick men had to be sent back from the front, and the illness was of a nature which left a man unfit for service for several weeks. Yet many men went back to the front when they felt far from well, and they carried on with that spirit of determination which animated our splendid army.

An attack known as the Hamel offensive, from Villers Bretonneux north to the Somme, was to be made by the Australians on 4th July, the assaulting units being one Brigade from each of the Second, Third and Fourth Divisions. Careful preparations for this operation, excellent co-operation by the tanks and aeroplanes, and the keenness of the attacking troops all contributed to a highly successful advance. All objectives were quickly gained. Over fifty enemy officers, 1500 men, 120 machine-guns, 5 minenwerfer guns, and 1 field gun were captured at small cost.

The 24th Battalion's task in this stunt was limited to carrying supplies and improving the defences after the attack. Parties carried forward Stokes mortar shells and deposited ammunition on the objective while the assaulting troops were mopping up. Rations were carried up to the advanced positions, and wire, picks, and a variety of material were placed at the forward dumps.

A party of our men under the works officer, Lieut. H. Baxter, dug a communication trench from the old front line to the new front line. The excavation was 300 yards in length.

Some of our men found time to improve the tracks for the stretcher-bearers carrying wounded back from the battlefield by constructing crossings over abandoned trenches. This and other work was done voluntarily under shell fire, and was one of the many instances in which the troops displayed a readiness to assist one another in their various duties.

As much rest as possible was taken by day in view of the heavy fatigue work to be carried out every night in getting supplies forward.

Two companies of American infantry had been attached to the Australians to assist in the attack. This was the first occasion on which the Americans had fought side by side with British troops, and the Sammies appeared to appreciate the fact that they were associated with Australians, who were regarded as storm troops of the first order. Before the action began an American colonel, addressing his troops, exhorted them to acquit themselves to the best of their ability. "Remember," he said, "you are going into action with lads who always deliver the goods." The Americans proved themselves brave and dashing soldiers, and with more experience would have been more than a match for the Hun.

An innovation which marked this advance was the use of aeroplances for carrying small arms ammunition to the asaulting infantry. The ammunition was dropped in parachutes by the 'planes and collected by the men in the lines. The successful work of the air service in this direction saved the infantry much hazardous labour, while the supplies were got forward expeditiously and with few casualties. Members of the Australian Flying Corps were highly successful in this work. The first box of ammunition was dropped within a few feet of the spot on the ground marked for the purpose. The Hun airmen imitated our flying men, and carried rations as well as ammunition to their infantry, but their judgment in dropping the material was not always perfect. On several occasions they emptied their loads on the lines occupied by our troops.

In addition to fatigue duty the 24th Battalion supported the front line troops, and were subjected to heavy shelling on the day following the advance. The dispositions of the companies were altered on this day. "B" Coy. reinforced "C" Coy. in the old front line, and "A" and "D" Coys. moved forward to Digger's Support.

A party of our men worked on the excavation of a deep dug-out for the Headquarters' staff in the line.

The Brigade was relieved on the night of the 6th. Our companies had experienced a busy and strenuous time during the three days at the front. Fatigue duty was a necessary and important part of a battle never appreciated by the men. On this occasion, like many others, the troops declared they would have preferred a place among the assaulting units.

Moving back to supports, the men were able to indulge in swimming again in the Somme.

At this time a party of our men, under Lieut. E. H. D. Edgerton, D.S.O., M.M. and Bar, was selected to represent the Battalion at a review of Allied troops at Versailles, but the numbers were reduced, and Lieut. Edgerton and Cpl. D. McKinnon, M.M., were sent as our representatives. Lieut. Edgerton commanded the Australian troops at the review.

Work on the front continued, including the laying of a buried cable to Villers Bretonneux.

At 8.20 p.m. on the 10th, after a fairly quiet day, our command ordered a general "stand to," and all units immediately prepared for action. The 24th Battalion quickly took up its defensive positions, two companies being in the Aubigny system and two companies at Alarm Post, near Blangy. "Stand down" was given at 1 a.m.

The care taken to keep all sections of the unit up to a high standard of efficiency, even in the forward area, was indicated by the awarding of prizes for the best-kept company cooker at this time. An inspection by the C.O. and other officers resulted in the following awards of merit:—First prize, "A" Coy.; second, "C" Coy.; third, "D" Coy.; fourth, "B" Coy. Many similar competitions were held from time to time, and the rivalry was so keen among the cooks that the cookers were always kept in first-class order. Honours were evenly distributed, as the first prize seldom went to the same company on two consecutive occasions.

A bombardment of our positions east of Blangy on the 12th caused us to hurriedly seek a safer spot for the time being.

Fatigue duty on the laying of cables, the excavation of deep dug-outs, and the extension of defences kept the troops busy by night.

A presentation of decorations was made by Lieut.-General Sir John Monash at a Brigade parade on the 13th. The troops were in high spirits after the victory of the 4th, and the General was pleased with the morale displayed on all sides.

While on this sector the 24th Battalion Association (formed by members of the unit who had returned home from active service) forwarded a sum of £25 as a gift to our regimental funds, and a message of appreciation was sent by the C.O. to the Association.

The 14th July was France's national holiday, and although the war had to be carried on, we were able to send representatives in response to a pressing invitation, to a celebration held in the field by the Third Zouave Regiment, which held sports and a dinner in honour of the occasion. In an unofficial way many of the French and Australian troops managed to fraternise during the day, and wherever the representatives of the two countries came together the entente cordiale was marked by the singing of the "Marseillaise" and other national airs.

Villers Bretonneux was at this time subjected to heavy bombardments with enemy gas shells, and our companies in the support positions were involved in the deadly atmosphere. Frequent encounters with gas had thoroughly trained our men in the methods of defence against these fumes, and although it was not a pleasant experience to have one's head "bagged" in a respirator, the boys were taking no avoidable risks. Their wariness saved us from casualties which carelessness or inexperience would have entailed, and which might easily have been disastrous to the unit. In spite of all precautions our men suffered a good deal, and a percentage of evacuations from time to time was unavoidable. The units on our left suffered correspondingly.

Lieut. C. A. A. Ellis, M.M., was now acting adjutant, Capt. Selleck having been attached to the Brigade staff as staff captain trainee.

The Seventh Brigade was at grips with the Hun on the 14th, and the 24th Battalion was called up to support the line.

The 24th Battalion took over the support line from the 28th Battalion on the 19th, the disposition of the companies being:—"B" Coy. in the old front line, "C" Coy. in deep dug-outs and trenches, "D" Coy. in dug-outs, and "A" Coy. in trenches. Several posts were manned. German airmen dropped bombs among our parties whilst this operation was in progress.

This was the first occasion on which we had been in liason with the French in the line. The Regiment on our right here was the Second Tirailleurs (Algerian troops). Our officers spoke highly of the alertness and efficiency of the French soldiers. A spirit of warm comradeship was displayed by our men and our allies. "C" Coy. men traded with bully-beef for wine. Bully-beef was currency with the Frenchmen.

Our Headquarters were established in a chalk pit, and the companies settled down to duty in their respective positions. There was much strenuous labour for the men every night, the heaviest task being the digging of a communication trench from the old German front line through Monument Wood towards Syria Trench. This work was hampered by heavy enemy shell fire, which was particularly severe at night in this area. Ammunition had to be carried to the front line troops, and many other duties kept the men fully occupied. An interesting incident here was the exploit of a British tank, which went into Monument Wood and hauled out a German tank which had been put out of action. A light artillery barrage was employed to drown the well-known sound of the tank engines, in order that the Germans, who were in close proximity, would not detect the adventure. The German tank was named "Mephisto," and was ornamented by a design in which a devil was depicted walking off with a British tank in his clutches. Alas for "Mephisto!" His performance was not up to expectations.

Monument Wood was so named because in it there stood a monument erected to commemorate a battle in the war of 1870.

The night of the 22nd was rough and noisy. Villers Bretonneux and the positions in contiguity to the town were subjected to a heavy bombardment by high explosives and gas. Working parties suffered heavily. A party of our men were at work in Monument Wood, and the only member of the whole batch not affected by gas was the officer in charge (Lieut. G. M. Ingram). The men were obliged to pass over low-lying ground, which was reeking with poisonous fumes, and in spite of the protection offered by respirators, which had to be worn continually, they had a trying experience. Other sections of the Battalion were also involved, and it was only the observance of the strictest discipline and the good sense of the men that prevented serious casualties.

Work was almost entirely suspended in consequence of this heavy gas attack. The following day was devoted to relieving the troops as far as possible from the discomfort of the situation. A number of men had to be evacuated, and others were in need of medical attention. One of the worst features of this gas was that men could be seriously affected before they realised it. Hours after contact the poison would do its painful work.

An interesting discovery was made in a chalk-pit where our Headquarters had been established. A German buzzer installation was found at this spot, and there was much speculation as to what information this instrument had conveyed to the enemy, as this buzzer was designed to record all conversations in the vicinity and transmit them to the Hun. It was, needless to say, quickly dismantled.

American troops were at this time attached to British units in order to gain experience, and we had a regimental staff and four platoons of the 3rd Battalion, 129 Reg. U.S. Infantry with us, a platoon being attached to each company.

The Villers Bretonneux road, by which our transport section brought us rations and other supplies, was often heavily shelled by enemy guns, but our drivers generally managed to escape injury.

The liberality with which the Hun was bestowing his gas shells upon us at this time provoked our artillery to reciprocate these gifts. On the night of the 29th over 20,000 gas shells were fired by our guns into the German positions, and all next day it was observed that the Hun stretcher-bearers were working overtime. Our artillery galloped forward and took up temporary positions while carrying out this bombardment. Later, when the Germans shelled these positions, our guns had gone.

We took over the front line from the 28th Battalion on the night of 30th July, the change over being accomplished successfully in spite of the activity of the German guns. The position was the right Brigade sector, south-east of Villers Bretonneux. "A," "C" and "D" Coys. each had three platoons in the line and one in support, while "B" Coy. was placed in support to the whole of the Battalion Sector, which extended over a front of 2000 yards, one-third facing east and two-thirds facing south, and including the recently captured Syria Trench, in front of which lay many German dead. The north boundary was the railway, by which was a mound where an excellent observation post was established. Between the railway and Syria Trench was Monument Wood, and also a mass of shattered trenches. The Boche wasted large stocks of shells on this locality, believing he was killing off our troops. We had no particular objection to his devotion to this duty, as none of our men had been posted there.

Due south of our positions were Monument Wood and the famous Hangard Wood, at the apex of which the enemy still held on to an uncomfortable salient in his line.

The enemy troops opposing us here were the 148th I.R., badly shaken, and the Second Grenadier Regiment, of better quality. These units were rather passive, and showed no desire to fight.

The Americans with us were eager to get a view of the enemy, and were straining their eyes on the look out for him. Their curiosity was apparently observed by the Boche, who began sniping at the exposed heads. Then the Americans returned the fire and Fritz slackened his activity. So the Sammies claimed a victory even if it was not important enough to immediately affect the issue of the war.

On our right we had the Third Zouaves Regiment (French), who proved staunch and exceedingly cordial comrades. They were enthusiatic in their praises of the Australians. In their trenches they posted the following notice:—"Vivent les Australiens, qui nous donnent des cigarettes!"

Our first day here was not particularly eventful, but at dawn on the 1st August the front was enveloped in a thick fog, which obscured our vision and kept us on the qui vive lest the enemy should attempt a surprise. It was more likely, however, that the Boche expected us to take the initiative, and he was not wholly disappointed. During the early hours of the morning platoons led by Lieut. Edgerton and 2/Lieut. C. J. R. Newton pushed forward with machine-guns, and opened fire on German working parties and ration limbers in the vicinity of Syria Trench. Our Lewis guns cross fired alternately, confusing the Hun and scattering his men. No working parties were afterwards observed to venture out on that spot.

Hostile artillery fire increased during the day, and was maintained at night, inflicting casualties on our carrying parties, who were taking forward ammunition for the Stokes mortars. Our guns returned the enemy fire, and the night was far from peaceful.

Rain commenced on the 3rd August and continued until the field was in a thoroughly sloppy and muddy state. That night the 13th Battalion moved in and relieved us. We handed over readily, and as we moved out the men had

visions of a more comfortable position. But we were only
leaving Hell to go into Hades. Our orders were to move
to a position on the left and relieve the 17th Battalion as
supports to the 23rd Battalion. Had we been given our
choice we would have remained where we were, for the support line at Bretonneux was the least desirable place in the
world. In intense darkness, and through rain, mud, slush
and shell fire, we groped our way to the new position.

The Americans with us, unused to the strain and disappointments of war, began to confess that the business was
"sure rotten," and they had a feeling "that the gar darn
Kaiser and his crew of brass hats ought to be right there
in the muck to see how they liked war from the soldier's point
of view." Possibly some of the Sammies, having been in
the trenches some while, imagined that it was time they had
a decent spell. To come out of the line and go straight
in again at another point was too much of a good thing.
Our boys, although they felt much the same as the
Americans, could not resist the temptation to pretend that
it was a common experience, and that they might look
forward to many equally pleasant periods!

Making the best of the uncomfortable conditions, we prepared for the front line again, and 48 hours after we had
left the right Bretonneux sector we took over the firing line
from the 23rd Battalion on the left sector, after being in the
line for five days. As we moved forward through the
ruins of the town the Germans shelled heavily with 5.9's and
other high explosives, and made the operation extremely
difficult. The bombardment was continued until 11 p.m.,
but the relief was completed by 1 a.m.

The Battalion sector here was slightly over 2000 yards,
which was an extraordinarily long line for one unit. The
men accepted the compliment of the trust reposed in the
Australians by the command, and explained the situation by
sarcastically remarking, "Oh, the Australians can do it!"
The opinion of the high command was that no attack was
likely here, and this supposition proved to be correct.

The American troops were withdrawn from us at this
stage, leaving us to hold the 2000 yards of front with our

strength reduced to about 60 men per company. The thin line caused the C.O. to remark that we were "holding the front by Christian science!"

In consequence of the wet conditions on the field supplies of dry socks and other clothing and extra hot meals were ordered from the quarter-master for the troops. The weather was squally, with rain at frequent intervals.

Our transport section rendered particularly good services at this period. Rations and other supplies were brought five or six miles, often under shell fire, and deposited within half a mile of the line. It was an unusually dangerous area for transport activities, but the rations were always delivered on time and in good order.

While we were at Bretonneux the German artillery, by accident or intention, "found" the rendezvous of two British tank Battalions in an orchard behind our lines. About 60 tanks were "parked" at this rendezvous, and when a German shell started a fire among these war machines there was some excitement among the tank crews. Armour plate is not particularly inflammable, but petrol and oil are dangerous elements where explosives are falling. The fire raged furiously for a while, and the glare was visible all over the field. When it subsided a dozen tanks had been burnt out, and trees had been badly scorched.

Fatal casualties in the Battalion had not been numerous on this sector, but the killed included L/Sgt. L. J. Morrison, who fell on 3rd August.

The main features of our operations on the front were reconnaissances and sniping, with lively artillery work on both sides.

The activity which had been going on behind our line for some days indicated that there was something important in the air, and the chief topic of conversation among the men was the number of guns being added to the artillery strength, the presence of numerous tanks, and the unmistakable preparations for a battle on a large scale

The keen interest of the men in these preparations grew to excitement when they learned that the Canadians were on the front on the right, and that arrangement had been made for the whole of the five Australian Divisions to operate together in the impending advance. This privilege had never been given to the Australians before, and the troops were enthusiastic over the prospect, whatever the task might be. "Furphies" filled the air, and expectancy was almost at fever point. The receipt by Battalion commanders of orders and maps for a great advance on 8th August settled all speculation.

TANKS GOING FORWARD TO BATTLE.

The Great Advance.

The 24th Battalion was holding a sector of the front line at Villers Bretonneux under extremely unpleasant conditions on 8th August when the Allied armies launched the grand assault which started the Germans on their way back to the Rhine. For the first time in the history of the A.I.F. the five Australian Divisions were to operate together as the Australian Army Corps, and their front in this great attack extended from Villers Bretonneux to the Somme.

The units holding the line on the night of 7th-8th were to prepare the way for the attack at dawn and afterwards follow the assaulting forces and carry on the advance. On the night of 6th-7th we cut the wire behind our front line, and on the night of 7th-8th we similarly treated the wire in front of our forward positions, leaving the way clear for the advance.

At dusk on the evening of the 7th the attacking forces began to assemble. Platoon after platoon swung along the roads in the moonlight, company after company, battalions and brigades, until whole divisions were on the front. For hours the processions of eager, confident troops kept coming up from the rear. Dozens of tanks crawled forward over the fields, and thousands of guns were ready for action, while a few batteries fired all through the night to give the field an air of normal activity. Aeroplanes droned overhead, flying low to drown the sound of the approaching tanks. For ten miles behind the line there was a hustle of troops and transport. Everything was moving. Engineers, Pioneers, Tunnellers, Bridging Trains. and every section of the army was ready. Our 8in. guns had been brought up within a mile of the line, and troops had been ordered to keep under cover during the barrage owing to the short range at which many of the guns were firing.

The old method of advancing on a set objective, gaining it, and staying there to be blown out was done away with. This was to be a real advance, with commanders directing their units, deploying and manoeuvring as the battle progressed. Brains as well as machines were to have a chance. It was meant to be the commencement of the march to Berlin, with as few stops as possible.

The British were on the north flank, the Australians between the Somme and the Villers Bretonneux railway, the Canadians south of Amiens, and further south the French.

At 4.20 a.m. on 8th August the barrage was launched, and ten minutes later the waves of infantry all along the front, supported by tanks, were sent against the German positions.

The guns electrified the atmosphere with their fire. A continuous deafening rumble reverberated over the field, and screeching shells filled the air with a noise like a high wind in a forest. Men waiting in supports blocked their ears with their fingers to shut out the deafening pandemonium.

More tanks waddled up to join in the drive, and aeroplanes were on the wing in hordes.

The German lines were rolled back under the force of the blow. In less than an hour our field guns were galloping forward to cover the advance, the eyes of the drivers flashing with the exhiliration of battle as they had longed to see it. The German guns had made no reply. The weight of the barrage and the dash of the assault had silenced all opposition. By 10 a.m., when a fog, which had enveloped the field all the early morning, lifted, the country as far as the eye could see was in our hands, and Pioneer Battalions were already busy preparing roads for our guns and transport.

Prisoners were sent back in hundreds, and before many hours passed the numbers had increased to thousands. Our men assisted in collecting the Huns and escorting them off the battlefield.

At midday the 24th Battalion moved forward and assembled in the No-man's-land of yesterday, and on the 9th we followed up through Marcelcave and Weincourt, and rested near Guillaucourt and Harbonnieres, alongside the railway. Here there was evidence of the destructive work performed by our airmen during the past few weeks. German ammunition trains and shells had been scattered broadcast along the railway.

The complete success of the attack that morning was demonstrated by the absence of casualties among the assaulting troops, whose losses had been remarkably small.

The night we spent near Harbonnieres was enlivened by German aircraft bombing the railway. On the morning of the 10th the Australians brought an 11in. gun and a number of waggons loaded with ammunition along the railway past our bivouac. This gun had been used by the Huns to shell Amiens. It was sent to Paris and exhibited there, and afterwards sent out to Sydney.

Three days after the commencement of the advance the 24th Battalion was again in the firing line between Rainecourt and Framerville, where we relieved the 18th Battalion on 11th August. From this line we moved to some old French trenches, and then, pushing on, established a line parallel with the Framerville-Proyart road. The village of Framerville was crumbling to ruins under a German bombardment, and our men, in the ravine below, were kept busy adjusting their respirators owing to frequent gas alarms.

Near the Proyart road the enemy had abandoned a huge dump, where his stacks of material, it was estimated, were worth one and a half millions sterling. The Germans, being unable to remove the dump or destroy it before they were driven back, were now endeavouring to bring about its destruction by shell fire, and the locality was decidedly unhealthy.

Around Framerville there was abundant evidence of the successful operations of armoured cars which had been employed against the enemy. These cars had dashed into the German positions and had got well behind their lines. Cookers had been caught on the roads before they could be pulled out. The horses lay dead on the tracks, and many of the cooks had met a similar fate, while some of the cookers had been overturned—probably by the horses taking fright.

At this time we lost one of our most distinguished soldiers, and one of the most promising of all our brilliant young officers. Lieut. E. H. D. Edgerton, D.S.O., M.M. and Bar, was killed on the night of 11th-12th August. He was a soldier who, if all the brave deeds of war were rewarded, would have been decorated with several V.C.'s. Only 21 years of age, Lieut. Edgerton had been with the Battalion from its inception, and had served on Gallipoli and in France and Belgium through all the hard battles of the long campaign. His gallantry knew no bounds. Attacking German strong-posts, facing the greatest danger, leading his men in the face of deadly fire, he covered himself with honour. A gentleman at heart, a most lovable man among his comrades, beloved by his men and admired by his senior officers, he was the ideal soldier. It was just one of the examples of the hardness of fate that this gallant young officer, after coming through many a desperate battle in which men hardly hoped to live, should be killed by a stray bullet while standing in a trench on a comparatively quiet night. No member of the Battalion was more deeply mourned.

At Rainecourt, on the 14th, we lost another popular officer —Lieut. C. C. Burge—a brave man whom other men were proud to follow, and one of the most popular and successful members of the Battalion football team.

Pushing on from Rainecourt, the Battalion swung across the open country in front of Herleville, where our Headquarters were established in dug-outs, which had apparently recently been German Corps Headquarters. A valley here contained additional quantities of enemy stores hurriedly abandoned.

At this stage the advance was held up by strong enemy resistance in St. Martin's Wood, which caused a good deal of trouble on our right flank. The Hun was endeavouring to check the advance, at least temporarily, to enable him to withdraw guns and stores and to reorganise his troops. Herleville was strongly held by enemy forces, who had the advantage of a deep sunken road, which afforded splendid protection for the garrison. Our heaviest gun fire could barely affect this position. Lieut. E. S. Baldock, with "B" Coy., in the centre of our line, had pushed forward, after making a thorough reconnaissance of the position, and it was decided to swing the line forward on the right of the village in the hope of causing the Boche to evacuate in consequence of this partially enveloping move. Our "D" Coy. (Capt. Ball, D.C.M.) was occupying a position in a quarry, and "A" Coy. (Lieut. W. B. Gow) was posted in an orchard. "C" Coy. (Lieut. G. D. Pollington, M.M.) was on the right.

The attack on Herleville took place at 4.15 a.m. on 18th August. Instead of the usual continuous barrage, a "box" barrage, in which the artillery fired on specified points, such as strong-posts and machine-guns, was employed. The result was unsatisfactory, as many of the German strong points were untouched, and the Boche was able to offer strong resistance to our infantry.

The 22nd Battalion attacked on our right, and further to the right the 23rd Battalion was also advancing. Our left flank was to act as a pivot till the line swung round on the opposite flank, but our right had to be pushed forward in conjunction with the 22nd Battalion. "C" Coy. had the biggest part of our share in these operations.

The attack was launched successfully, but the strong enemy forces, under the protection of the deep sunken road, and with many machine-guns strongly posted, held up the attack at several points on our right. Our right flank party, under Lieut. H. A. Rigby, gained their objective, but found themselves without sufficient support, and the Germans, moving under the cover of the sunken road, gradually hemmed them in. Our men had mounted their machine-gun, and they put up a gallant fight against tremendous odds. They had crossed a low ridge and were out of sight, but we could hear their machine-gun firing desperately. For three hours they held on, although several of their number had been put out of action. The pressure gradually increased as the enemy closed in upon them under cover of hedges and banks, and the German machine-guns beat them down with cross fire. When the advance was continued later this party had disappeared. It was subsequently learned that the few who were not put out of action had been taken prisoners.

Several of our other posts were in a precarious position for some time. Sgt. McLear and L/Cpl. J. Artis with small parties of men hung on bravely to their posts until they were able to withdraw. L/Cpl. Artis had seen Lieut. Rigby's party surrounded by the Huns, and his post was then our extreme right flank, where his party defied the enemy for some hours. Sgt. McLear and L/Cpl. Artis were awarded the D.C.M. for their valour in this engagement.

Up till this time the 24th Battalion had not lost more than half a dozen men as prisoners during the war, in spite of the many tight corners in which sections of the unit had found themselves from time to time. This fact speaks eloquently for the tenacity and bravery of our troops. In the case of Lieut. Rigby's party, however, the position was hopeless, as they were overwhelmed in daylight, without hope of escape.

Although the Brigade's attack on Herleville was not immediately and wholly successful, the completion of the operation was not long delayed, and the advance was continued. The attack had yielded 188 enemy prisoners on the Brigade front.

On the night of 18th August we were relieved by the Argyll and Sutherland Highlanders, of the 32nd British Division.

After the relief we proceeded to Harbonnieres, where we were to be picked up by motor waggons. A lively bombing raid by German airmen caught the motor transport column on its way to Harbonnieres, and after two of the 'buses had been put out of action, the column decided that it would be safer (for the 'buses) to hold off a few miles from the rendezvous, and the troops consequently had that distance added to their march from the line. At a late hour the Battalion got aboard the waggons, and was conveyed back to Daours, arriving there at about 7 a.m. on the 19th. The greater portion of the Battalion was accommodated in a large woollen mill on the banks of the Somme. The large building, from which all the machinery had been removed by the Germans, afforded good shelter, though much labour had to be expended in cleaning up the place and making it habitable. The troops displayed a keen interest in the ruins of the mill where the looms (the only part of the plant remaining) were daily inspected by hundreds of soldiers from different units in the area. The river afforded excellent swimming, and the boys made the most of this convenience. A swimming carnival, cricket matches, and other recreations made life worth living. Concerts and band performances added enjoyment to the pleasant evenings.

It was at Daours that our Battalion Press commenced its publications in the field.

We had been here just a week, and were beginning to feel that it was a highly desirable place of abode, when our happy days were suddenly brought to an end. The eventful day was Sunday, 25th August. A Brigade church parade was held in the morning, and everybody set out to spend a pleasant afternoon, when unexpected orders were received to move to the line. The rest of the day was marked by scenes of hustle and preparations for battle.

A concert had been arranged for the evening, and when the unit was ready for action and awaiting orders to move, the entertainment proceeded. With their fighting equipment gathered round them, the boys abandoned themselves to an hour's fun, as if they had never heard of war. As a matter of fact, war had become a regular business, and while there was time for amusement men could not afford to worry about shells and bullets. A spare hour for a little diversion was to be accepted and availed of as a busy business man appreciates an hour's leisure in the course of his daily occupation. Thus had men come to accommodate themselves to the great unending war.

Then came orders to embus on the road, and the troops turned their thought once more to scenes of strife.

Miles of motor waggons loaded with troops trailed through the village amid clouds of dust, till rain set in and changed the scene, and when night fell men were still loading themselves on the waggons and moving off to the front.

At this time motor waggons crowded the roads day and night. Whole Divisions of infantry were thus transported from place to place behind the lines. It was a speedy method of travel, and the troops had no objection to the system, for route marches, which were still frequent enough, had hitherto been one of the worst features of the campaign.

That night, in the rain and intense darkness, it was only by a mischance that the motor column lost its way and gave us a longer ride. The route was through Fouilloy and Villers Bretonneux and along the main road to the vicinity of Herleville.

The Battalion went into a section of a trench system prepared by the French many years earlier for the defence of Amiens. Early next morning we moved forward past Chuignolles and Chuignes, and took over the line at Fontaine-les-Cappy, where the Sixth Brigade relieved the First Brigade. The enemy dead on the field here bore testimony to the First Brigade's determined advance.

The advance commenced on the 8th had been followed up so successfully that the enemy was still falling back. Our job now was to keep on the Boche's heels. Rain fell while we hurried away to the front, and we found the ground fairly muddy.

The Battalion's fighting strength at this time was rather low, the trying period at Villers Bretonneux (where gas affected many of the troops) and the effects of the influenza epidemic having been responsible for a large number of evacuations, causing the C.O. (Lieut.-Colonel James) a good deal of anxiety. The companies were now commanded by Lieut. W. B. Gow, Lieut. E. S. Baldock, M.C., Lieut. A. V. Sedgwick, and Capt. A. A. Ball, D.C.M. Lieut. A. E. Middleton had succeeded Lieut. C. A. A. Ellis, M.M., as acting adjutant.

PEACEFUL PENETRATION.

The command had adopted a method of advance which was known as "peaceful penetration." The term would imply an absence of the reputed characteristics of war, but in reality this penetration of the enemy's positions, which went on every day along the whole front, was often marked by sharp fighting, with heavy shelling and bombing on the part of the enemy. What was a departure from the ordinary method of attack, however, was the absence of artillery preparation (or barrage) on our part. Farms, ruins of factories, sunken roads, woods, and other objectives in the general advance were attacked by the infantry without the assistance of guns. Sometimes little resistance was offered; at other times vantage points were hotly contested or heavily shelled by the enemy after they had been occupied. It was heartening, however, to know that the Hun was being kept on the move, and the troops were keen on the task of expediting his retreat.

On the night of 26th-27th August the unit on our left advanced their line, and our "D" Coy. moved forward accordingly.

At 2 p.m. on the 27th our "B" Coy. (under Lieut. E. S. Baldock, M.C.) attacked and occupied a sugar factory, but owing to heavy shelling by the enemy with 15 cm. guns and an attempted enveloping movement by the Boche, had to temporarily withdraw. The company had 2 men killed and 8 wounded. The Boche shelled violently until about 6 p.m. Then his guns began to ease off, and eventually ceased. It appeared that the Germans, endeavouring to adapt themselves to our "peaceful penetration," had attempted to lay a trap for us at this factory, but they were too slow in closing the door, and the "mice" got out. In disgust Fritz picked up his traps and moved on.

"A" Coy. (Lieut. Gow) had meanwhile made some progress. In the evening "C" Coy. (Lieut. Sedgwick) advanced through Dompierre, and the other companies followed through this village. Heavy enemy shell fire made the movement of troops difficult, and positions had to be frequently changed during the night to avoid heavy casualties.

The advance was held up on the 28th by machine-gun fire from the direction of Assevillers, and the Hun violently bombarded Dompierre. Three patrols, each consisting of 1 officer and 20 other ranks, were sent forward to establish contact with the enemy. The first patrol, under Lieut. Baldie, moved along Gaudaloupe Alley and returned without meeting opposition. The second party, led by Lieut. P. E. Smythe, moved up Martinique Alley, and in Atilla Trench captured three Germans and a machine-gun. In this exploit Lieut Smythe personally displayed marked coolness and bravery, and he was awarded the M.C. for his achievement. The third patrol, under Lieut. Salmon, advanced along Bouchnot Alley and met heavy machine-gun fire from the direction of Assevillers. Two men of this party were killed and one wounded.

On the information supplied by these patrols the companies moved at night to occupy the Herbecourt-Assevillers line. Machine-gun fire hampered their progress, but at 2 a.m. the Germans were found to have retired, and our companies then advanced and occupied the line.

The Boche continued his retreat during the night, and on the morning of the 29th the Seventh Brigade passed through our line, and continued the advance almost to the Somme where it turns south at Peronne. The 24th Battalion moved into reserve to the Fifth Brigade in trenches between Herbecourt and Mereaucourt Wood. Two of our sergeants were killed during these operations. Sgt. C. Bennett, M.M., fell on the 27th, and on the 28th Sgt. A. C. Cooper, M.M., was killed.

During the advance from Fontaine-les-Cappy the troops had been treated to a unique and welcome change of diet. On the Somme near Friese, where the Battalion transport lines were established, the French had in pre-war days constructed a number of eel traps, which had yielded large hauls of eels, and had evidently been a profitable industry. During the German occupation the business had been carried on by the Hun army, which had smoked the eels and supplied them as rations to its units in the field. The Australians in turn took up the business, but entirely independent of the commissariat, and although they soon tired of eels, for a week or two waggon loads of cooked eels were daily distributed among the troops of the different Divisions. The voluntary duty of skinning and cleaning the eels, so far as the 24th Battalion was concerned, was undertaken by the members of the band, and after the cooks had done their part, the daily supplies were forwarded with the rations and distributed to the companies. After a few days on eel, however, the men were ready to go back to the ordinary fare, and even to look with favour on a tin of bully-beef.

An incident at the front, which reflected the unquenchable humour of the army, even in battle, was the capture by a unit on our left of a German steam roller, used by the enemy labour units on the roads. We found it inscribed, "Captured for the 24th road-makers." This inscription was afterwards erased, and the prize bore the notice, "Captured by the A.I.F. padres."

MT. ST. QUENTIN.

The Second Australian Division's most brilliant achievement was now about to be written on the pages of the war's history. The German army along the whole front had been hurled back with remarkable suddenness, but now the Hun was on a stronger line, and doubtless had no intention of retiring further. His dominating position of Mt. St. Quentin was his strongest fortress, and it was the key to the country from Peronne to the Hindenburg line. During the Allied advance begun in the summer of 1916 and carried on till the German retreat in 1917, the French had hammered at Mt. St. Quentin and Peronne for two months. Even then it had not been taken by direct force of arms. The Australians captured the Mount and Peronne in two days. The part played by the 24th Battalion in this historic victory is recorded with pardonable pride.

The 30th August, 1918, found the Battalion bivouacked in an old system of French trenches, which, in the early days of the war, was a front line, some 4000 yards to the west of Mt. St. Quentin, where the troops were refitting and resting after the exhausting moving battle of the previous weeks.

That morning rumour had it that we were about to support an attack by the Fifth A.I. Brigade on Mt. St. Quentin. At about 5 p.m. a conference took place between the colonel and the company commanders, at which the latter were informed that the Fifth Brigade was attacking the Mount the next day (31st August). The Sixth Brigade was to move forward on to the slopes of the Mount and act as supports after its capture.

At 12 noon on 31st August the 24th Battalion moved from its bivouac in the old French trenches, and crossed the River Somme by means of a long foot-bridge situated near and to the west of the village of Clery. This bridge was half-a-mile in length, and being a frail structure, sup-

MONT ST. QUENTIN.—Scene of the Sixth Brigade's brilliant operation on 1st Sept., 1918.

ported by pontoons (some of which had ceased to float), and accommodating only a single file of men, had subsided in places till it was below the level of the water. It had been built by the Germans, and was strained and rickety. It was no rialto, and our passage across it was tinged with an element of adventure. For that reason it was regarded by the troops as a highly suitable structure. A steel bridge would have been much less interesting. The river and swamps safely crossed, the Battalion halted for dinner amongst our 18-pounder guns, which at the time were in action against the Mount. The C.O. received news that the Fifth Brigade attack on the Mount had not entirely succeeded. Another conference of officers was at once called.

The Fifth Brigade, it appeared, had attacked and captured the Mount, but owing to the reduced strength of the Battalions at the time of the assault, followed by heavy casualties and overwhelming and sudden counter-attacks by the enemy, had been obliged to withdraw in the main. Elements of this excellent Brigade, however, had held their ground, and at that moment were somewhere on the western slopes and crest of the Mount, some of them completely cut off and well behind the most advanced Germans. The village of St. Quentin, on the crest of the Mount, was again in the enemy's hands. Consequently the Sixth Brigade's advance was seriously handicapped by the direct observation of the Hun and his artillery fire.

At 1.30 p.m. the Battalion, led by Major W. H. Ellwood, M.C., and in parties of half platoons, 100 yards apart, moved forward. In this formation we followed the railway line along the bank of the Somme past the village of Clery to the point where the river turns south to Peronne. Here we halted within 800 yards of the enemy, and took shelter behind the high banks of the river.

The lack of information concerning the position delayed us until about 6 p.m.

In the meantime we had sustained our first casualties in the "new stunt," as we regarded it at the time. Two 4.2 shells had "found" us. Luckily, the Huns fired high.

Scores of shells, just skimming the bank above us, plunged into the muddy water 30 feet away.

Further information and orders at length arrived, and once again we picked up our equipment and the hundred and one odds and ends that go to complete the modern soldier's kit, and continued our trek into the line.

An advance party under Lieut. G. M. Ingram, M.M. (afterwards V.C.), had preceded us and reported "Brasso Redoubt" empty. This, our immediate destination, was a system of old shallow trenches on the slope of the Mount and about 1000 yards from the summit. Capt. Bowden and Lieut. Stuart, with runners, also made a reconnaissance.

At about 7 p.m., with an hour of daylight remaining, we worked our way up the redoubt, filing along two shallow trenches leading towards the enemy, and reached Gottlieb Trench, which ran at right angles to the redoubt trenches, and which was comfortably deep and homely.

Alas for our first impressions! Within an hour two heavy enemy shells had landed amongst our men packed in the trench, and had inflicted casualties of about 18 killed and 25 wounded.

The troops were extended right and left along the trench, making a continuous line facing the enemy. This done, we settled down to consolidate the position. Men not required as sentries and for other necessary duties scraped "possies" in the bottom of the trench, and curling up, most of them were soon asleep.

We had imagined that this trench was to be our "home" for the tour in the line. A small slip of paper brought to the company commanders at 11 p.m. by a hot and weary runner dispelled that illusion. By the flickering lights of half-a-dozen matches this is what the paper revealed:—

"Warning order. The 24th Battalion, in conjunction with the 23rd Battalion, will attack Mt. St. Quentin tomorrow, 1st September—A A A—Zero time 6 a.m.—A A A—Further orders to follow."

Truly a bolt from the blue!

Our right flank was not yet linked with the 23rd Battalion, and Lieut. P. E. Smythe, with his platoon, spent much anxious time endeavouring to locate that unit.

At 3 a.m. on 1st September the attack orders arrived, and then ensued a quiet bustle all along the line. Rifles and Lewis guns received a final rub with oily rags, equipment was readjusted and lightened as much as possible, and everything done by each man in the way of a hasty preparation for his part in the coming "hop over."

At about 4 a.m. the officers in charge of companies—Lieut. W. B. Gow, Lieut. A. Stuart, Lieut. E. S. Baldock, M.C., and Capt. G. J. Bowden—met and decided the tactical details of the attack

"C" and "D" Coys. were to lead the assault, followed by "A" and "B" Coys. The left boundary of the Battalion front was the Canal du Nord, and our right embraced the Mount, which we were to attack, with the 23rd Battalion on that flank. The village of Feuillaucourt, on "D" and "B" Coys' left, was only a short distance from the J.O.T., and this village was to be mopped-up as the troops advanced. They were then to push on over the main Peronne road and a tramline to the objective. "C" and "A" Coys' ground, after passing the main road, had a sunken road on the slope of the Mount, but otherwise offered no shelter from enemy fire. The whole position was strongly fortified with German strong posts and many machine-guns, with riflemen in large numbers on the whole front.

The Mount dominated the whole of the ground, and looked an almost impregnable fortress. Our companies were, for such a task as they had in front of them, painfully weak in numbers. "C" Coy's. strength was 80, counting all ranks, while "D" Coy. numbered only 70. The other companies were correspondingly small. "C" and "D" Coys. each had a front of 400 yards. The attack was to be made in three waves, the first wave in extended order, and the other two in artillery formation, with spaces of 50 yards between the groups. When the companies formed up, "C" and "D" Coys each had a front wave of 30 men, with 16 yards between each man. Every casualty in the first line therefore meant a gap of 32 yards.

The time dragged heavily as we waited in Gottlieb Trench. The last hour seemed a day. A profound hush appeared to come over everyone, relieved at intervals by cheerful sallies from that hero—the man who jokes at such times to keep up the spirits of his comrades!

The trench presented an unusual appearance owing to our small numbers. For stretches of 20 yards the trench was empty. Then there was a knot of half a dozen silent, grim-faced men puffing at pipes and cigarettes, and looking vacantly at the parapet in front of them. The same thought was probably in every mind. In the early glimmer of dawn the sight of the huge, black, steep slope of the Mount in front of us, and the knowledge of our weak numbers and the strength of the massed Huns holding the heights, impressed upon us the truth that we were "up against it," and that this stunt promised to be tougher than all the hard tasks we had previously encountered at Pozieres, Bullecourt, Ypres, and other places.

A sudden and terrific hail of machine-gun bullets cracked on the parapet, the earth shook with the concussion of the first Hun artillery salvoes, the heights in front of us were suddenly transformed into a madhouse of hundreds of chattering machine-guns, and we looked at our watches—5.45 a.m.! Was this the preparation of a Hun assault, or had the Boche divined our intention of attack? A moment's reflection, and we realised that our movements of the previous day had warned the Boche, and that he was now getting to work to stop us.

Rain fell at the critical hour, making visibility poor.

The minutes crawled.

Six a.m.! Our solitary battery of field guns fired a salvo, and thereafter each gun of that battery fired independently. We had expected a heavy backing of our artillery. We waited a minute for the guns to open fire, but in vain.

The officers roared "Over!" and as one man the long and very thin line of khaki jumped over the parapet. The hill in front was alive with machine-guns, and every man instinctively advanced in short rushes from one shell hole to another. Owing to our scarcity of men and the enemy's wire entanglements, a concerted advance was impossible. A number of officers and N.C.O.'s were hit directly the attack started, and this helped to throw every man on his own initiative. This perhaps was in no small way the secret of our extraordinary success. The close control needed so urgently where an attack is made behind a heavy moving barrage was here unnecessary. As it was, small batches of men, generally with a Lewis gun, found themselves apparently alone, but just plugged along up the hill.

This is the kind of fighting in which many V.C.'s are earned and not awarded, because the deeds of bravery are not seen by the necessary witnesses.

Two enemy mines, one on our right and one on the left, were exploded in an attempt to disorganise the attack.

As we advanced through the village of Feuillaucourt the Germans concealed in the ruins brought down a number of our men, including Lewis gunners, who were endeavouring to gain superiority of fire. Nevertheless, the village was taken in our stride, and the boys pushed on. L/Cpl. E. L. Ford, a Lewis gunner, of "B" Coy., distinguished himself early in the attack by engaging and overthrowing a German strong-post.

At about 6.30 a.m. Lieut. A. V. Sedgwick, who was leading the first wave of "C" Coy., came into close contact with strong enemy forces, and after a lively engagement at point blank range (about 30 yards), he realised the futility of advancing with his few men. He therefore withdrew to the junction of the sunken road and the main Peronne road.

The attack was eventually held up by a withering point blank machine-gun and rifle fire, and the company commanders posted their men behind the shelter of a low bank above the sunken road. The situation was reported to Headquarters.

The Germans who had been driven off by our advance were now observed coming back in strong force—fully 10 to 1 against us.

Lieut. Towner, of the 2nd M.G. Battalion, got forward with two Vickers guns, and with these and a machine-gun we had already captured from the enemy, opened a destructive fire on the Germans in front of us, putting four or five of their machine-guns out of action.

After a delay of about two hours orders were received

from Headquarters to reorganise and prepare to attack again at 1.30 p.m., when we would be assisted by an artillery barrage.

The key to the position was a crater-like strong-hold, packed with German machine-guns and men, on the summit of the Mount. Our artillery was to bombard this crater at 1 p.m. with the object of reducing the garrison. But our gunfire made little impression on the position, and the enemy fire continued unabated.

We were now within 150 yards of this crater, and on a suggestion from Headquarters it was resolved to advance on the strong-hold by moving in file along a trench which led from the sunken road up the Mount. One company of the 21st Battalion was sent in to assist in this effort. Lieut. Sedgwick organised a mixed party of 24th and 21st Battalion men, numbering about 20, and led the attack, supported by other parties at distances of 20 yards. Lieut. Towner's machine-guns, on the sunken road, enfiladed the other German trenches on the hill to keep down the fire of the Germans in these positions while our men rushed the crater. One platoon of our riflemen meanwhile engaged the German machine-gunners and reduced their fire.

The effort, so weak in comparison with the enemy strength, appeared almost hopeless; indeed it seemed absurd, and could only be compared to throwing peas at a whale. It was, however, a wonderful testimony to the daring and optimism of our troops.

When the attack was launched the German machine-gunners opened with a deadly blast of bullets, but they were almost silenced by the waiting riflemen. The Huns on the hill stood up to fire on our attacking party, and were cut down by our machine-guns. Lieut. Sedgwick and his men, with fixed bayonets and bombs, gained the crater with a final rush, and after a stubborn hand-to-hand fight, in which the attackers were outnumbered by at least ten to one, they secured complete possession of the strong-hold. Many of the Huns bolted, throwing away arms and equipment as they fled, and providing excellent targets at 150 yards range for our men on the left. All over the Mount the Germans

Lt. SEDGWICK, M.C., and Party awaiting the attack on the crater, Mont St. Quentin.

were making off. Many of them got out of their trenches and ran round in circles, baffled and unnerved by the fire of our rifles and machine-guns and the presence of our troops on the summit of the hill. As the remnant of the garrison ran down behind the spur, our "D" and "B" Corps, on the left, completed the rout by direct fire. One trench by which the Germans sought to escape from the Mount was blocked with their dead. They had endeavoured to make off by following a trench leading towards the canal, where there was an exit to their next line. To foil this move "D" and "B" Coys. sent parties to block the exit.

The seemingly impossible had been achieved. The capture of the crater was a coup which decided the battle, as it cleared the enemy from the heights and permitted our further advance with fewer casualties. Thus Mt. St. Quentin was outflanked and captured. The 23rd Battalion mopped-up the greater part of the village.

With the way open for a further advance, Sgt. E. J. R. Dart ("B" Coy.) and another man went forward to ascertain the enemy strength in Plevna Trench, the German line immediately in front. They found some Huns in dug-outs here, and rounded them up. Sgt. Dart guarded the prisoners while his companion went back to report. The companies advanced and occupied the line.

"C" and "A" Coys., on the right, advanced and took possession of the Mount.

Plevna Trench, on the left flank, entered another called Kolovna Trench, which was strongly held by the Boche. However, as we had already achieved a great success, and as our handful of survivors were physically exhausted, we contented ourselves with consolidating the ground gained, and then settled down to hold it against counter-attack. Our line then ran from the Canal du Nord on the left along Plevna Trench to the crater on the Mount, and thence along the summit to the forward end of the village of St. Quentin on the top, where our right joined the left flank of the 23rd Battalion.

When General Sir Henry Rawlinson, the Army Commander, received the report that Mt. St. Quentin was in our hands he could scarcely believe it was true, and when the victory was confirmed beyond doubt he did not disguise his amazement and delight.

The fall of this fortress opened the way for a more speedy advance than the command had anticipated. The English press hailed the capture of Mt. St. Quentin as one of the classic achievements of the war.

Mt. St. Quentin was such a commanding eminence that from its summit a view could be obtained of the country for miles in every direction. Even Amiens was visible from that splendid elevation.

The factors which contributed mainly to our success were the speed and daring with which our men attacked the crater under Lieut. Sedgwick's gallant leadership, the excellent shooting of our riflemen and Lewis-gunners in beating down the enemy, the capable management and effective work of Lieut. Towner's machine-guns in the enfilading fire, and the loss of nerve on the part of the strong German garrison.

One of our company commanders afterwards expressed himself thus:—"The capture of Mt. St. Quentin covers with honour the few men of the Sixth Brigade who took it, and it is an everlasting disgrace to the Germans for allowing them to do it, especially as the Huns were picked troops."

The German losses were extremely heavy. The large numbers of enemy dead bore grim testimony to the effectiveness of our shooting.

Our own casualties were not light, but had we depended upon numbers instead of strategy the capture of such an important fortress would probably have been regarded as satisfactorily achieved had our losses been four times as heavy.

The 24th Battalion casualties were:—Killed, 5 officers, 43 other ranks; wounded, 3 officers, 88 other ranks. The more than usual proportion of killed to wounded was due to the fact of there being little or no shelter for a man when once hit.

The German prisoners taken, apart from the large number of the enemy killed or wounded, exceeded our casualties.

The 23rd and 24th Battalions captured no fewer than 400 German machine-guns, and also a large quantity of ammunition.

Our officers killed were Lieuts. E. M. Martin, C. J. R. Newton, P. W. Salmon, A. G. Gilchrist, and P. T. McCarty. Captain Bowden was among the wounded.

The N.C.O.'s and men who fell included some of our bravest soldiers. During the preparations for the attack we lost three N.C.O.'s. These were Coy.-Sgt.-Major W. Love, Coy. Q.M.-Sgt. V. J. Jolly, and Cpl. H. W. Martin. Pte. C. L. Doble, one of "A" Coy's. original and popular boys, was also killed. The fighting on 1st September robbed us of a number of brave and promising N.C.O.'s. The killed on this day included Cpl. R. Roff, M.M., Cpl. C. Ryan, Cpl. J. L. G. Makin, Cpl. R. J. Andrew, Cpl. S. C. Fishwick, Cpl. D. Dearth, and L/Cpl. J. R. F. Byrne. On the day following the attack, when we were holding the new line, we lost other good soldiers, among the killed being Sgt. J. Cumming (a prominent footballer) and Pte. D. F. Sullivan. Dan. Sullivan, a youth in years, but a veteran in valour and battlefield experience, was an original member of the Battalion. He had been wounded and evacuated four times during his long service with the unit, but was always eager to get back to the front and "carry on," even when he might have remained away from the field. Such men were deeply mourned by their comrades, and their loss to the unit could not be expressed in words.

Although all the brave men at Mt. St. Quentin did not receive decorations, the number of distinctions awarded indicated the gallantry with which all ranks played their parts in the battle. Major D. D. Coutts, the Battalion's medical officer, who had displayed marked valour and devotion in many engagements, was awarded the D.S.O. Three of the company commanders (Capt. G. J. Bowden, Lieut. A. Stuart and Lieut. W. B. Gow) and Lieut. A. V. Sedgwick (who led the attack on the crater) received the Military Cross. Lieut. E. S. Baldock, M.C. ("B" Coy.), who rendered equally meritorious service, had already won a decoration. The distinctions granted to N.C.O.'s showed what an important part the Non-Coms. played in the defeat of the enemy. Four D.C.M.'s were awarded, the recipients being Sgt. J. H. Bond, Sgt. E. J. R. Dart, Sgt. E. Holloway, and L/Cpl. E. L. Ford. The following N.C.O.'s and men who had already won Military Medals were each awarded a bar to that decoration:—Sgt. D. McL. McKinnon, M.M., Pte. A. S. Adolfsson, M.M., Pte. L. Herman, M.M., L/Cpl. F. M. Walker. M.M,, and L/Cpl J. W. Cooke, M.M. A large number of Military Medals (recorded elsewhere) were also awarded to N.C.O.'s and men.

Lieut. Towner (2nd Machine Gun Battalion), and also Sgt. Lowerson (21st Battalion), who was with Lieut. Sedgwick in the attack on the crater, were honoured with the V.C.

Our stretcher-bearers, true to their reputation for devotion and bravery, had again distinguished themselves, and several of them were among the medal winners.

The runners played their important part in the battle with their customary resourcefulness and valour. The Headquarters runners—soldiers like C. R. Lepp, E. W. Dardel, T. Drake, F. H. Hamilton, M. Bernier and A. V. Denier—could always be relied upon to do their work faithfully and intelligently. As the adjutant once remarked, an operation order could have been entrusted to them verbally. These runners all won decorations. (Dardel later received a commission in the Australian Flying Corps).

We held our position in Plevna Trench until the morning of 3rd September, when the Seventh Brigade passed through our line and continued the attack successfully. At 11 a.m. that day we received the welcome order to move back.

The commander of the Sixth Brigade (Brigadier-General J. C. Robertson, C.M.G., D.S.O.) received the following message from General Birdwood:—"My personal and hearty congratulations on the really good work done by your Brigade in the attack on Mt. St. Quentin. I feel that the work done there is just about as good as any that the A.I.F. has put in, and you must be proud of your men, as I am sure they are of their commander."

A memorial at Mt. St. Quentin, erected in honour of the Second Division, marks the scene of one of the greatest victories of the A.I.F.

RESTING AT CAPPY.

After an uneventful march of about six miles, on our way back from Mt. St. Quentin, the Battalion reached Cappy, on the Somme Canal, where we were to bivouac during a short period of rest and reorganisation.

At the parade on the following day the C.O. expressed to all ranks of the unit his admiration of their splendid achievements at Mt. St. Quentin, the importance of which was fully appreciated by the Allied commanders.

The troops, thoroughly skilled in the art of constructing shelters, carried large quantities of iron and timber from the ruins of Cappy, and soon had terraces of cosy dug-outs along the Canal. A storm in the night was one of several notable episodes at this place. Violent wind wrought havoc with the frail habitations of the men, and shell-splintered trees crashed to the ground. A large tree stove in the roof of the orderly-room and imparted a shock to the staff asleep on the floor. Some of the dug-outs were submerged beneath heaps of fallen boughs. The loud rolling thunder and blinding flashes of lightning added to the fury of the night, but the boys, used to the sensation and the din of battle, remarked that it was a poor attempt on the part of the elements to imitate the scenes of war. During the storm the Q.M.'s. store (a large marquee) was lifted bodily and carried across the field.

The weather, however, was fairly agreeable for the greater part of our stay here, and the men were able to walk out of their dug-outs and plunge into the Canal for a morning bath. There was no greater luxury for soldiers living in "burrows" than a refreshing dip in a clear stream, and between the hours of the parades the Canal was the scene of hundreds of happy men from our own and other units disporting themselves in the water.

When army men shed their clothes, colonels and privates appear much the same kind of beings. So here at these swimming places senior officers who were not personally known to some of the men found themselves addressed as "Diggers," and were fortunate if they were not accorded less complimentary attention. But most Australian officers enjoy these experiences. Some even took the trouble to disguise themselves so that their rank would not be recognised.

The success of the last battle had put all ranks in good humour, and men romped and played in the highest spirits. A captain who had just received a new tailor-made uniform put on his fine clothes one evening and strutted along the Canal with a feeling that the war was progressing most favourably, and that personally he was more than holding his own now that he had his new suit. His pleasant reflections were interrupted by a party of his brother officers, who dragged him to the edge of the Canal, and seizing him by the arms and legs, swung him over the edge of the water, counting "one, two, three," and threatening to toss him into the stream. Something happened at a critical moment, and the captain dropped into the water, dragging another officer with him. While spectators cheered the pair, they struggled in the Canal, ducking each other in turn and eventually emerging well soaked.

When men were able to accept these experiences as amusement there was little danger of life becoming monotonous.

As soon as the troops had rested and forgotten the strain of battle, sports were introduced to stimulate their energy once more. Brigade and Divisional sports were held and provided rich enjoyment for all ranks.

At the Divisional sports a band contest (quickstep) was held for all bands of the Second Division, and out of eleven bands competing the 24th Battalion Band walked off with first honours, amid intense excitement and cheers. The bandmaster (Sgt. E. Bright) was personally congratulated by General Birdwood, who was in attendance, and who always enjoyed himself at the sports meetings held by the troops. The band's drill instructor was Lieut. W. D. Baldie. Drum-Major L. Roberts, M.M. (one of our regimental stretcher-bearers), led the band on the march.

At this time the Corps commander, under pressure from the War Office, had decided, owing to the seriously reduced strength of the Australian Battalions, to disband some of the units and build up others in order to enable the Corps to carry on. The hard and continuous fighting in which the Australians had been engaged since the beginning of April, when they stopped the German advance on Amiens, had not only worn the troops down physically, but had left the Battalions painfully weak in numbers. The Diggers, however, manifested very strong feeling on the question of disbandment. In the Sixth Brigade the unit affected was the 21st Battalion, one company of which was to be allotted to the 24th Battalion. Accordingly our "C" Coy. was broken up and divided among the other three companies in order to allow all the 21st men coming to us to enjoy some of their former identity as a separate company. Out of consideration for the feelings of the troops, and in view of an early resumption of hostilities by the units then resting, the disbandment was postponed.

The 24th Battalion decided to carry on with only three companies.

While at Cappy our Battalion press was established in a former German officers' billet in the village. A ballot by the troops for a title for the regimental newspaper decided in favour of "The Red and White Diamond" (the colour badge of the unit).

Another notable event at Cappy was the departure of the 1914 men on six months' furlough to Australia. Thank God, the veterans did not have to return to war.

While on a route march from Cappy the Battalion one day passed through Chuignolles, where the troops had an opportunity of examining the huge German gun which had been in action there, and which the enemy had partly destroyed when it was abandoned. This monster was covered with inscriptions written by Australian troops who visited the spot from day to day. Many units facetiously claimed the honour of capturing the gun. One humourist gave the credit to non-combatants. He had written on the gun in chalk: "Captured by the Military Police, assisted by the W.A.A.C.'s."

BEAUREVOIR.

While we had been resting at Cappy the great advance had gone on, and now the Boche was being hunted off his Hindenburg Line. The Second Division's turn for battle had come again, so we prepared for action, and on 27th September set off for the front. A march of eleven miles brought us to a position outside Le Mesnil, and on the 28th we pushed on to Tincourt, where we saw the smoke of the battle in which the Americans and Australians were attacking the Hindenburg Line on the St. Quentin Canal.

Next morning a party of "A" Coy. men were late on parade. They produced a note from the C.O. of the Casualty Clearing Station, in which that officer thanked them for their good work as stretcher-bearers during the night. They had voluntarily toiled all night carrying wounded at the hospital.

The Battalion marched from Tincourt to the Hindenburg Line on 2nd October, passing through Roisel, Hervilly, Hesbecourt and Villaret, and that night rested on the line from which an attack had been launched five days earlier. The large numbers of American dead on the field told a pathetic story of heavy fighting. The Hindenburg Line was still marked by wide belts of wire entanglements half a mile in depth.

Our men were elated at the evidence of German defeat, and they were in the best of spirits as they waited here on the line from which the Hun had believed he could not be ousted. But to the Germans the Hindenburg Line was now only a memory—a painful memory of battle and defeat.

The discovery of a supposed German corpse-conversion works in the Canal tunnel near Bellicourt excited the interest of everybody on the front. Hundreds of troops visited the spot to investigate the cause of the sensational reports in circulation. Newspaper correspondents made the most of the discovery, but the soldiers satisfied themselves that the gruesome chamber in the tunnel was nothing more than a

German cook-house where a party of Huns had been trapped and killed by bombs.

A German counter-attack against the 27th American Division had robbed the Sammies of some ground which they had won. This development made necessary an alteration in the plans for the continuance of the advance. The intention had been to launch the Second Australian Division and a force of cavalry against the German line at Beaurevoir with the object of making a big drive, but it was now decided to withhold the cavalry.

The Fifth and Seventh Brigades had attacked the German defences in the Weincourt-Beaurevoir system at 5.30 on the morning of 3rd October. This attack had met with a good deal of success, but strong opposition was encountered in the Beaurevoir system, and the assaulting Brigades had not been able to advance more than about 1000 yards east of this line. These Brigades had suffered casualties, but had inflicted much heavier losses on the enemy. There were evidences of bitter hand-to-hand fighting on the field at many points. Germans from no fewer than 23 different units were identified among the prisoners taken in this attack, indicating serious disorganisation of the enemy forces.

The village of Ramicourt, which had already been captured, and Beaurevoir, where the battle was still in progress, were made notable by the release of civilians by the advancing Allied army. Only the aged inhabitants had been left by the Germans, who had removed all the people able to work. The aged refugees, who were conveyed by ambulance cars to safer regions, welcomed their deliverers with great joy, and the troops fed them while they waited for conveyances. Many a digger denied himself a meal in order to appease the hunger of these unfortunate people, who described how for a week they had lived in the cellars of their houses, subsisting on raw vegetables.

At 2 p.m. on 3rd October the 24th Battalion was quietly resting on the broken Hindenburg Line, acting as suppotrs to the Fifth and Seventh Brigades. At 3 p.m. we were in fighting order and hurrying up "Watling Street" towards

Estrees. Orders had come with electrical suddenness. At 2 p.m. that day the 22nd and 24th Battalions had been placed under orders of the Fifth Brigade, commanded by Brigadier-General Martin, who ordered the 24th Battalion to move forward immediately to the Beaurevoir system captured by the Fifth Brigade (which had established a line in the ravine immediately in front of the village of Beaurevoir) and prepare to attack on that front. We had accordingly assembled the companies with the greatest possible speed and moved off in artillery formation from the Canal. Our orders were to be in position in the line on the left of the main Beaurevoir-Nauroy road by 4 p.m.

The company commanders now were:—"A" Coy., Capt. J. A. Mahony, M.C.; "B" Coy., Temporary Capt. G. D. Pollington, M.M.; "D" Coy., Capt. J. H. Fletcher. "C" Coy. (as already stated) had been merged with the other companies owing to the reduced strength of the unit.

The C.O. (Lieut.-Colonel James, D.S.O.) and the adjutant, (Lieut. A. E. Middleton), accompanied by a runner, moved ahead of the Battalion and made a reconnaissance of the Beaurevoir system. The C.O. then decided to remove the Battalion from the trenches to a more favourable position on a sunken road about 300 yards to the left of the main Nauroy road.

Enemy aeroplanes, flying low, must have reported our movements to the German artillery, as a heavy barrage was put down on the village of Estrees, through which we had just passed, and on the ground immediately in front of it. The enemy planes also fired on our troops. Sgt. McGillicuddy, a very brave soldier, was killed here. By 5 p.m. the Battalion was disposed along the sunken road about 2000 yards from the village of Beaurevoir.

Then the C.O. was called back to the headquarters of the 19th Battalion, in rear of Estrees, to receive orders. It was with extreme difficulty that this spot was located, and it was 6 p.m. before the C.O. was able to get into touch with Brigadier-General Martin, who ordered an attack on Beaurevoir at 6.30. The 24th Battalion was to attack on the left of the Brigade front, with the 22nd and 23rd

Battalions on the right. With only half an hour to get his men on the J.O.T., the C.O. hurried back to assemble his company commanders and give them instructions. "A" and "B" Coys. were ordered to lead the assault, with "D" Coy. supporting. The attacking companies, moving off in haste, had to race to reach the J.O.T. in time to follow our barrage. In spite of all our hurry the companies arrived just as the barrage ceased. By all the rules of war this might have been regarded as disastrous, and in many instances an attack on a strong position under such circumstances would have been postponed; but it was not so here.

In the dusk of the evening the men formed up in one line in the dry Torrens Canal, and were informed that the objective was the crest of the hill in front. At the command to advance the troops started up the slope. Soon the enemy machine-gunners and snipers opened fire, and our men dropped down and poured in a fusillade from Lewis guns and rifles. The Hun fire quickly subsided. Then with a yell our men swept up the slope and over the ridge, and in less than an hour from the time they began their advance they were established on the line of their objective in front of the village.

The attack was a brilliant success, and was completed with only six casualties (two killed and four wounded).

At 7.30 p.m. Capt. Mahony reported that 37 enemy prisoners and two machine guns were being sent back.

The suddenness with which the advance was made is indicated by an incident at Capt. Mahony's headquarters on the new line. Two German runners unexpectedly entered the dugout. Believing that the Huns were making a surprise counter-attack, our men snatched up their arms. But the two Germans were even more surprised. They had brought despatches and rations (tripe stew) for the commander of the German regiment which had held the line, not knowing that the position was in our hands, and in the dark had walked into captivity.

After the objective had been gained and the flanks linked up, the Sixth Brigade Battalions again came under the command of Brigadier-General J. C. Robertson.

At 9 o'clock that night (3rd October) the commander of a Manchester Regiment (which had just arrived from Italy) reported at our Battalion Headquarters and stated that he was to relieve us. (Telephonic communication with Brigade Headquarters had not then been established). Orders were subsequently received to hand over to this Regiment and to take up a position on the low ground immediately in rear of the 22nd Battalion on the right.

It was an unusual procedure to effect a flank relief immediately after an attack, but the change-over was successfully effected by 4 o'clock on the following morning.

The Second Division's operations at Beaurevoir had yielded 1100 German prisoners.

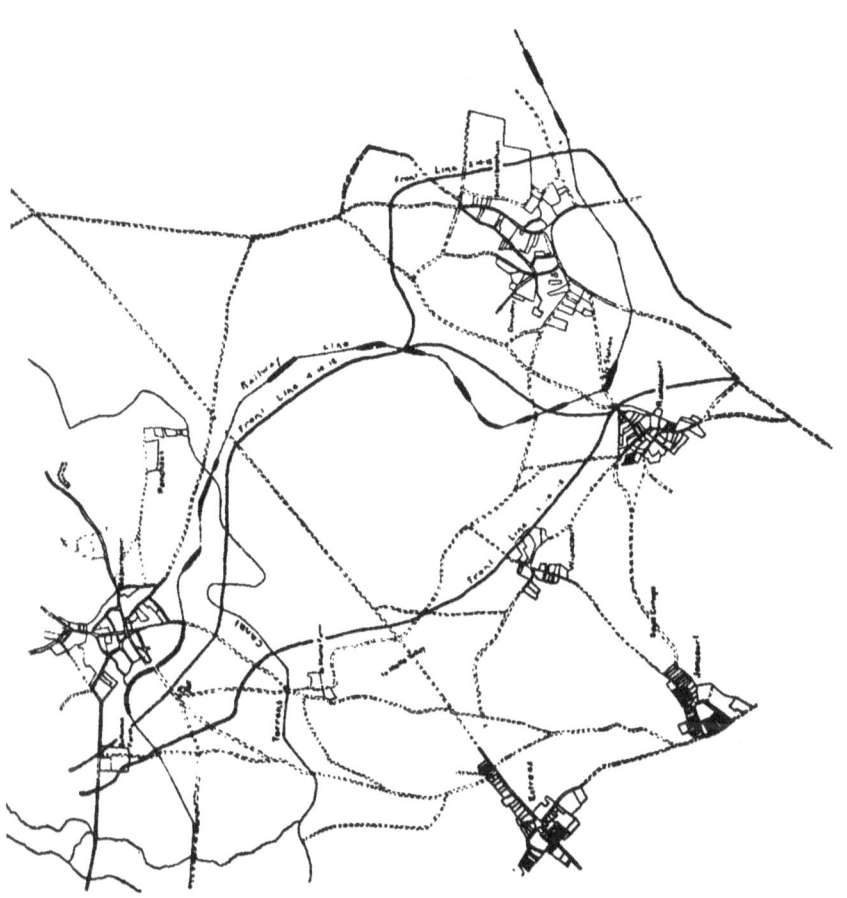

Beaureboir and Montbrehain: Scene of the final Australian Infantry attacks in the Great War.

MONTBREHAIN.

OUR LAST BATTLE.

At 6 a.m. on 4th October the 24th Battalion Headquarters were established in a new position in the Beaurevoir system. The Battalion remained quiescent for the greater part of that day, but a bombshell which did not come from the enemy was dropped upon us during the afternoon. This was an intimation that the Battalion was to make another assault on the following morning. The objective this time was Montbrehain and the high ground on a line with that village. The war had certainly taken on a vigorous and strenuous aspect! The troops quickly recovered from the shock of this news, and while they had the opportunity they amused themselves and displayed a wonderfully cheerful spirit. In an old German dugout nine officers were huddled together singing and jesting as if war were a huge comedy. Parodies on well-known songs were rendered impromptu with a highly entertaining effect. One of these efforts was:—

"A" takes the right flank, "D" takes the left flank,
But we'll be in Montbrehain before you.
We'll send up the white flares to show that we're tres bon
And we'll all go back to Abbeville in the morning.

(These words indicated that the troops were expecting the Corps to be relieved and sent back for a rest).

Another parody was on the army favourite "Parlez-vous":—

"The 24th are in the line—Parlez-vous,
They want Hock watches to tell the time—Parlez-vous,
The infantry, the infantry, who go before the guns;
The infantry, the infantry, who "rat" the poor old Huns;
The Cavalry, Artillery, and all the Engineers
Will never catch the infantry in a hundred thousand years.
Inky, pinky, parlez-vous."

Capt. Mahony and Capt. Fletcher sang "I'm Courting Bonnie Lizzie Lindsay Noo," and Capt. Fletcher sang " The Bells of St. Mary's."

Alas for the hopes of men in war! Within 12 hours four of these lighthearted, gallant men (including Capt. Mahony and Capt. Fletcher) were dead, and four others were wounded.

While the companies were getting their equipment in fighting order during the afternoon and making light of their serious business, the commanders assembled at Brigade Headquarters to discuss plans for the impending battle.

The attack on Montbrehain was fixed for 6.5 a.m. on 5th October. The German positions were known to be strongly held. It was later learned that the enemy had anticipated an attack here, and had sent in a strong garrison to defeat the assault.

The ground over which the advance was to be made was exceedingly rough, and was protected with wire and broken by trenches. These conditions made an uphill assault all the more difficult. Consequently the Divisional commander arranged for the assistance of a Tank Company. It was hoped that at least eight tanks would support the infantry.

The artillery barrage was to commence 300 yards east of the J.O.T., rest on that line for four minutes, and then move at the rate of 100 yards every four minutes to the final protective barrage line about 500 yards beyond the infantry objective. The J.O.T. was to be taped by the Sixth Field Coy. Engineers. The Battalion Intelligence Staff (Cpl. Geo. Harker and the Battalion scouts) rendered valuable assistance in this work. The 2nd Australian Pioneer Battalion was to relieve the 138th British Infantry Brigade holding our front line on the night of the 4th. The 21st Battalion (on the right) and the 24th Battalion (on the left) were to form up on the J.O.T. one hour before zero, behind the Pioneer Battalion. At zero minus 15 minutes, the Pioneer Battalion was to withdraw behind the 21st and 24th Battalions. At zero (6.5 a.m.) the 21st and 24th Battalions were to advance on Montbrehain and the high ground to the north and north-east of the village. The

Pioneer Battalion was to follow up and gradually form a defensive flank on the south side of the village facing southeast along the general line.

At 7 o'clock on the evening of the 4th the C.O. returned from Brigade Headquarters, and hastily summoning the company commanders, gave them verbal instructions for the assault. The company commanders were also ordered to make reconnnaissances of the field before the troops assembled on the J.O.T.

At 3 a.m. on the 5th our men were turned out of their shelters in the trenches and ordered to prepare for the attack. The morning was frosty, with the moon shining from a clear sky, and once they were astir the lads were eager for some activity to get their blood circulating with a little more warmth. A few hours later, when they were charging up the slope in the face of heavy fire, their blood was at boiling point.

On the way to the J.O.T. some gas was encountered, and many of the men were sneezing. By 5 a.m. the Battalion, spread out in one line, was on the tape ready for the assault. That meant that they had one hour to wait and shiver in the cold. "A" Coy. (Capt. J. A. Mahony, M.C.) was on the right. "B" Coy. (Temporary Capt. G. D. Pollington, M.M.) in the centre, and "D" Coy. (Capt. J. H. Fletcher) on the left. A gas barrage put down by the enemy at 5.15 made the position decidedly uncomfortable.

At 6.5 a.m., just as the sun was creeping over the horizon, our barrage opened, and the attackers jumped up from the ground and went forward. The village was 500 or 600 yards ahead. The pace of the barrage (100 yards every four minutes) did not permit a spirited charge at first. The troops could only wait and follow calmly.

The attack was launched without the tanks, which were late in coming up.

As the troops advanced the enemy barrage, which had responded promptly, shortened, irrespective of the position of his own troops. The German artillery, machine-guns and rifles poured in a heavy fire against our thin attacking line, and although men began to fall the rest went on determinedly. The first enemy posts were met on a railway line, but these were soon disposed of.

"A" Coy., on the right, brought their Lewis guns into action against enemy strong posts, and were endeavouring to beat down the enemy machine-gunners, when a tank came to their aid, making straight for the German strongposts and riding them down in a manner which delighted our men. As the enemy troops attempted to make off they came under our fire and suffered heavily. Gaining the edge of the village, the boys waited a while for our barrage to lift. Big shells from the German guns were falling among them here, but at the favourable moment they swept on over hedges, through orchards and demolished houses, and past the church, overpowering the enemy forces, cleaning out dugouts, and rounding up prisoners. Sgt.-Mjr. Rankin and other N.C.O.'s distinguished themselves during the attack.

The men of "B" Coy., in the centre, had to fight their way without the assistance of the friendly tank. Indeed, it appeared at one stage as if this company had an almost impossible task. From the high ground above German machine guns swept the slope, while snipers were picking off the men as they pulled themselves together in a small trench. Coy. Sgt.-Mjr. G. H. Cumming, M.M., was killed here. Capt. Pollington, realising that delay meant disaster and heavy casualties, ordered his men to prepare to charge in the face of the enemy's fire. The attacking line was weak in numbers—one man to every 15 or 20 yards—but at the word "Go" the company swept up the hill with a yell which must have unnerved the German machine-gunners. The Huns, with enough machine-guns and rifles to stop a brigade, were firing just over the heads of our men, who swept into the first enemy stronghold with a suddenness which alarmed the garrison. A sharp, short, hand-to-hand fight disposed of the Germans to a man, and then the attackers dashed on to the second strong-post, which also went down before the rush. Groups of German riflemen in shell holes were mopped up on the way.

Further ahead was a quarry, fortified (it was eventually

LIEUT. G. M. INGRAM, V.C., M.M.

discovered) with no fewer than 40 machine-guns and considerably ov a hundred men. Such a position would appear to be impregnable against an infantry attack, but, encouraged by their achievements so far, "B" Coy. was ready to tackle this fortress.

At this stage Capt. Pollington was badly wounded, and he handed the company over to Lieut. W. T. West, M.M.

It was in the heavy fighting which marked "B" Coy's. advance that Lieut. G. M. Ingram, M.M., won his V.C. The story of Lieut. Ingram's gallantry, as recorded in the "London Gazette," illustrates the strong opposition which his company faced in the attack:—

"Lieut. George Morby Ingram displayed most conspicuous bravery and initiative during the attack on Montbrehain. When, early in the advance, his platoon was held up by a strong point, Lieut. Ingram, without hesitation, dashed forward and rushed the post at the head of his men. Nine machine-guns were captured and 42 of the enemy killed after stubborn resistance. Later, when the company had suffered severe casualties from enemy posts, and many leaders had fallen, he took control of the situation, rallied his men under intense fire, and led them forward. He himself rushed the first post, shot six of the enemy, and captured a machine-gun, thus overcoming serious resistance. On two subsequent occasions during the advance he displayed great dash and resource in leading his men against enemy posts, where they inflicted many casualties and took 62 prisoners. Throughout the whole day he showed the most inspiring example of courage and leadership, and freely exposed himself regardless of danger."

The quarry previously referred to was one of the German strongholds against which Lieut. Ingram gallantly and successfully led his men.

By this time "B" Coy. had become isolated, and in face of very heavy fire established a line of posts on the objective, at the same time making efforts to get in touch with the companies on the flanks. The situation was probably observed by the enemy, who dropped a heavy barrage between our right and centre companies, and inflicted heavy casualties on both groups.

J

Lieut. Ingram was enthusiastic in his praise of the N.C.O.'s and men of his company. He specially commended the bravery of Sgt. D. W. Witherden, M.M., who played a brilliant part in the attack.

"D" Coy., on the left, after going some distance, had been held up by the enemy's heavy fire, which had robbed the company of all its officers, the commander, Capt. Fletcher, being among the killed. A tank had come to the company's assistance, but was quickly put out of action, and the troops were left to overcome the enemy resistance by their own strength. Two of the platoon commanders (Lieut. J. F. Gear, M.C., and Lieut. E. L. Forbes) made an effort to outflank a particularly strong enemy position, one party going right and one left. Lieut. Gear fell, shot through the heart, and Lieut. Forbes was wounded. As this plan did not succeed, Coy. Sgt.-Mjr. A. Burke, who took command of the company when all the officers had been put out of action, decided to dig in on the line which the company was then holding, just short of the crest. Later Lieut. Calvert was sent from "B" Coy. to take charge of "D" Coy, and the company gained its objective and eventually linked up with the flanks.

When our men got through the village they observed numbers of Germans retiring over the high ground ahead, but when the enemy found that our advance had stopped and that our numbers were small he reorganised his troops and sent them back to engage the posts which we had established on the line of our objective. The German artillery and machine-guns also concentrated on our posts, and our already small forces were further reduced by heavy casualties. With the small number of men at our disposal it was difficult to link up the whole of the front, and the enemy, recognising our difficulty, pushed a strong party of his men in between our right and centre companies. Two of our advanced posts were consequently withdrawn and established on a sunken road.

English troops on the right of our Brigade had attacked simultaneously with our assault with the object of covering our Brigade's exposed right flank after the village had been captured. The English troops, however, had been unable to gain their objective, and the enemy forces holding Mannequin Hill were able to direct enfilading and reverse fire on our men in Montbrehain. But for the good work of the 2nd Australian Pioneer Battalion in protecting this flank, the 21st and 24th Battalions would probably have been enveloped by an enemy advance from the south into the village. Twelve hours before the attack the Pioneer Battalion had been scattered on various duties, and they had to be assembled and sent forward in haste. Major W. H. Ellwood, M.C., was attached to the Pioneers to assist in directing their operations and co-operating with the other units in action on the Brigade sector.

Casualties in the 24th Battalion were so heavy during the day that two companies of the 27th Battalion were placed at our disposal as close supports. The enemy was fighting determinedly after recovering from the first shock of the attack, and his artillery fire was particularly destructive. Two companies of the 28th Battalion had also been made available for our assistance, and these men carried up supplies of ammunition and helped to consolidate several posts. The 18th Battalion was also sent in as supports to the new line.

Although the enemy did not launch an organised counter-attack during the day, he made many attempts to cut off our advanced posts. Had he succeeded in these efforts he would doubtless have endeavoured to regain the high ground beyond the village. It was not until 8 p.m. that the whole of our line on the objective had been securely linked up and consolidated, and it had only been accomplished by great determination in the face of heavy fire and in spite of numerous casualties.

The German machine-gunners fought gamely at many points throughout the whole of the day's hard battle. During our advance the strong enemy posts (manned in some cases with 40 to 50 men and numerous machine-guns) kept up their fire until our troops came to hand-to-hand conflict with them and after our objective had been gained determined parties of machine-gunners came back under our fire in an effort to retake some of the posts.

The incessant fighting during the day was a heavy tax upon our supplies of ammunition in the forward posts, and often when our ammunition was exhausted the men used the captured German machine-guns, rifles and revolvers to keep up the fire until supplies arrived.

The general testimony of our men was that they had never seen so many enemy dead on so small an area. While our own losses were heavy, the casualties inflicted upon the enemy were far greater. Our artillery and Vickers guns contributed largely to the enemy's losses. Judging by the number of prisoners taken and the known enemy casualties, the German garrison at Montbrehain must have been well over 1500 men, who were supported by strong artillery forces, hundreds of machine-guns, and a number of trench mortars. Prisoners from ten different German regiments were captured during the day. The confusion of units, and the failure of the Boche to launch an organised counter-attack, were indications of the disorganised state of his forces, a condition which was at this time in evidence along the whole front on the enemy side. The German garrison at Montbrehain had been ordered to hold on to their positions at all costs.

Montbrehain was a severe defeat for the Boche, and it paved the way for a successful advance by the Americans when the offensive was resumed a few days later. The enemy prisoners captured on the Sixth Brigade front numbered 623, including 17 officers.

Brigadier-General Robertson took the first opportunity to congratulate the troops under his command on the pronounced success of the battle.

The success of the operations at Beaurevoir and Montbrehain proved once more that the Australian soldier was not a man to be deterred by difficulties. The country was strange to the troops, and there was no time to gain acquaintance with the conditions of the field or the positions of the enemy. The men were thrown into the attack at Beaurevoir almost at a moment's notice, and they had barely gained their objective when they were withdrawn and sent round to make another assault on other ground which was

MONTBREHAIN. - The scene of the Battalion's last engagement on Oct. 5th, 1918.

also unknown to them. Their commanders could only say, in effect, "There is your objective (the crest of a ridge or a village as the case might be); take it and hold it."

Two attacks and a difficult flank relief in 36 hours were a severe test for a unit sadly reduced in numbers, but the success achieved, in spite of many difficulties, demonstrated that the Battalion in its final battle was fighting as well as it had ever fought in its days of unimpaired strength. That the German army was at last suffering its well-deserved but long-deferred defeat was an inspiration to our war-weary men.

News that Turkey had capitulated and had accepted the Allies' terms for an armistice was another indication that the day of victory was not far distant.

The 24th Battalion casualties at Montbrehain were:— Killed, 4 officers, 43 other ranks; wounded, 5 officers, 75 other ranks. Eight men were reported "missing." The officers killed were Captain J. A. Mahony, M.C., Captain J. H. Fletcher, Lieut. J. F. Gear, M.C., and Lieut. W. D. Baldie.

Capt. J. A. Mahony, M.C., one of our finest soldiers, who had risen from the ranks, had distinguished himself as a brave leader and a most successful company commander. His long record of faithfulness and gallantry in battle had won the complete confidence of his men, who were always ready to follow him or obey his orders. Capt. Mahony's remarkable coolness under fire was always an inspiration to his troops. He never went into action without his walking stick, which was his constant companion. While shells and bullets burst and whistled he moved about as if no danger were near. He was almost as fearless of danger as was the stick he carried. In our football team he had played a part as brilliant as his part in battle, while as a comrade he was beloved of all ranks. His death would have been keenly felt at any time, but the hardness of fate, which cut him down when our work was almost completed, was a blow which went deeply to the hearts of all.

Capt. J. H. Fletcher had embarked from Australia with the original Battalion as a private, and had served on

Gallipoli and in France and Belgium through many hard battles. He had received his commission in Egypt, and had won his captaincy by ability, faithfulness and gallantry. It was a sad coincidence that he and Capt. Mahony, whose regimental numbers in the original Battalion were 1056 and 1057, should both rise to the rank of Captain, both go into action as company commanders on our last day in action, and both lay down their lives when our work was almost completed. Such are the fortunes of war!

Lieut. J. F. Gear, M.C., another well-known and gallant officer who died that day, had left Australia with the Battalion's third draft of reinforcements, and joined the unit on Gallipoli. In addition to his fine soldierly and manly qualities, Lieut. Gear was one of our most successful athletes in field sports. As a student at the Continuation School, Ballarat, he had several times gained distinction as sports champion. Before enlisting for active service he had been a successful candidate for Duntroon, but although of perfect and athletic proportions, an inch of measurement denied him this ambition. He enlisted as a private when the call for service came, and he won his stars and his distinction by his undoubted ability and gallantry. He was another of the brave men who had been spared to serve through the long campaign, and then, when victory was in sight, had made the supreme sacrifice to crown their work. Lieut. Gear had temporarily commanded "D" Coy. at Cappy and Tincourt.

Coy. Sgt-Mjr. Cumming M.M., joined the Battalion in Egypt, and had seen long service as a capable sergeant in his company. In action he always proved himself a soldier with coolness and courage, and at all times he had the esteem and confidence of the junior N.C.O.'s and men.

Other N.C.O.'s who fell at Montbrehain were Sgt. L. S. Rainson, Sgt. W. Watson, Cpl. N. A. Grant, and Cpl. E. L. Ford. Pte. J. W. Blankenberg, popularly known as "Russia," a soldier who had served faithfully and gallantly with the unit in many engagements, was killed in the attack.

On the night of the 5th the 118th American Brigade came up to relieve us, and by 2.30 a.m. on the 6th our men had been withdrawn. The Sixth Brigade was the last Australian Infantry Brigade in action in the war. After relief we moved back to Nauroy.

Montbrehain was a hard battle, especially as it followed so closely our attack on Beaurevoir, only 36 hours earlier. It proved to be our last fight. The success achieved that day was a fitting conclusion to the Battalion's long period of service in the war, but the heavy losses suffered made it a sad finale to our many and varied operations. Men who had left Australia with the unit and had served with constancy and gallantry through the long campaign with all its trials laid down their lives a few hours before the Battalion fired its last shot.

The bravery displayed by all ranks at Beaurevoir and Montbrehain earned distinctions for officers, N.C.O.'s and men. The C.O., Lieut.-Colonel W. E. James, was awarded a Bar to his D.S.O. Military Crosses were gained by Temporary Captain G. D. Pollington, M.M., Lieut. W.T. West, M.M., and Lieut. H. W. Clough, M.M. The N.C.O.'s, whose gallantry was always largely responsible for the Battalion's success in action, won five D.C.M.'s, the recipients being Coy. Sgt.-Mjr. W. E. Rankin, Sgt. D. W. Witherden, M.M., Sgt. W. G. Rintoull, Cpl. H. J. Willoughby, and Cpl. F. Saffin, M.M.

The good work of the Battalion transport section on this field kept our troops well supplied with rations when other units were not so well provided for.

A CORPS REST.

The Australian Corps had been so reduced and fatigued that further offensive operations were impracticable without rest and reorganisation. The Australian Divisions had been fighting strenuously since they were thrown in on the Somme early in the spring to stop the German swoop on Amiens, and now that the summer had passed, and the German army, like the leaves on the trees, was falling into decay, it was felt that the Australian Corps could well afford to take a rest.

When we left the field at Montbrehain we did not know, of course, that our last battle had been fought. If the war had gone on the Australians would have been in the thick of the fighting again before the close of the year. But the German military machine fell to pieces earlier than we anticipated.

The morning after we were withdrawn from the line at Montbrehain we marched to Jeancourt, and the following day moved to Roisel. From this area we travelled by train on 7th October to the Amiens district, then many miles from the battle front.

The 24th Battalion was allotted to billets at La Chaussee (Tirancourt), a quiet little village one kilometre from Picquigny, on the Somme. Detraining at St. Roch, a suburb of Amiens, on the night of the 7th, the Battalion marched 12 miles to our new home. At La Chaussée the troops soon settled down to enjoy the serenity of the peaceful countryside. Light training, with sports and entertainments, an increased allotment of "Blighty" leave, and frequent opportunities for visiting Amiens, Abbeville and adjacent towns filled in the days agreeably, and the men were quickly restored to their wonted vigour and high spirits.

General Sir Henry Rawlinson, commander of the Fourth Army, issued a message of appreciation to the Australian Corps, which was under his command for a considerable period. The General said:—

"I have watched with the greatest interest and admiration the various stages through which the Australians have passed from the hard times at Flers and Pozieres to the culminating victories at Mont St. Quentin and the great Hindenburg system at Bony, Bellicourt Tunnel and Montbrehain. During the summer of 1918 the safety of Amiens has been principally due to their determination, tenacity and valour. The story of what they have accomplished as a fighting army corps, of the diligence, gallantry and skill which they have exhibited, and of the scientific methods which they have so thoroughly learned and so successfully applied, has gained for all Australians a place of honour among nations and among the English-speaking races in particular. No one realises more than I do the very prominent part they have played, for I have watched from day to day every detail of their fighting, and learned to value beyond measure the prowess and determination of all ranks. In once more congratulating the corps on a series of successes unsurpassed in this great war, I feel that no mere words of mine can adequately express the renown they have won for themselves and the position they have established for the Australian nation, not only in France, but throughout the world."

France added her praises. M. Clemenceau, who later presided over the Peace Conference at Versailles, had travelled to the front to tell the Australians how much France admired them and how greatly she appreciated their achievements. He said France had judged the Australians by a high standard, and was not surprised that that standard had been reached and exceeded. "The French people knew that the Australians would fight a real fight," said M. Clemenceau; "but they did not know that from the beginning the Australians would astonish the whole continent by their valour."

While we were at La Chaussée the postponed disbandment of some of the Australian Battalions was put into effect, but now that the end of the war was in sight the troops were less concerned about their identity as separate units. The 21st Battalion was attached to the 24th Battalion, and remained as part of our unit until the demobilisation took place. The sympathetic action of Lieut.-Colonel James in allowing the men of the 21st Battalion to retain their own colour badges on their uniforms was greatly appreciated by the red and blacks.

Capt. F. P. Selleck, M.C., returned from Brigade Headquarters on the 23rd of October, and resumed duty as adjutant of the 24th Battalion.

REGIMENTAL INDUSTRY.

At La Chaussée the regimental pioneers were busy making crosses for the graves of our men who fell at Beaurevoir and Montbrehain. When the crosses were ready five of the pioneers left for our last battlefield to erect the Battalion's tribute to the memory of its dead. The distance was about 60 miles, and the difficulties met and overcome on the journey furnished a typical example of the faithfulness with which our pioneers always carried out their work, which to them was a labour of love. The party set out with 90 crosses for the graves of 21st and 24th Battalion men. At Amiens an officious R.T.O. refused to allow them to proceed further by rail, as no provision had been made officially for the carriage of the material. So the pioneers "bought" a "Tommy" motor driver and his lorry, and had the crosses conveyed by road to Estrees, which was reached at midnight. Next morning an old German waggon was commandeered, and with two horses borrowed from the Third Division Artillery the party eventually reached Montbrehain. Rough handling and exposure to the mud on the way had besmeared the crosses so badly that they had to be repainted. After days of hard work the 90 crosses were erected, each bearing the name and number of the fallen soldier, his Battalion colours, and the date of his death.

The 24th Battalion memorial cross at Pozieres, erected in July, 1917, was another example of the good work of the Battalion pioneers. The cement used for the base of the memorial was collected barrel by barrel from various sources, and was all given free in response to the solicitude of our pioneers, who were second to none in their devotion to the graves of our soldiers. Every grave that was accessible had a neat and substantial cross. In all the military cemeteries where our men are buried the 24th Battalion graves are easily recognised. The crosses are of uniform size and design, and on every head piece the red and white diamond stands out conspicuously. At Pozieres, Grevillers, Ypres, Warloy, Heilly, Mt. St. Quentin, and many other places our crosses remain as silent witnesses to the bravery and sacrifice of our fallen troops. The pioneers, who also buried most of our dead, conveyed some of the bodies many miles in order to inter them in a military cemetery, and where this was impossible the graves were tended with the fullest devotion. The pioneers searched the country for the best material for the crosses, and in many cases they were able to secure fine old oak timber for the purpose. During the week the Battalion was at Daours no fewer than 70 crosses were made, and were erected on graves on the Somme battlefields.

The pioneers included several all-round useful tradesmen. Other work at which they were employed from time to time included general repairs to property in billeting areas, the making of fittings for canteens and offices, the manufacture of rifle grenade cups out of old shell cases, also waddies and rattles for raiding parties, baking and frying dishes for the cooks, megaphones for sports, the mending of primus stoves, and even repairing damaged band instruments. Being keen and resourceful men, they were given a free hand as far as possible, and the manner in which they secured material for their requirements often won the admiration of the commanding officer.

Other tradesmen carried on important institutions in the Battalion. At the workshop of the armourer sergeant rifles, revolvers, and Lewis guns were kept in repair, bicycles were mended, and a variety of useful work executed. The bootmaker sergeant and the company bootmakers had the responsible and strenuous duty of keeping the soldiers' boots in order. Route marches and football helped to keep the bootmakers "up to their eyes" in work. The regimental tailors, whose equipment included a sewing machine, were always rushed with work, altering uniforms to make large garments fit small men, sewing on colour badges, blocking crushed hats, and generally improving the personal appearance of the troops while they were in rest areas.

The most important institution in the Battalion's establishment, however, was the Quartermaster's store, where the daily rations were allotted to the Companies, and all equipment, including clothes, issued to the troops according to requirements—when the goods were available. In the distribution of material the Company quartermaster sergeants came into the business as the middle men (so far as the Battalion was concerned). Their part in the provisioning of the unit was about the hundred and first stage of army transportation and distribution, and by the time the goods reached them there was never anything to spare. A printing office, a small store or canteen, and a farrier's shop at the transport lines were all included in the Battalion's industrial activities. The regimental post office, which received and despatched our mails and parcels, was an institution which we could not have done without. The Battalion Orderly-room, where the executive work of the unit was transacted, and where defaulters paraded to answer for their sins, was a place which the average Digger tried to avoid.

CEASE FIRE!

While we rested at La Chaussée, the German forces continued to fall back all along the line before the sweeping advance of the Allies. The end of the war came at last with unexpected suddenness.

The Armistice, on 11th November, 1918, found us preparing to return to the front. The First Division was already on the way.

It was a wonderful day. Messages were flashing over the field that hostilities would cease at 11 a.m. It was too good to believe at first. War had seemed so permanent, so unending all through those four and a half years of terror, pain and death, that the troops wondered what would happen if it ceased. No sound of guns, no rifle fire, no crashing bombs, no wounded, no more dead on the fields, no more "hopping over," no more wading through muddy trenches, no more ration fatigues to the line? It could not be! It was impossible that peace had come.

But the band turned out, the people ran up and down the streets shouting excitedly, flags appeared on the buildings, work ceased, the streets filled with soldiers and civilians.

And 11 o'clock came, and the order had gone forth— "Cease fire!" It was victory as well as peace.

Men looked into each other's faces, gripped each other by the hand, and felt what they could not speak. And then they set out to celebrate the great day.

The armistice was an admission of Germany's defeat. The celebration in Amiens was as much Australian as it was French. The 24th Battalion was accorded a great honour that day, when our band was chosen by the Corps Commander, General Sir John Monash, to proceed to Amiens as the representative band of the Australian Army.

When the band arrived in the city the populace had already reached a high pitch of excitement. The buildings and streets were ablaze with flags and decorations, and thousands of Australian troops had joined the rejoicing throng. The appearance of the Australian band was the signal for a heart-stirring demonstration in honour of the Australian Army. As the band played the Marseillaise and the National Anthems of the other Allied nations a wave of intense patriotic fervour swept over the crowd, which made no effort to restrain its feelings, but rejoiced with the utmost abandon and ecstasy. Our band led a huge procession which marched through the battered streets for hours, winding in and out in every direction till the whole place had been aroused to new life and liberty.

An American band brought up the rear of the procession, but in front, where our band at times could scarcely keep its tunes going on account of the women and girls embracing the bandsmen, a large Australian flag, with its Southern Cross unfurled in the breeze, was held aloft by a proud Mademoiselle elevated on the shoulders of two stalwart Diggers.

From the windows and balconies of the buildings flags and flowers were showered upon the troops as they marched about shouting in their excitement.

Australians had pride of place in all the speeches that were made by the representatives of France and that city, they had the first kisses of the excited women and girls, they had free wine and free meals, and everything that a grateful people could bestow upon them. The public men of the city and the Diggers of the A.I.F. shook hands and embraced one another in the keenest delight, and the boys kissed France's daughters till they had all been kissed, and then started all over again.

The National Anthems of the Allies rang through the streets all day and through the night, and the people sang whatever words they knew of Australian airs.

In every French home in the district the day was celebrated by a feast, and Australia was represented at every festive board.

A souvenir of Armistice Day, an eight-page booklet entitled "Fin de la Guerre," was printed by the 24th Battalion Press at La Chaussée, and a copy was presented, through the Maire, to every household in our billeting area.

Then came preparations to follow the Boche's broken, stampeding army to the Rhine. The Australians were to form part of the army of occupation, and we got ready to enter Germany with all the pomp we could assume.

With band and banners we set off from La Chaussée at 9.30 a.m. on the 23rd, with hopes that we would soon be in Germany. The morning was frosty, but the sun was shining. The residents of the village turned out to give us a parting cheer, while a few of the girls stood at the doors of the houses wiping tears from their eyes. Cupid had been busy during the past few weeks. The knowledge that the Allied Armies were on their way to the Rhine gladdened the hearts of the French people, and provoked them to impart all kinds of advice to the boys respecting "Mamemoiselle Boche." The lads laughed, and assured their friends that the French girls had no real cause to be concerned.

A short march brought us to Vignacourt, where we entrained, and then travelled slowly through Amiens, Villers Bretonneux, Peronne and Cambrai. The old battlefields were viewed with the keenest interest by the troops, who pointed out the scenes of conflict with the enemy and reflected on the long campaign, now crowned with victory, with the satisfaction that comes to the victors after a hard-fought struggle.

Darkness found us journeying on slowly in the rough, jolting trucks. Trains on this line crept along like worms feeling their way. German mines still lurked in many places, in spite of the search which had been made for these potential "surprise packets." (On the same line a few days later a leave train exploded one of these mines, and 30 men were killed, while many others were injured.) It was well for our peace of mind while we "groused" about the snail-like movement of the train that night that we did not realise our danger.

A freezing temperature had the boys scouting for braziers and coal at every stopping place. All through the frosty night the men huddled around the smoky fires in the trucks, singing and telling their funniest stories, and when, at 6.30 next morning, the train arrived at Bertry and we took to the road, many of us were black with soot.

The steaming cookers had a cheery look about them when we assembled for breakfast on the road, where everything but the cookers was covered with thick frost or ice.

Breakfast over, the Battalion formed up in column of route, headed by the regimental colours and the Australian Flag, and to the music of the band started on a victory march towards Germany. Busigny was passed on the way to Bohain, where we went into billets for two nights.

Bohain was a town of no mean size. Thousands of troops were resting here on their way to the Rhine, and the whole district, in spite of its desolation, was aglow with the elated spirits of the victorious soldiers. Battalion after Battalion, with bands and banners, marched into the town and took up quarters in the deserted houses. (Only the poorer inhabitants had stayed to endure the hardships of German occupation.)

Winter was with us once again. Rain made the roads and streets muddy and cheerless, and the nights were cold, but the severest weather only added a relish to the sweetness of victory. Trenches, exposure, wounds and death had passed away like the horrible nightmare they had been. It was good to live, to remember what had been endured, and to shelter from the rain and cold at night and reflect on what war had meant under such conditions.

The Hun had left the country poor and afflicted. All stock of any use to him had been commandeered. Not a cow remained. Horses, sheep, goats, pigs, and fowls had been seized by his army when it held the country or carried away when it left. In some of the towns the people were found half starved and poorly clad, and the unwelcome offspring of German soldiers had been left behind to increase the burden of the afflicted people. The inhabitants had harrowing stories to tell of the severity of German rule, but their thin faces lit up with hope and smiles when they spoke of the enemy's undignified departure.

At Bohain one old lady, who delighted to have Australian soldiers drink of her scant supply of coffee and hear them tell of their far off country where no war had ever been, described to us how in April a German officer who had taken possession of her best room used to say he would be in Paris in a few days. And when the time elapsed and he was still at Bohain, she said to him, "Why do you not go to Paris? Perhaps the gate is shut!" And then she would hold out to him a bunch of keys that he might find one to open the gate. And the Boche would scowl and slam the doors and stalk out in a bad temper.

And when our boys called her "mother," and she patted their cheeks, tears came to her eyes. She was thinking of two of her own sons who would never come back. Her young grandson came in with an armful of wood gathered from the ruins of a nearby house. The boy was happy now. While the Germans were there they compelled him to work from daylight till dark every day in the fields, where they grew vegetables for their army. There had been no school there for over four years, for the Germans had taken the school buildings for military purposes and used the children as their servants. When they left they mined the public buildings and utterly destroyed them.

Soldiers of the Allied Armies who had been prisoners in the hands of the enemy and civilians who had also been in captivity drifted back in hundreds, riding on army motor waggons when they could find room, and walking when there was no better means of travel. Many of the Army Ambulance cars were employed to carry the liberated prisoners of war back to comfort. The army had to feed civilians as well as soldiers, for all ordinary means of supply had vanished. Waggon loads of provisions were sent forward daily to feed the inhabitants.

From Bohain some of the troops walked to Montbrehain to view the scene of their last battle. The graves of two men, one 24th Battalion and one 21st Battalion, on the objective at the apex of the village remained as monuments to the determination and success of our last assault. French civilians had placed on these graves " everlasting " wreaths as a tribute to their deliverers.

On 26th November the Battalion started on a nine-mile march to St. Souplet, again passing Busigny, and we pitched camp for the night in tents at a spot closer to our detraining point (Bertry) than we were at Bohain! Straw spread over the wet ground enabled the men to sleep with fair comfort, although the country was white with snow. Next day we were off again for Favril, 11½ miles distant. On the way we passed the last No-man's-land of the war, where shell holes and other signs indicated the severity of the fighting on the closing days of strife. The Canal du Sombre, which runs through Mauberge, was crossed on the march.

In a cellar of a ruined house in the Rue de Bois at Favril we found an elderly woman who had lived in this hiding place for five days while the closing battle of the war was in progress around her. Her house had been in No-man's-land, and while she sheltered in the cellar, the guns had blown away her dwelling over her head. When she saw that we were British troops she said, "My heart is cheerful now, and I owe much to the English."

Ten miles, through Prishoes and Cartignies, on 28th November, brought us to Boulogne-sur-Helpe, where we remained for a fortnight, and found the short days and long nights dragging heavily owing to the lack of amusements and the quiet seclusion of the locality. A dance in heavy boots on a brick floor was not an ideal form of enjoyment, even with the band playing in the loft above, but it was better than going to bed at 6 p.m. Parties of men travelled to Avesnes (once German General Headquarters), where the Anzac Coves performed nightly.

On 10th December motor waggons were sent out with a commission to "search France" in quest of supplies for the approaching Christmas dinners, which were expected to eclipse all previous celebrations of the festive season.

On 17th December the Battalion moved on again, heading for the Charleroi area, in Belgium, where brighter conditions were promised. Marching about 15 miles on the 17th, we arrived at Solre le Chateau, where comfortable billets were found in a former German hospital. Next day we pushed on to the pretty little village of Solre St. Gery, a journey of 11 miles taking us across the Belgian border. A march of 12 miles on the third day, along the magnificient valley on the Eau d'Heure, on our way to Walcourt, was full of interest and charm. Walcourt possessed a famous old church, from which the Huns had removed its wonderful tower and carried it to Germany.

Our destination was Nalinnes, which was reached on 20th December. This village was 11 kilometres from the City of Charleroi, which was connected by tram. The whole of the country here bore a peaceful aspect, with well-preserved buildings of superior architecture, and the Belgian people welcomed us with great cordiality. Hitherto they had known little of Australia or her men, but they were to be speedily and thoroughly educated on these important subjects.

The troops were now in the best billets which they had ever been privileged to occupy, for here they lived not in barns and sheds, but in the spare rooms of the houses. It did not take them long to win their way into favour with the people, and many of them slept in real beds with white sheets and clean blankets; some of them dined with the Belgian families, paying a nominal board in some cases, and in others living as honoured guests.

Our "march to the Rhine" ended here. The Australian Army Corps, it was now decided, would not form part of the army of occupation, as arrangements were being made for early demobilisation. This was a disappointment to some of the men, but the prospect of getting home the sooner more than compensated for the loss of the opportunity of seeing Fritz and his family at home. Nevertheless, some of the troops did cross the Rhine (on unauthorised excursions), and when they saw the British flag at Cologne they felt that France and Belgium and the British Empire were safe.

With the object of allowing the soldiers to see as much of Belgium as was possible while awaiting demobilisation, unlimited leave was granted to all ranks, while passes for "Blighty" and Paris were also handed out freely. Lack of money was the only difficulty which faced many would-be tourists. The Commonwealth Bank in London had never been so busy in its existence, and the cable lines to Australia were almost monopolised by urgent messages for bank drafts.

Many of our men journeyed to Brussels and saw the gay city that had never wholly lost its animation; they gazed on the field of Waterloo and wondered what the soldiers who fought there would have thought of the war that had just closed; and they went on to Antwerp and many other places, viewing everything with keen eyes and contrasting the old world with their young country in the south.

Every man who had been to Paris would have hailed with delight another opportunity of seeing that fair city, of being petted again by the handsome women whose dainty ways and wonderful frocks had charmed them so much. Men longed to promenade again in the boulevards and the Avenue des Champs-Elysées, to ride in the Bois de Boulogne, to sit in the glorious Opera House listening to its soul-lifting music, to gaze on the wonderful palaces, to dine in the bright cafes, and to live as only Paris knows how to live. And every man who had not been there regretted he had missed the opportunity or that it had never come to him. Still, home was more than Paris, and the regret was only a fleeting thought. Already the all-absorbing talk among the troops was of boat-rolls, ships and Aussie.

In the city of Charleroi, where the attractive shops were stocked with wares of all descriptions and bore every evidence of peace, even if the high prices reflected the effects of war, the troops had a gay time. Dancing was the popular amusement. The soldiers had free use of the trams, and gave them liberal patronage.

A dance held by the Sixth Field Ambulance and the 24th Battalion at Charleroi was a highly successful social function. Our unit had always been on the most friendly terms with the Sixth Field Ambulance, and this gathering was marked by the highest goodwill and true comradeship.

German money was still in circulation, and was handed out to us as change by the shops and cafes. The Boche had made the rate of currency in his own favour, and the mark was almost twice the value of the Belgian franc. Many of our soldiers during the period of hostilities had handled handfuls of German money,and had discarded it as worthless. The army, of course, was paid in Belgian currency, as the military did not recognise German money at the Boche's own valuation. While at Nalinnes we were honoured on more than one occasion by the presence of H.R.H. the Prince of Wales, who was then attached to the staff of the Australian Corps, and who became exceedingly popular with all the Australian troops in the Charleroi area. A number of our men who had won distinctions were decorated by the Prince on the 24th December.

General Birdwood reviewed the Battalion on the square in Nalinnes on 3rd January. The General, in a happy speech, thanked the troops for unfailing service throughout the long campaign, and wished them a happy return to Australia. One of the remarks made by General Birdwood that day was, "One always felt safe when one had the old 24th on the job."

Christmas had come again—now with its old message, "Peace on earth," and everybody resolved to be merry as well as happy. The motor waggons which had been sent in search of supplies for the Christmas dinners had come back heavily laden, and with the assistance of the hospitable Belgian people the soldiers were able to make the celebrations worthy of the glad season. This was the fourth Christmas the Battalion had seen on active service, and the knowledge that it would be the last gave us all cause for rejoicing. A sum of £250 from the Sixth Brigade Comforts Funds and £25 from the 24th Battalion Association were timely and highly appreciable gifts. The Australian

A ROYAL INSPECTION.

H.R.H. the Prince of Wales inspecting the 24th Battalion at Nalinnes, Belgium. The C.O. (Lt.-Col. James) is accompanying the Prince, and in their rear are Brig.-General J. C. Robertson, General Holmes and General Rosenthal.

Comforts Fund, which had been a boon to the troops during the war, provided us with 12 cases of goods for the festivities.

Each Company had its own Christmas dinner, managed by its own officers and N.C.O.'s and prepared by its own cooks. In all the toasts and speeches the happiest note was the prospect of an early return to Australia. Yet the troops did not forget their comrades who had fallen in the fight. At all the festive gatherings the memory of the gallant dead was affectionately honoured.

The good friendship established by the troops and the Belgian residents of Nalinnes was demonstrated when the 24th Battalion entertained about 250 children at the school hall on 4th January. In the afternoon the children sat down to a tempting feast, the brightly decorated tables being heavily laden with a variety of dainty dishes and sweets. The officers and men who waited upon the happy little guests persuaded the small boys to "keep going" until they could not "go" another mouthful, and then the boys readily resorted to the expedient of filling their pockets. At this stage the girls were at a disadvantage. Many parents, who had brought along their toddlers to the banquet, looked on with extreme delight, and enjoyed the music of the band while the youngsters abandoned themselves to the disposal of the edibles. After the feast the parents and children were treated to a cinema show. It was a happy day for the juveniles and a pleasant celebration of the liberation of their country from the bondage of German tyranny. The younger children had only known the world as a world at war, for they could not remember the days when peace had reigned, while some had been born while the guns boomed and soldiers marched to fight. Now, at all events, they would remember the Australian soldiers as part of the grand army that had brought deliverance.

DEMOBILISATION.

The first draft of the 24th Battalion to leave the field was a small party of original members of the unit, who took their departure on 24th December, 1918. These old hands included Lieut. C. R. Boyd (a 1914 veteran who had voluntarily remained on service when the 1914 men took their departure for Australia several months earlier), Coy. Sgt.-Mjr. W. E. Rankin, D.C.M., Coy. Q.M. Sgt. E. V. Rattle, M.S.M., Sgt. P. Dunham, and a number of privates. The party was tendered a send-off at the Nalinnes school hall on the evening of 23rd December. Addressing the departing troops the C.O., Lieut.-Colonel W. E. James, D.S.O., referred to the long and faithful service of the men. He said there had been and still were in the Battalion faces which they had learned to love. When at times they had lost some of these faces it had taught them that in spite of losses they must carry on. They had all embarked on a great adventure, and during the long campaign a strong bond of comradeship had been created. For nearly four years the only home they had known had been the old Battalion with its familiar faces and staunch comrades. No man need hang his head because of anything the 24th Battalion had done; indeed, they could afford to hold up their heads because of the Battalion's achievements. It had been a hard and long struggle, and many times the strain had pressed well nigh to breaking point. But now the job was done they had the great satisfaction of knowing that they had "stuck it" right through, and he hoped they would be rewarded for their constancy by many years of happiness. Brigadier-General J. C. Robertson, C.M.G., D.S.O., also extended his good wishes to the party.

On 24th December the party was given an enthusiastic send-off. After a parade on the village square, where an address was delivered by Brigadier-General Robertson, the band led the party to Marchienne au Pont, where other parties from the Division were assembling. Owing to the congested state of the French railways at this period the departure of the draft from Marchienne was delayed until the 28th.

The first large draft from the Battalion, composed of all ranks who had embarked from Australia prior to 1st July, 1915, was despatched on 24th January, 1919. This draft had been organised for several weeks, and was known as the A1 Company. A farewell dinner, held at Nalinnes on 31st December, was one of the most successful and enjoyable functions of this happy season. On the 24th the Company paraded on the square at Nalinnes, and the whole unit assembled to honour the occasion. The Brigadier and his staff also attended. The departing troops were led out of the village by the band, while women waved handkerchiefs and shed tears which they did not try to hide. Five kilometres out on the Charleroi road a halt was made, and the company was addressed by the C.O., who commended the gallant and faithful service of the men during the years of war, and wished them a pleasant voyage to Australia. The rest of the Battalion, which had marched with the departing company to this spot, then formed an avenue, and the party marched through this guard of honour, carrying the Battalion colours, and cheered till they passed out of sight. The regimental colours had been presented to the Battalion through Mrs. W. M. Hughes (wife of the Prime Minister) and Mrs. Andrew Fisher (wife of the Australian High Commissioner in London).

A few days later the 24th Battalion band proceeded to England and toured the Australian hospitals and soldiers' clubs in and around London, where programmes of music were rendered. The tour included two performances at the Aldwych Theatre. While in London the band was entertained by General Sir Ian Hamilton at his residence, Hyde Park corner.

The weather became extremely cold at the end of January. A heavy fall of snow gave the troops and their Belgian friends opportunities for spirited recreation in the form of snowballing. Many vigorous but friendly battles were fought in the streets of Nalinnes and Charleroi.

The last of the Sixth Brigade football competitions was played in this area. The final match between the 23rd and 24th Battalions, on 4th January, was one of the most exciting of the many excellent games played in the field. When the excited crowd of soldier barrackers was waiting for the final bell the 24th team was leading by one point, but in a scuffle near the sticks the umpire gave the 23rd a mark, and amid loud protests from the 24th supporters our opponents scored a goal and won by five points. This match was witnessed by General Rosenthal (Commander of the Second Division) and a number of other officers of high rank.

The third draft of our troops for demobilisation left Nalinnes on 2nd February. This company was also sent on its way rejoicing.

On 12th February the Battalion moved from Nalinnes to Marcinelle, a suburb of Charleroi. The march was made over frozen snow, and was productive of many involuntary acrobatic feats as the troops slipped and sprawled on the glassy roads.

At Marcinelle the billets were even better than those at Nalinnes, and the Belgian people equally as sociable and good hearted. The troops who awaited their turn for demobilisation found themselves agreeably accommodated, and many more friends were added to their pleasant acquaintances.

The C.O. was called to a command at one of the demobilisation camps in England, and Captain E. V. Smythe, M.C., was promoted temporary Major and left with the adjutant (Captain F. P. Selleck, M.C.) and assistant adjutant (Lieut. R. Rail) to complete the demobilisation of the unit in the field.

Each draft in turn travelled by train to Le Havre, and then crossed the Channel to England, where the troops awaited in camp at Sutton Veney, near Salisbury, their turn for troopships to carry them home.

Relieved now of their fighting equipment, the men felt they were moving towards liberty at last. But ships were scarce, and there were irksome delays. Men travelled to

Scotland, Ireland, and all over England, bidding their relatives and friends farewell, came back to camp, waited, went off again, returned, and still waited. Some were busy with brides or prospective brides; some had gone out on non-military employment (or as it was more correctly termed, non-military "enjoyment"); some were filling in the time with educational courses, and some had actually pushed off on the wide seas.

Boat rolls were worse than the roll of the ocean, for many names "rolled" off the lists when kits were ready for the voyage, and hopes were high. And so the days passed, with other drafts coming across from the Continent and crowding camps.

In London the men promenaded the Strand and Piccadilly more numerous than they had ever been known in the great metropolis before; and down at the ports soldiers with wives and children waited for that blissful creation known as the family ship.

On the anniversary of Anzac Day the Australian Divisions marched through London with fixed bayonets (an honour not accorded to every section of the British Army), and were cheered by admiring crowds.

When the Dominion troops marched through London the Australians were represented again. They had learned to love the Mother Country, just as many of the Mother Country's daughters had learned to love them. On this march the troops of the Second Australian Division were commanded by Lieut.-Colonel James, D.S.O., and led by the 24th Battalion band.

As more ships became available the soldiers at the camps became fewer. Gradually the troops made their way back to their homeland in the south, some travelling via the Cape, and some by the Suez route. Some returned on family ships with wives and children, and some on hospital ships under the care of nurses and doctors who had served with the army in the field.

From port to port the boats passed round the Australian coast, distributing their soldier passengers on the way, and bringing joy unspeakable to hearts that had ached while distance separated the men from home, and dangers hung over their heads.

Australia gave her soldiers a royal welcome as every ship came in, and the troops rejoiced because the day for which they had longed had come at last. They were ready to say, "There's no place like home!"

A TRIBUTE.

To our gallant men of all ranks; to those who gained distinctions; to those who deserved distinctions, but in the fortunes and misfortunes of war did not receive them; to those who went through the campaign and came back to love and home; to those who bear the marks and endure the afflictions of wounds, but most of all to those who laid down their lives in the great cause, all honour and praise.

In a military hospital in France some of the troops and the nurses collected a small sum of money, which they proposed to hand as a gift to a soldier who had given his healthy strong blood for infusion into the weak body of another. When the money was offered the man replied—" No, I cannot take money. I did not sell my blood; I gave it."

That was the spirit of every man who laid down his life for his country.

And this tribute is offered—

"Lest we forget."

APPRECIATION.

Now that the war is over and the army has come back to peace, we desire to record our appreciation of all the gifts received by the Battalion from our friends at home while the men were abroad. To the Australian Comforts Fund, the Sixth Brigade Comforts Fund, the Red Cross, the Salvation Army, the Y.M.C.A., and the 24th Battalion Association, we tender our sincerest thanks. The hard life of the soldiers at the front would have been infinitely harder but for the many comforts and the cheering gifts provided by these zealous and patriotic institutions. To all the women who devoted so much time to the making of shirts, scarfs, socks, and other garments; to the school children who gave their pennies and laboured so enthusiastically on behalf of their soldier fathers and brothers; to the thoughtful correspondents who wrote so regularly to "lonely soldiers," and to all who played their parts in helping the army to "carry on" and to achieve decisive victory, we here record our gratitude.

The author desires to acknowledge, in connection with the compilation of this history, the services of Lieut. E. J. Pittard, M.C. (secretary of the Publication Committee), Capt. G. S. McIlroy, M.C. (president of the 24th Battalion Association), Capt. S. G. Savige, D.S.O., M.C., and Capt. F. P. Selleck, M.C., whose initiative, keen interest, and untiring labours have been mainly responsible for the publication of this book, which has been achieved in spite of many difficulties. Other members of the Battalion have helped in the work of supplying data for the story, which has been put together piece by piece from various sources. There are many details which official records could not supply, and the author is conscious that the story does not represent the full glory of the Battalion as a fighting unit, or the highest honour of its members individually. Yet it is offered with the hope that it will in some measure satisfy the desire for a printed record of our days of active service in the long and trying campaign.

24th Infantry Battalion, Australian Imperial Force.

ROLL OF THE FALLEN
List of Decorations, Awards, &c.

These details have been compiled at the Base Records Office. Every effort has been made to produce accurate lists, but if any errors or omissions have occurred the Publication Committee tenders its regrets to those concerned. Owing to unavoidable circumstances, it nas been found impossible to publish a complete Nominal Roll of the Battalion.

APPENDIX.

VICTORIA CROSS.
Lieut. G. M. Ingram, M.M.

COMPANION OF THE ORDER OF THE BATH.
Colonel W. W. R. Watson.

COMPANION OF THE ORDER OF ST. MICHAEL AND ST. GEORGE.
Colonel W. W. R. Watson.

ORDER OF THE BRITISH EMPIRE.
Capt. H. C. Brinsmead, M.C.

MEMBER OF THE BRITISH EMPIRE.
Major E. V. E. Neill.
Capt. G. M. Carr.

DISTINGUISHED SERVICE ORDER.
Lieut.-Colonel W. E. James (and Bar).
Major (T/Lt.-Col 23rd Batt.) W. K. Fethers.
Major D. D. Coutts (R.M.O.).
*Major G. M. Nicholas.
Major W. M. Trew.
Capt. S. G. Savige, M.C.
Lieut. J. C. Scales, M.M.
*2nd-Lieut. E. H. Edgerton, M.M. and Bar.

*Killed in action.
Rank given first is that at date of award.

MILITARY CROSS.

2nd-Lieut. (Lieut.) E. S. Baldock.
Capt. G. J. Bowden.
Capt. (Lt.-Col. A.F.C., O.B.E.) H. C. Brinsmead.
*Lieut. J. B. N. Carvick.
Lieut. H W. Clough, M.M.
Capt. (Major) W. E. Ellwood.
Lieut. J. L. Fawcett.
*Lieut. J. F. Gear.
*Capt. T. C. E. Godfrey.
Lieut. W. C. Godfrey.
Chaplain-Capt. Goldanich.
Lieut. W. B. Gow.
Lieut. W. Graham.
Capt. J. Hardy (R.M.O.).
Lieut. A. Hughes.
Capt. (Major) J. E. Lloyd (and Bar).
*2nd-Lieut. (Capt.) J. A. Mahoney.
*Capt. G. L. Maxfield.
Capt. G. S. McIlroy.
*2nd-Lieut. B. F. Nicholas.
*Lieut. R. Pickett.
Lieut. E. J. Pittard.
Lieut. J. T. Pocknell.
Lieut. (Capt.) G. D. Pollington, M.M.
Capt. S. G. Savige.
Lieut. A. V. Sedgwick.
Capt F. P. Selleck.
Capt. (T/Major) E. V. Smythe (and Bar).
Lieut. P. E. Smythe.
Lieut. A. Stuart.
Lieut. W. West, M.M.

*Killed in action.
Rank given first is that at date of award.

APPENDIX.

DISTINGUISHED CONDUCT MEDAL.

4292—Pte. J. Artis.

377—Sgt. (Capt.) A. A. Ball.

3773—Sgt. J. H. Bond.

834—C.S.M. A. L. Burke.

2609—Cpl. E. J. R. Dart.

6309—*Cpl. E. L. Ford.

1529—Cpl. (Lieut. 22nd Batt.) W. M. Green.

5363—Sgt. A. Harris.

2487—Sgt. E. Holloway.

Sgt. S. H. Kirby.

*L.-Cpl. C. Lousada.

88—Cpl. C. J. Mitchell.

125—Sgt (Lieut.) F. McCooey.

6354—Cpl. C. O. McLear.

791—C.S.M. W. E. Rankin.

1029—Sgt. W. G. Rintoull.

3915—Pte. R. N. Robinson.

6388—Cpl. F. Saffin (M.M.)

1742—Cpl. G. W. Torney.

307—Sgt. (Lieut.) E. V. White.

Sgt. (Lieut.) A. E. Whitear.

3956a—Sgt. D. W. Witherden (M.M.).

333—Sgt. R. L. Williams.

3666—Cpl. H. J. Willoughby.

*Killed in action.
Rank given first is tnat at date of award.

APPENDIX.

MILITARY MEDAL.

5291—L.-Cpl. A. S. Adolfsson (and Bar).
3946—*Pte. H. A. Anderson.
1547a—*Sgt. A. B. Arnel.
3755—Pte. J. E. Ashley.
1782—Pte. A. G. Baker.
4067—*Pte. H. H. Bell.
6035—*Sgt. C. Bennett.
4068—Pte. M. Bernier.
6784—L.-Cpl. G. Blyth.
4363—*Pte. J. W. Blankenberg.
5797—L.-Cpl. J. L. Bowe.
3990—Pte. H. A. D. Brown.
1665—Sgt. J. F. Burton.
2133—Sgt. R. McL. Campbell.
4378—L.-Cpl. J. Carmichael.
4300—Pte. E. Catton.
4675—Pte. D. Clarke.
611—Sgt (Lieut.) H. W. Clough.
4388—Sgt. J. M. Collery.
4680—Sgt (Lieut.) M. E. Consedine.
5319—Cpl. J. W. Cooke (and Bar).
2868—*Sgt. A. C. Cooper.
4303—*Pte. E. A. Cooper.
1764—*Pte. (Lieut. 21st Bat.), H. H. Corney.
2354—*C.S.M. G. H. Cumming.
1523—Pte. (Lieut: A.F.C.) E. W. Dardel.
2609—Cpl. E. J. R. Dart.
1815—*Cpl. R. W. Davidson.
6303—Pte. M. L. Dawson.
3312—Pte. A. R. Dodemaide.
959—Pte. T. A. Dwyer.
801—Sgt. (Lieut.) N. V. Dyte.
1524—Cpl. (Lieut., D.S.O.) E. H. Edgerton (and Bar).
2036—Sgt. (Lieut.) C. A. A. Ellis.
1509—Sgt. W. A. Elmore.
2037—L.-Cpl. T. H. R. Frost.
3823—Pte. W. G. Gardiner.
5122—Sgt. R. O. Goldsmith.

741—L.-Cpl. G. A. Graham.
2642—L.-Cpl. N. L. Greaves.
1518—L.-Cpl. F. Hallam.
5025—Pte. H. J. Hallawell.
2153—Pte. F. H. Hamilton.
3840—Cpl. G. E. Harker.
2386—*Pte. C. Harris.
2465—Pte. W. J. Harvey.
5151—Pte. L. Hermon (and Bar).
434—L.-Cpl. J. A. Holdman.
2380—Pte. R. Holloway.
5126—L.-Cpl. H. R. Hunter.
2455—Pte. W. G. T. Hutchinson.
5919—L.-Cpl. (Lieut., V.C.) G. M. Ingram.
207—Sgt. (Lieut.) R. Irving.
2192—L.-Cpl. M. Jackson.
5362—L.-Cpl. D. W. Johnson (and Bar).
2186—Sgt. E. W. Johnson (and Bar).
96—Sgt. A. R. Keith.
562—Cpl. E. C. Kennedy.
754—Pte. T. H. Kerr.
2283—Sgt. H. A. Lacey.
1960—Sgt. E. F. Lamont (and Bar).
903—*Cpl. H. Lang.
   Sgt. W. Lang.
4136—Pte. W. Lee.
2199—Pte. C. R. Lepp.
452—Cpl. V. N. Letman.
5154—L.-Cpl. W. Lincoln.
4722—*Pte. T. Lovell.
1798—Pte. F. Madden.
912—Pte. H. S. Maddern.
468—Pte. J. J. Madigan.
1550—*Sgt. P. J. Molloy.
5163—Pte. J. E. Morrissey.
425—Sgt. P. Mortimer (and Bar).
1734—T.-Sgt. A. Mundell.
3873—*Pte. N. C. Munro.
953—L.-Cpl. F. A. Murray.

*Killed in action.
Rank given first is that at date of award.

APPENDIX.

1544—Cpl. J. A. McEvoy.
1537—*Pte. C. L. Mackay.
919—Sgt. W. H. McKeon.
1798—Cpl. D. M. McKinnon (and Bar).
1742—Sgt. (Lieut.) J. M. McLachlan.
1696—Pte. C. S. McLeish (and Bar).
1741—Pte. E. A. McLeod.
6351—Pte. J. F. R. McRae.
744—*Pte. A. C. Neale.
4018—Cpl. C. Newman.
    Sgt. (Lieut.) L. Nicholls.
363—Sgt. (Lieut.) R. G. Nichols.
2422—A.-Cpl. E. O'Neill.
6114—Cpl. A. W. Parker.
5163—L.-Cpl. H. Parsons.
568—*Pte. H. F. Pillow.
2735—Cpl. J. Pitts.
2972—Sgt. (T.-Capt.) G. D. Pollington.
482—Sgt. W. G. Price.
933—Sgt. A. G. Prime (and Bar).
760—Pte. G. S. Primrose.
262—Sgt. J. J. Radley.
4757—Pte. D. W. Reid.
99—Pte. W. Richards.
1725—Pte. A. L. Roberts.

5895—L.-Cpl. J. S. Robinson.
4762—*Cpl. R. Roff.
267—L.-Cpl. J. W. Rookes.
3242—Sgt. H. Ross.
6388—Cpl. F. Saffin.
    Cpt. (Lieut., D.S.O.) J. C. Scales.
    Cpl. (Lieut. 21st Batt.) W. G. Scales
4771—Pte. H. W. Scott.
3621—Pte. G. H. Sell.
570—*C.S.M. N. H. Shepard.
2246—Pte. F. Smith.
950—Cpl. M. F. Smith.
3912—Pte. H. M. St. Clair.
1734a—Pte. J. H. Stewart (and Bar).
6390—Cpl. C. S. Stonehouse.
    *Sgt. (Lieut., M.C. and Bar, 21st Batt.), J. Sullivan
    Cpl. (Lieut. 21st Batt.) W. L. Taylor.
1128—Pte. A. E. Temple.
2452—Pte. J. Thyne.
6405—Pte. B. H. Tuckett.
4545—L.-Cpl. F. M. Walker (and Bar)
1033—Sgt. E. J. Wilson
3956a—Sgt. D. W. Witherden.
    Sgt. (Lieut., M.C.) W. West.

MERITORIOUS SERVICE MEDAL.

*Lieut. P. S. Carne.
2159—C.Q.M.S. H. J. Duffy.
2146—Sgt. H. V. Griffiths.

38—Sgt. J. R. Parker.
527—C.Q.M.S. S. Tough.

CROIX DE GUERRE (FRENCH).
4388—Sgt J. M. Collery (M.M.).

CROIX DE GUERRE (BELGIAN).

384—R.S.M. J. W. Green.
222—Sgt. R. Laidlaw.

88—Cpl. C. J. Mitchell (D.C.M.).
6354—Cpl. C. O. McLear (D.C.M.).

LEGION D'HONNEUR CHEVALIER (FRENCH).
Colonel W. W. R. Watson, C.B., C.M.G.

*Killed in action.   Rank given first is that at date of award.

APPENDIX.

MENTIONED IN DESPATCHES.

28—Cpl. H. J. E. Bamfield (one occasion).
Lieut. H. Baxter (one occasion).
Lieut. N. R. Calvert (one occasion).
2nd.-Lieut. P. S. Carne (one occasion).
Major D. D. Coutts (one occasion).
2nd.-Lieut. E. H. Edgerton (one occasion).
Major (Lt.-Col.) W. K. Fethers (one occasion).
Lieut. W. B. Gow (one occasion).
1529—Cpl. W. M. Green (one occasion).
Sgt. H. V. Griffiths (one occasion).
2043—Sgt. L. T. Henderson (one occasion).
Cpl. S. Horton (one occasion).
Lieut.-Colonel W. E. James (two occasions).
96—Pte. A. R. Keith (one occasion).
1534—Pte. J. H. Kemp (two occasions).
Major C. E. Manning (one occasion).
Lieut. I. A. Macindoe (one occasion).
36—Driver G. McIntyre (one occasion).
Major E. V. E. Neill (one occasion).
Major G. M. Nicholas (one occasion).
38—Sgt. J. R. Parker (one occasion).
Captain S. G. Savige (three occasions).
Lieut. J. L. Scales (one occasion).
Capt. F. P. Selleck (one occasion).
Major W. M. Trew (one occasion).
2274—Sgt. J. T. Trewhella (one occasion).
Lieut.-Colonel W. W. R. Watson (two occasions).

(Rank shown in parenthesis is that on discharge.)

APPENDIX.

24th BATTALION, A.I.F., ROLL OF HONOUR.

No. & Name	Date of Death.	No. & Name	Date of Death.
66—Pte. S. Kohn	28/5/15	1134—Pte. C. Altman	29/11/15
756—Pte. L. Kirk	28/5/15	458—Pte. A. Macbeth	29/11/15
860—Pte. A. Cassidy	29/5/15	1303—Pte. R. G. Beaston	29/11/15
1147—Pte. P. McKinnon	25/5/15	1785—Pte. W. E. Werner	29/11/15
600—Pte. W. H. Brown	25/5/15	1049—Pte. R. L. Ellis	29/11/15
835—Pte. G. Bennett	1/6/15	1613—L.-Cpl. G. C. Duncan	29/11/15
1133—Pte. F. Fletcher	14/6/15	Lieut. A. C. Fogarty	29/11/15
9—Q.M.S. D. McIntyre	16/6/15	686—Cpl. F. C. Puddephatt	29/11/15
708—Pte. F. A. Stewart	26/6/15	1660—Pte. T. Burnet	29/11/15
1321—Pte. H. R. Brittain	14/7/15	1138—Pte. H. H. Abbott	29/11/15
1804—Pte. J. Boulton	8/8/15	1505a—Sgt. G. F. Rumbol	29/11/15
847—Bglr. J. Christensen	19/9/15	836—Sgt. W. Buchanan	29/11/15
344—Pte. W. P. O'Brien	16/9/15	794—Sgt. S. F. Daw	29/11/15
488—Pte. G. Parnaby	15/9/15	561—L.-Cpl. R. N. Emery	29/11/15
1157—Pte. R. H. Gray	16/9/15	1540a—Pte. J. L. Maas	29/11/15
964—Pte. W. Turnbull	21/9/15	1514a—L.-Cpl. S. T. Bormann	29/11/15
85—Pte. F. A. O'Loughlen	16/9/15	427—Pte A. S. Hughes	29/11/15
1164—Pte. A. E. McLennan	17/9/15	523—Pte. G. W. Roberts	29/11/15
445—Pte. F. Keighery	11/9/15	1566—Pte. A. J. Voller	29/11/15
711—Pte. S. G. Sunderland	29/9/15	582—Sgt. P. E. B. Sheppard	29/11/15
388—Pte. H. J. Cox	23/9/15	869—Pte. G. W Donnelly	29/11/15
466—Pte. W. D. F. Mowat	23/9/15	736—Pte. J. A. M. Power	29/11/15
910—Pte. P. Lynch	30/9/15	1512a—Pte. W. D. Gibb	29/11/15
789—L.-Cpl. J. A. Geddes	20/9/15	99—Pte. N. Gambetta	29/11/15
1588—Pte. T. H. Mills	28/9/15	1563—Pte. J. L. Taylor	29/11/15
565—Pte. F. L. Usher	20/9/15	501—Pte. F. Stevens	29/11/15
637—Pte. W. Hepburn	19/9/15	1590—Pte. E. Gunning	29/11/15
343—C.S.M. H. F. S. Tippet	18/9/15	169—Pte. W. D. Clydesdale	29/11/15
444—L.-Cpl. J. G. Kirkland	22/9/15	1122—Pte. H. J. Lynch	29/11/15
1787—Pte. J. J. Webb	23/9/15	413—Pte. — Green	29/11/15
1591—Pte. D. Enright	1/10/15	456—Pte. A. W. Mihan	29/11/15
90—Pte. J. W. Stanley	6/10/15	2495—Pte. T. J. Nesbitt	29/11/15
192—Pte. F. H. Forster	9/10/15	354—Sgt. J. W. Stagoll	29/11/15
129—Sgt. L. J. Finning	4/10/15	297—Pte. H. M. Thompson	29/11/15
342—Pte. H. A. Clover	4/10/15	172—Pte. W. Dean	29/11/15
1571—Pte. E. Wilson	4/10/15	1095—Pte. H. V. Ferguson	29/11/15
812—Pte. J. H. Atkinson	24/10/15	1654—Pte. A. Armstrong	29/11/15
576—Cpl. J. T. Redfern	13/10/15	440—Pte. H. Jackson	29/11/15
1906—Pte. J. W. J. Hindaugh	30/10/15	1341—Pte. H. N. Rothery	29/11/15
2409—Pte. R. Morrall	7/10/15	1685a—Pte. D. T. Cousins	29/11/15
1519—Pte. H. Collett	14/10/15	Lieut. W. S. Finlay	29/11/15
337—Pte. S. Fenton	13/10/15	691—Pte. R. W. Poole	18/12/15
1035—Pte. A. J. Rawlinson	12/10/15	1024—Cpl. J. H. Eddy	16/12/15
603—Pte. J. F. Breen	23/10/15	25—Pte. T. P. Jones	12/12/15
437—Pte. E. J. Mortimore	20/11/15	981—Pte. A. J. Forster	12/12/15
370—Pte. H. H. Bowie	13/11/15	1009—Pte. E. Bell	8/12/15
1587—Sgt. H. C. Ross	8/11/15	702—Pte. W. Richardson	25/12/15
Lieut. F. M. Coffey	18/11/15	1330—Sgt. E. Grice	12/12/15
875—Pte. R. T. Farish	20/11/15	608—Pte. A. J. Condon	12/12/15
1152—Pte. N. J. Fielding	29/11/15	1560—Pte. A. J. A. Stewart	26/12/15
1542—Pte. H. L. Hardy	14/11/15	3368—Pte. W. J. McCormack	29/1/16
560—Cpl. G. W. Rushton	14/11/15	1902—Pte. C. D. Daniels	1/1/16
1525—Pte. E. G. Taylor	28/11/15	833—Pte. W. H. Brown	1/1/16
425—Pte. L. J. T. Hart	30/11/15	569—Sgt. G. D. Blanch	4/1/16

APPENDIX.

No.	Name	Date of Death
2712	Pte. W. H. McClelland	15/1/16
3011	Pte. A. Brand	1/1/16
3100	Pte G. H. Gunn	18/2/16
4394	Pte. J. D. L. Davidson	27/3/16
1915	Pte. M. T. Kennedy	28/3/16
658	L.-Cpl. H. Lamont	27/5/16
3061	Pte. H. L. Cathie	29/5/16
985	Pte. H. C. Jennings	24/6/16
1593	Pte. A. Watson	30/6/16
1960	Pte. M. E. O'Neill	30/6/16
952	Pte. S. Strahan	30/6/16
319	Pte. R. D. Jack	30/6/16
2456	Pte. A. Roth	30/6/16
1784	Pte. J. H. Farley	1/7/16
3609	Pte. T. B. Shaw	3/7/16
2367	Pte. J. Horne	2/7/16
828	Pte. G. Bradley	28/7/16
973	Pte. C. Wilson	28/7/16
1159	Cpl. G. B. Swanton	28/7/16
	Lieut. A. J. Kerr	27/7/16
888/7	Cpl. C. B. Hall	29/7/16
420	Pte. N. Guest	29/7/16
1522	Pte. R. J. Curtis	29/7/16
2109	Cpl. A. W. Armstrong	29/7/16
2432	Pte. L. J. Phillips	28/7/16
636	Pte. H. Harding	30/7/16
3653	Pte. P. A. Tweedie	29/7/16
1750	Pte. W. J. F. Whiteway	29/7/16
3540	Pte. E. A. Humphrey	29/7/16
1653	Pte. R. Baker (alias E. Scholes)	29/7/16
1507	A.-Cpl. J. F. Ryan	29/7/16
3593	Pte. N. C. Richards	29/7/16
989	Pte. A. Smith	29/7/16
533	Pte. T. Urquhart	29/7/16
531	Pte. L. H. Thornton	29/7/16
439	Pte. J. W. L. Johnson	29/7/16
1055	Cpl. J. D. Jaguers	29/7/16
982	Pte. W. G. Gardner	30/7/16
648	Pte. F. W. Jones	29/7/16
662	Pte. T. Mackrell	29/7/16
2141	Pte. J. Fenotti	29/7/16
884	Pte. W. J. Gingell	30/7/16
3812	Pte. G. E. Evans	29/7/16
1790	Pte. W. A. B. Bowley	29/7/16
1771	Pte. G. T. Steele	27/7/16
3658	Pte D. Vooght	27/7/16
1550a	Pte. H. Richmond	27/7/16
2361	Pte. H. V. Dogral	27-29/7/16
1675	Pte. F. G. S. Healey	28/7/16
2124	Pte. H. Collins	28/7/16
1713	Pte A. T. Noakes	28/7/16
3762	Pte. A. P. Byass	28/7/16
599	Pte. J. S. Butcher	29/7/16
2834	Pte. F. R. Buckle	29/7/16
822	L.-Cpl. A. L. Benjamin	29/7/16
3988	Pte. P. Monaghan	30/7/16
2252	Pte. W. C. Missen	28/7/16
2276	Pte. R. N. Matthews	29/7/16
1698	Pte. A. E. Magnus	29/7/16
447	L.-Cpl. F. L. Lugton	29/7/16
65	Pte. J. A. Jones	29/7/16
2342	Pte. A. Batchelor	—
1955	Pte. A. B. D. Neal	29/7/16
2720	Pte. R. H. Nebbit	29/7/16
2105	Pte. A. Armstrong	29/7/16
475	Pte. J. Neely	29/7/16
2729	Pte. W. J. O'Shea	29/7/16
1716	Pte. J. D. Patterson	29/7/16
244	Pte. W. E. Newson	29/7/16
936	Cpl. A. J. Reville	29/7/16
97	Pte. W. J. Hill	30/7/16
407	Pte. J. Fitzgibbon	29/7/16
724	Pte. J. G. Tinkler	5/8/16
953	Pte. G. Sussens	5/8/16
2210	Pte. G. Sims	5/8/16
977	Sgt. A. Roebuck	5/8/16
923	Pte. H. Nelson	5/8/16
3194	Pte. E. Mason	5/8/16
3195	Pte. J. A. McCormick	5/8/16
3853	Pte. R. G. Knox	5/8/16
2389	Pte. C. Johnson	5/8/16
206	Pte. M. J. Heagney	5/8/16
885	Pte. W. Gorrie	5/8/16
2272	Pte. E. Francis	5/8/16
2626	Pte. A. S. Ewart	5/8/16
3621	Pte. E. M. Rolfe	5/8/16
2000	Pte. K. A. Sutherland	5/8/16
969	Pte. W. Veney	5/8/16
2086	Pte. W. R. Stirling	5/8/16
803	Sgt. A. Ross	5/8/16
3973	Pte. H. W. Rowe	5/8/16
931	Pte. C. Phillips	5/8/16
2438	Pte. G. Robertson	5/8/16
2249	Pte. V. Rogerson	5/8/16
688	Pte. C. F. Paine	5/8/16
683	Pte. J. O'Connell	5/8/16
26	Pte. H. O. Pain	5/8/16
896	Pte. V. Jackson	5/8/16
3839	Pte. J. Hutchison	5/8/16
247	Pte. G. W. Norwood	5/8/16
716	Pte. R. Smith	5/8/16
2375	Pte. G. Hargreaves	5/8/16
2148	C.S.M. A. G. Hawkins	6/8/16
886	Pte. F. R. Golburn	5/8/16
3950	Pte. J. J. Flynn	5/8/16
176	Pte. F. Dean	6/8/16
3787	Pte. H. N. Coventry	5/8/16
135	Pte. N. W. MacKinley	5/8/16
1700	Pte. J. C. Michael	5/8/16
606	Pte. G. Camilo	5/8/16
2224	Pte. T. H. Ashley	5/8/16
4019	Pte. T. Leach	5/8/16

APPENDIX.

	Date of Death.
2169—Dvr. J. Hutchinson	5/8/16
1668a—Pte. T. F. Egan	5/8/16
5066—Pte. W. H. Brown	5/8/16
3775—Pte. W. Benton	5/8/16
443—Pte. H. W. Johnson	4/8/16
1751—T.-Cpl. R. A. Nicholson	5/8/16
3235—Pte. J. N. Robinson	5/8/16
2437—Pte. J. Patterson	4-6/8/16
144—Pte. J. Bickley	5/8/16
3777—Pte. R. H. Bailey	5/8/16
308—Pte. G. Woodhouse	8/8/16
16—Dvr. G. T. Davis	1/8/16
3199—Pte. W. L. McKenzie	2/8/16
32—L.-Cpl. J. W. Jones	6/8/16
3632—Pte. H. G. Tarr	3/8/16
2nd-Lieut. F. R. Hays	8/8/16
2nd-Lieut. J. R. Clarke	4/8/16
2nd-Lieut. A. G. Goodson	3/8/16
Capt. W. H. Tatnall	7/8/16
Major C. E. Manning	7/8/16
Capt. H. F. H. Plant	7/8/16
Lieut. J. B. N. Carvick (M.C.)	7/8/16
3896—Pte. P. H. Read	7/8/16
1566/2566—Pte. J. G. Baensch	8/8/16
591—Pte. C. A. C. Atkinson	6/8/16
4020—Pte. P. J. Murray	5/8/16
3865—Pte. W. G. Laker	6/8/16
2479—Pte. W. R. Wheeler	4/8/16
3904—Pte. S. W. Schilling	3/8/16
1572—Pte. W. E. Wilson	6/8/16
2207—Pte. F. H. Roberts	6/8/16
479—Sgt. J. Ould	8/8/16
1894—Pte. A. M. Crook	6/8/16
4115—Pte. B. Gregson	7/8/16
4017—Pte. R. McInerney	6/8/16
3794—Pte. G. F. Carwardine	2/8/16
2351—Pte. D. Campbell	2/8/16
1327—L.-Cpl. A. F. Campbell	3/8/16
4462—Pte. A. J. Meyer	5/8/16
2491—Pte. T. J. Ryan	22/8/16
5291/5341—Pte. W. J. Garnham	13/8/16
2067—Pte. J. T. Taylor	22/8/16
1690—Pte. J. McDonald	24/8/16
2328—Pte. G. Waters	22/8/16
2055—Pte. R. H. Marchant	27/8/16
4430—Pte. F. H. Murphy	28/8/16
2708—Pte. B. McKay	27/8/16
4010—Pte. R. A. Johnson	27/8/16
3253—L.-Cpl. H. Steel	23/8/16
1630—Pte. R. J. Hunter	24/8/16
2269—Pte. E. Burke	23/8/16
1155—Cpl. W. Quade	19/8/16
3489—Pte. A. Evans	18/8/16
3046—Pte. H. Condron	18/8/16
819—L.-Cpl. T. L. Baxter	24/8/16
1342—Pte. A. Reeves	28/8/16
435—Pte. C. Hollies	29/8/16

	Date of Death.
3756—Pte. T. P. Arthur	29/8/16
2112—Pte. A. Anderson	25/8/16
2nd-Lieut. R. N. Thomas	27/8/16
Lieut. W. A. Coward	23/8/16
3816—Pte. A. E. Folks	14/8/16
2772—Pte. F. J. Smith	14/8/16
2348—Pte. G. A. Bell	14/8/16
706—Pte. J. Smyth	12/8/16
4138—Pte. P. E. Living	16/8/16
2749—Pte. A. Quirk	12/8/16
733—Pte. C. A. Way	26/8/16
4315—Pte. H. J. Hughes	22/8/16
709—Pte. F. Sell	22/8/16
1564—Pte. G. W. Thomson	22/8/16
2024—Pte. S. Wilson	22/8/16
2392—Pte. E. Johnson	22/8/16
2181—Pte. F. Jones	22/8/16
1669—Pte. C. Beckwith	22/8/16
1547—Sgt. A. B. Arnel (M.M.)	23/8/16
3792—Sgt. H. C. Charman	24/8/16
3553—Pte. T. Johnston	25/8/16
2230—Pte. T. H. Mummery	26/8/16
638—Pte. W. L. Hyder	26/8/16
900—Sgt. J. C. Kerr	25/8/16
3135—Pte. H. A. Hogan	26/8/16
902—Pte. K. P. T. King	26/8/16
870—Cpl. A. C. Dixon	26/8/16
625—Pte. A. Gardiner	26/8/16
1729—Pte. W. E. Sheedy	25/8/16
1996—Pte. C. P. Smith	25/8/16
1163—Sgt. T. Murphy	25/8/16
529—T.-Cpl. H. C. Tyrer	23/8/16
689—Pte. A. W. Pink	26/8/16
2159—Pte. T. H. Hallworth	26/8/16
4181—Pte. J. J. Pollock	25/8/16
2386—Pte. C. Harris, M.M.	25/8/16
888—Pte. A. Hansen	25/8/16
879—Pte. A. W. Frohlich	25/8/16
1676—Pte. R. M. Bain	25/8/16
4494—Pte. J. R. Patterson	25/8/16
1773—Pte. R. L. Stagoll	24/8/16
1600—Pte. J. L. Foley	24/8/16
2433—Pte. L. J. Paget	24/8/16
4159—Pte. J. R. McClintock	24/8/16
3800—Pte. F. H. Cooper	24/8/16
157—Cpl. A. S. Burvett	24/8/16
2457—Pte. R. Armstrong	24/8/16
1783—A.-Cpl. W. J. Bannan	24/8/16
2165—Pte. W. R. Hardwick	26/8/16
1723—L.-Cpl. E. Law	25/8/16
3907—Pte. A. E. Simmons	27/8/16
590—Sgt. R. J. Robertson	26/8/16
4185—Pte. B. J. Pretious	27/8/16
2419—Pte. P. O'Loughlin	26/8/16
107—Pte. C. R. Joselin	22/8/16
3757—Pte. A. Arnold	23/8/16

APPENDIX.

No. — Name	Date of Death.
2205—Pte. M. T. Paley	22/8/16
852—Pte. W. C. E. Cox	22/9/16
1040—Cpl. R. H. Foers	24/9/16
4410—Pte. L. G. Grayland	28/9/16
623—Pte. F. W. Edwards	27/10/16
4405—Pte. J. T. Duncan	8/11/16
667—Pte. D. S. McIntyre	9/11/16
Major G. M. Nicholas, D.S.O	14/11/16
102—L.-Cpl. F. Bird	21/11/16
4516—L.-Cpl. A. J. Russell	6/11/16
4588—Pte. J. Barry	6/11/16
4417—Pte. M. J. Fogarty	6/11/16
2470—Pte. K. J. McDonald	6/11/16
1956—Pte. A. Nicholson	6/11/16
4113—Pte. W. E. Garvie	19/11/16
4377—T.-Cpl. C. K. Camp	13/11/16
4096—Pte. E. S. Duncan	13/11/16
2676—Pte. A. E. James	14/11/16
695—L.-Cpl. R. Ross	14/11/16
1995—Pte. W. C. Silver	15/11/16
4000—Pte. J. L. Barker	14/11/16
2791—Pte. T. B. Sullivan	15/11/16
880—Pte. P. Fraser	19/11/16
2003—Pte. J. Saw	18/11/16
877—Pte. R. Fiddes	31/12/16
4175—Pte. W. Oliphant	25/12/16
5381—Pte. C. F. Meeking	24/12/16
3886—Pte. H. J. Pounds	24/12/16
3870—Pte. C. A. Minniece	7/1/17
4493—Pte. G. Patterson	8/1/17
820—Cpl. P. T. Beadel	17/1/17
4359—Pte. W. B. Begelhols	6/1/17
4427—Pte. L. Grattidge	6/1/17
786—Sgt. J. A. Jones	6/1/17
4537—Pte. N. Thomas	6/1/17
6347—Pte. A. McMurtie	18/2/17
5439—Pte. B. J. Warren	5/2/17
1772—Cpl. A. J. Shaw	5/2/17
4261—Sgt. R. E. Gell	16/2/17
6359—Pte. J. P. O'Leary	16/2/17
2069—Q.M.S. A. F. Wainwright	28/2/17
6327—A.-Sgt. J. R. Kennedy	26/2/17
2486—Pte. G. Welsh	4/3/17
4982—Pte. P. W. Blake	26/2/17
4024—Sgt. E. Harrison	13/3/17
5704—Pte. W. J. Lydiard	9/3/17
3627—Cpl. A. Ross	3/3/17
3804—Pte. H. C. Dickinson	19/2/17
341—T.-Cpl. M. McL. Dobbie	22/2/17
4592—L.-Cpl. H. W. Harrison	25/2/17
1011—Cpl. J. E. A. Bruce	25/2/17
378—Pte. H. D. Baylis	3/3/17
6155—Pte. F. J. White	3/3/17
270—Cpl. W. Snadden	8/3/17
4682—Pte. S. Cremean	16/3/17
5789—Pte. J. Babbage	15/2/17
4513—Pte. A. K. Robertson	28/3/17
4420—Pte. E. L. George	15/3/17
1734—Sgt. A. Mundell, M.M.	14/3/17
4173—Pte. G. O'Brien	14/3/17
298—Pte. L. Trezise	14/3/17
5106—Pte. C. G. West	13/3/17
4306—Pte. G. J. Darcy	13/3/17
4089—T.-Sgt. A. J. Clegg	13/3/17
4993—Pte. C. T. Chandler	13/3/17
4983—Pte. P. D. Boddy	13/3/17
5699—Pte. W. H. Gammon	11/3/17
4476—Pte. H. J. McCarthy	14/3/17
4721—Pte. R. C. Little	15/3/17
5605—Pte. J. Inkson	9/3/17
5630—Pte. W. D. Neagher	23/4/17
4604—Pte. D. T. G. Reid	16/4/17
6314—Pte. J. W. Gniel	17/4/17
4472—Pte. L. H. McPherson	19/4/17
4519—Pte. J. R. Rutterford	18/4/17
4669—Pte. B. E. Callaghan	18/4/17
2420—L.-Cpl. N. E. O'Brien	21/4/17
2203—Pte. C. J. Miller	16/4/17
4652—Pte. W. E. Allen	18/4/17
718—Pte. R. D. Taylor	19/4/17
5686—Pte. L. C. White	16/4/17
5319—Pte. A. J. Coglin	22/4/17
5707—Pte. S. F. Richmond	5/5/17
5332—Pte. F. L. Du Rieu	3/5/17
3772—Pte. A. Boyd	4/5/17
5632—Pte. M. Meenan	4/5/17
4522—Pte. A. W. Sadler	4/5/17
1545—Cpl. F. C. Mathews	4/5/17
6076—Pte. T. R. Jones	15/5/17
5657—Pte. T. Rolfe	4/5/17
Lieut. P. G. D. Fethers	3/5/17
5550—Pte. A. J. Bennett	7/5/17
705—Pte. G. Swanson	4/5/17
5925—Pte. C. M. Bell	4/5/17
4053—Pte. C. G. Armour	4/5/17
5328—Pte. A. W. Dean	3/5/17
4414—Pte. A. G. Enticott	14/5/17
1657—C.S.M. M. Cronin	6/5/17
6061—Pte. N. G. Goode	3/5/17
2401—Pte. M. L. Kinane	3/5/17
5459—L.-Cpl. H. J. Johnston	3/5/17
630—Cpl. C. F. Harrison	3/5/17
109—L.-Cpl. W. J. Fitzpatrick	3/5/17
4310—Pte. P. Fitzsimmons	3/5/17
5144—Pte. W. H. Forster	3/5/17
2631—L.-Cpl. G. C. Fossey	3/5/17
5791—Pte. S. F. Barber	3/5/17
5296—Pte. L. J. Beale	3/5/17
5419—Pte. G. R. Blackwood	3/5/17
5323—Pte. A. E. Creighton	3/5/17
612—Pte. W. A. Connelly	2/5/17
4568—Pte. G. Dell	4/5/17

APPENDIX.

	Date of Death.
5680—Pte. F. R. McNaughton	4/5/17
1127—Pte. R. F. Young	3/5/17
1551a—Sgt. P. H. Taylor	3/5/17
5425—Pte. J. E. Snee	3/5/17
1757—Cpl. H. L. Pollard	3/5/17
Lieut. Rynehardt	3/5/17
5677—Pte. L. G. Tout	3/5/17
5904—Pte. E. A. Vallance	3/5/17
4785—Pte. W. A. Waltho	3/5/17
6043—Pte. J. Commins	3/5/17
5385—Pte. S. G. Murphy	3/5/17
5437—Pte. L. J. Upton	3/5/17
5959—Pte. J. Rennie	3/5/17
4139—L.-Cpl. E. E. Littlewood	3/5/17
2030—Cpl. J. R. Burns	3/5/17
6058—Pte. E. L. Curran	3/5/17
4792—Pte. E. C. V. White	3/5/17
Capt. G. L. Maxfield (M.C.)	3/5/17
1763—Pte. A. Runting	3/5/17
5153—Pte. J. E. Lincoln	3/5/17
221—Pte. F. E. Lindsay	3/5/17
908—Pte. D. E. Lohman	3/5/17
4802—Pte. M. R. Macbeth	3/5/17
5375—Pte. T. H. Manallack	3/5/17
5879—Pte. R. T. McLoskey	3/5/17
584—C.S.M. A. W. Petch	3/5/17
2748—Pte. C. C. Priddle	3/5/17
5081—Pte. J. A. Robinson	3/5/17
4040/416—Pte. W. Rosewarne	3/5/17
3625—Pte. J. L. Rolls	3/5/17
4981—Pte. R. H. Blair	3/5/17
1325—Pte. S. Chamberlain	3/5/17
3324—Pte. W. A. Creswick	3/5/17
1815—Cpl. R. W. Davidson (M.M.)	3/5/17
4407—Pte. A. E. Eckford	3/5/17
769—Sgt. L. F. Dobson	3/5/17
1797—Pte. J. Driscoll	3/5/17
930—Pte. R. Perry	3/5/17
4700—Pte. F. C. Gordon	3/5/17
1806—Pte. R. W. Haig	3/5/17
5616—Pte. W. D. King	3/5/17
5076—Pte. R. W. Ramage	2/5/17
5119—Pte. P. Brennan	3/5/17
5310—Pte. J. Campbell	3/5/17
3780—Pte. L. Cohen	3/5/17
4686—T.-Cpl. A. P. Dobinson	3/5/17
4465—Pte. J. Mitchell	3/5/17
5050—Pte. A. W. Mallette	3/5/17
903—Cpl. H. Lang, M.M.	3/5/17
289—Pte. G. A. W. Turnbull	5/5/17
5165—Pte. R. W. H. White	3/5/17
4204—Pte. A. L. Stewart	3/5/17
4520—Pte. W. J. Rutterford	3/5/17
5423—Pte. F. R. Smith	3/5/17
5901—Pte. R. Swalwell	3/5/17
5434—Pte. E. Taylor	3/5/17

	Date of Death.
6027—Pte. A. Arrowsmith	3/5/17
6165—Pte. J. A. Flack	3/5/17
6034—Pte. J. A. Burns	3/5/17
547—Pte. H. E. Young	3/5/17
2340—L.-Cpl. A. J. Boak	3/5/17
4448—Pte. H. H. Johnston	3/5/17
5347—Pte. J. S. Hayden	3/5/17
4749—Pte. G. L. Paxin	3/5/17
578—Cpl. E. C. Millward	3/5/17
5643—Pte. F. B. McCurran	3/5/17
5623—Pte. P. Manzie	3/5/17
5946—Pte. V. W. Litchfield	3/5/17
4135—Pte. J. Lee	3/5/17
1652—L.-Cpl. W. H. Alloway	2/5/17
1586—L.-Cpl. A. Simpson	3/5/17
3883—Pte. J. W. Nesbit	4/5/17
5428—Pte. W. H. Stanton	4/5/17
535—L.-Cpl. J. W. Sadler	4/5/17
6136—Pte. R. Smith	3/5/17
(Correct name H. J. Cullinger.)	
Lieut. J. Harris	3/5/17
5802—Pte. W. E. Burke	3/5/17
4713—L.-Cpl. W. J. Hunter	8/5/17
6052—Pte. E. J. Ewen	3/5/17
5626—Pte. W. Manderson	5/5/17
4298—Pte. A. Burnip	24/5/17
5869—Pte. T. M. Murphy	1/6/17
5693—Pte. J. H. F. Wright	1/6/17
6399—Pte. J. R. T. Telfer	11/6/17
4128—L.-Cpl. T. W. Joyce	1/6/17
2737—Pte. W. Parkes	22/9/17
6384—Pte. H. Stevens	23/9/17
5114—Pte. J. Wright	22/9/17
2794—Pte. A. H. Thompson	21/9/17
3781—Pte. F. Curtis	21/9/17
664—Pte. C. L. Michael	22/9/17
6056—Pte. C. A. Gray	20/9/17
4189—Pte. W. F. Rowland	22/9/17
4534—Cpl. R. Sproull	21/9/17
4761—Pte. A. H. Roberts	21/9/17
2236—Pte. G. W. Reilly	21/9/17
484—Pte. W. R. Peach	21/9/17
5619—Pte. G. T. Lees	21/9/17
641—Sgt. S. W. Johnson	21/9/17
735—Pte. R. Zula	20/9/17
5443—Pte. A. G. W. Williams	20/9/17
5823—Pte. F. Gibbs	20/9/17
4303—Pte. E. A. Cooper, M.M.	20/9/17
3795—Cpl. G. Castle	20/9/17
4492—Pte. T. E. Patterson	21/9/17
4717—Pte. W. Jackson	5/10/17
(Alias H. Grainger.)	
6058—Pte. A. Griffiths	7/10/17
541—Pte. J. J. White	5/10/17
Lieut. F. W. J. Murphy	4/10/17
Capt. T. C. E. Godfrey, M.C.	4/10/17

APPENDIX.

	Date of Death.
Capt. G. Harriott	4/10/17
5688—Pte. S. M. Williams	7/10/17
601—Pte. P. Briggs	—
Lieut. A. Wilcock	4/10/17
824—Pte. A. G. Billingham	7/10/17
2nd-Lieut. E. S. Worrall	4/10/17
932—Pte. R. Plowright	4/10/18
5615—Pte. R. B. Kilvert	5/10/17
5536—Pte. J. Quinlan	5/10/17
3244—Pte. J. Boyd (Alias J. Roberts.)	—
6424—Pte. J. Wilkinson	4/10/17
5325—Pte. T. H. Cross	6/10/17
2155—Pte. H. W. Pettit	6/10/17
5587—Pte. R. T Gooding	4/10/17
4433—Pte B. Harris	4/10/17
1548—Pte. W. A. Bradshaw	4/10/17
383—Pte. F. W. Cridge	4/10/17
5012—Pte. J. F. Dunkerley	4/10/17
6180—Pte. A. E. Marshall	4/10/17
6175—Pte. A. E. Tucker	2/10/17
6192—Pte. G. J. A. Gordon	4/10/17
4452—Pte. L. F. Lamb	4/10/17
5858—Sgt. P. H. Lingford	5/10/17
5076—Pte. S. W. Opie	4/10/17
4976—Pte. J. C. Bell	4/10/17
5803—Pte. V. F. Carey	4/10/17
6311—Pte. N. J. Fegan	4/10/17
5359—Pte. W. Hyams	4/10/17
5380—Pte. F. T. Mauer	4/10/17
4747—L.-Cpl. C. G. Orchard	4/10/17
5708—Pte. J. R. Rantman	4/10/17
4593—Pte. R. Hayes	4/10/17
5095—Pte H. D. L. Sutherland	4/10/17
1963a—Pte. G. G. Watson	4/10/17
5418—Pte. W. C. Simpson	4/10/17
5424—Pte. J. H. Smith	4/10/17
5444—Pte. F. G. Wilson	4/10/17
5856—Pte. P. R. V. le Roux	4/10/17
5018—Pte. S. Fisher	4/10/17
4722—Pte. T. Lovell, M.M.	4/10/17
5889—Pte. P. Parkinson	4/10/17
4773—Pte. A. Shimmen	4/10/17
2215—Cpl. S. Welsh	4/10/17
1324—Cpl. A. Banks	4/10/17
2032—Pte. N. Cornthwaite	5/10/17
4507—Pte. A. V. Pippard	5/10/17
279—Sgt. E. Scrivener	5/10/17
2857—Pte. A. E. Tolley	5/10/17
616—Sgt. H. C. Dickens	4/10/17
1536—Pte. J. J. Egan	4/10/17
197—Pte. J. Gunn	4/10/17
632—Pte. W. H. Henley	4/10/17
208—Sgt. A. M. Henry	4/10/17
646—Pte. J. V. Jacobson	4/10/17
4170—Pte. G. Murray	4/10/17
1702—Pte. W. H. Marshall	4/10/17
746—Pte. F. Robinson	4/10/17
1985—T.-C.S.M. W. A. Russell	4/10/17
4200—Pte. H. V. Stait	4/10/17
3633—Pte. H. Taylor	4/10/17
5575—Pte. J. T. Doherty	4/10/17
4602—Pte. W. E. Proctor	4/10/17
6072—Pte. C. E. Hing	4/10/17
5298—Pte. S. C. Betts	4/10/17
5315—Pte. C. P. Clarke	4/10/17
1813a—Sgt. V. O. Cleghorn	4/10/17
5364—Sgt. M. Jones	4/10/17
1223—Pte. R. A. McColl	4/10/17
4184—Pte. S. T. W. Preston	4/10/17
3803—Pte. T. Campion	9/10/17
2135—Sgt. D. W. S. Cumper	9/10/17
103—Pte. E. East	9/10/17
5015—Pte. D. E. W. Findley	26/10/17
6096—Pte. F. Montgomery	9/10/17
4569—T.-Sgt. W. Ellis (Correct name W. R. M. Hallas.)	9/10/17
4709—Cpl. S. M. Hill	9/10/17
4154—Cpl. L. R. Mace	9/10/17
4734—Pte. R. Montgomery	9/10/17
4484—Pte. A. H. Ockwell	9/10/17
1964—Pte. O. W. T. Orchard	9/10/17
3888—Pte. R. C. Pilven	9/10/17
934—Pte. A. F. Prior	9/10/17
1526—Pte. H. S. Ray	9/10/17
570—C.S.M. N. H. Shepard, M.M.	9/10/17
3210—Pte. W. H. Watt	9/10/17
2488—Pte. W. Z. Welsh	10/10/17
4075—Pte. F. W. Bulling	9/10/17
6443—Pte. J. Stonehouse	9/10/17
5601—Pte. L. F. Hummerston	9/10/17
6028—Pte. N. L. Armstrong	9/10/17
6078—Pte. C. C. Jewels	8/10/17
6087—Pte. V. G. Lewis	9/10/17
375—Pte. W. J. B. Bott	9/10/17
4681—Pte. R. Cooper	9/10/17
6453—Pte. E. Forbes	9/10/17
2377—Pte. S. A. Heathcote	9/10/17
4711—Pte. C. Hosking	9/10/17
4453—Pte. J. H. Lane	9/10/17
661—Pte. C. F. Minehan	9/10/17
6471—Pte. A. Scroggie	9/10/17
Capt. C. M. Williams	9/10/17
2nd-Lieut. N. C. Nation	9/10/17
Lieut. B. F. Nicholas, M.C.	9/10/17
Lieut. R. J. Pickett, M.C.	9/10/17
5311—Pte. E. E. Capp	10/10/17
4402—Pte. M. Donovan	12/10/17
6055—Pte. R. J. Gamble	8/10/17
6086—Pte. J. C. Littlefield	8/10/17
6029—Pte. S. C. Andrews	9/10/17
6166—Pte. V. V. Collin	9/10/17

APPENDIX.

	Date of Death.
5666—Pte. A. A. Smith	9/10/17
6374—Pte. H. Rolton	8/10/17
5560—Pte. W. T. Clements	9/10/17
5582—Pte. E. J. Field	9/10/17
5783—Pte. A. R. Pope	9/10/17
8082/1759—Pte. C. W. Sykes	9/10/17
6409—Pte. C. R. Vennell	9/10/17
4787—Pte. J. Watts	9/10/17
6094—Pte. W. W. Murphy	9/10/17
2022—Pte. C. Wightman	8/10/17
4109—Pte. J. P. Gemmell	9/10/17
855—Pte. F. P. Conroy	8/10/17
2369—Cpl. C. L. T. Hey	8/10/17
1749—Cpl. W. L. Norman	8/10/17
260—Pte. W. Porteus	8/10/17
1755—Pte. F. World	8/10/17
2266—Pte. E. G. Bolton	9/10/17
3765—Pte. W. M. Burke	9/10/17
1733a—Cpl. E. E. Stainsby	10/11/17
56—Cpl. P. H. Knight	10/11/17
5445—Pte. H. A. J. Woods	29/11/17
4859/4589—Pte. W. J. Bradley	6/1/18
4412—Pte. M. Elliot	7/2/18
4712—Pte. R. J. Hughes	10/3/18
1144—Pte. H. S. Butterfield	8/3/18
2027—Cpl. S. Frankel	15/3/18
3574—Pte. J. Murphy	15/3/18
6373—Pte. H. E. Rawlins	22/3/18
6423—Pte. T. S. Welsh	8/3/18
4995—Cpl. E. Collinson	22/3/18
3604—Pte. R. J. O'Leary	28/3/18
4753—Pte. W. J. Popple	22/3/18
1741—Pte. F. Toomey	24/3/18
4087—Pte. J. H. Chamberlain	27/3/18
6401—Pte. W. J. Tickell	25/3/18
548—Pte. W. E. Williams	27/3/18
1339—Pte. W. Peterson	27/3/18
6190—Pte. H. O. Crabtree	9/4/18
5313—Pte. J. Charters	9/4/18
6959—Pte. W. R. Tyers	16/4/18
5170—Pte. W. Robins	16/4/18
6782—Pte. P. Berry	9/4/18
6305—Pte. J. M. Dwyer	9/4/18
4945—Pte. P. H. Laing	16/4/18
6415—Pte. W. H. Williamson	9/4/18
6430—Pte. H. Winters	21/4/18
6188—Pte. P. W. Young	11/4/18
6954—Pte. R. Colgate	21/4/18
89—Cpl. V. Hughes	20/4/18
4738—Cpl. W. M. McDonald	23/4/18
245—Cpl. W. G. Nichols	19/5/18
6858a—A.-Cpl. M. Nathan	23/5/18
Lieut. G. E. B. Munro	22/5/18
592/573—Sgt. O. A. Collins	15/5/18
2889a—Pte. G. Jackson	12/5/18
5033—Pte. J. W. Hillgrove	19/5/18

	Date of Death.
6789a— — R. H. Commons	19/3/18
4101—Pte. L. V. Emerson	19/5/18
6834a—Pte. D. F. Matheson	19/5/18
7558—Pte. E. Newbound	19/5/18
6881—Pte. W. Scott	19/5/18
6893a—Pte. H. Stobo	19/5/18
6133—Pte. A. J. Strudwick	31/5/18
2047—Pte. W. Kressen	31/5/18
4317—Pte. J. Mackenzie	31/5/18
386—Pte. C. D. Coleman	3/6/18
6877a—Pte. S. C. Robinson	12/6/18
6907—Pte. J. T. Turner	11/6/18
2119—Pte. J. C. Black	12/6/18
6830—Pte. A. Livermore	15/6/18
3873—Pte. N. C. Munro (M.M.)	12/6/18
6878a—Pte. C. Sandford	15/6/18
3935—Sgt. J. A. Fisher	16/6/18
(Alias J. A. Daly.)	
6378—Pte. A. S. Real	16/6/18
6933—Pte. R. J. Goodisson	11/6/18
1550—Sgt. P. J. Molloy (M.M.)	8/6/18
6772a—Pte. H. M. O'Donoghue	16/6/18
255—Cpl. C. M. Paget	16/6/18
1161/1357—L.-Cpl. F. L. Bell	15/6/18
6791a—Pte. E. W. E. Darling	14/6/18
6813—Pte. J. Ellis	14/6/18
4695—L.-Cpl. G. Gavens	15/6/18
6819—Pte. W. J. Jennings	14/6/18
766a—Pte. C. H. Matthews	14/6/18
6775a—Pte. A. R. Boots	14/6/18
2143a—Pte. J. G. Woodfield	7/7/18
854—T.-Cpl. C. H. Collins	4/7/18
6773a—Pte. M. R. Black	6/7/18
4461—Pte. J. G. Matthews	25/7/18
6063—Pte. H. Harrison	23/7/18
675a—Pte. H. W. Haynes	23/7/18
2214—Pte. J. A. C. Godward	2/8/18
763—Pte. N. Butcher	25/7/18
6909—Pte. C. Toner	25/7/18
6828a—Pte. I. L. Lewtas	8/8/18
5120—Pte. V. J. Marocco	7/8/18
Lieut. C. C. Burge	14/8/18
Lieut. E. H. D. Edgerton, D.S.O., M.M. and Bar	12/8/18
6879a—Pte. L. W. Schrader	8/8/18
6802a—Pte. W. R. Firebrace	15/8/18
228—L.-Sgt. L. J. Morrison	3/8/18
483—Pte. A. G. Pilley	15/8/18
6874a—Pte. G. L. Reeves	12/8/18
6400—Cpl. L. C. Thomasson	12/8/18
4788—Pte. F. C. Webb	12/8/18
149a—Pte. W. Chibnall	20/8/18
2458—Pte. R. H. Paterson	3/8/18
594—Dvr. G. E. Brown	28/8/18
568—Pte. H. F. Pillow (M.M.)	18/8/18
1146a—Dvr. H. E. Ashworth	18/8/18

APPENDIX. 339

	Date of Death.
392—Pte. T. Butler	17/8/18
2274—Pte. L. C. Millman	18/8/18
6839—Pte. S. G. Jarrett	18/8/18
6414—Pte. C. Wilson	18/8/18
6863a—Pte. T. O. Olsen	28/8/18
859—Cpl. J. Cuddy	22/8/18
227—Pte. A. Neville	28/8/18
6035—T.-Sgt. C. Bennett (M.M.)	27/8/18
2nd-Lieut. A. G. Gilchrist	1/9/18
Lieut. E. M. Martin	31/8/18
2nd-Lieut. C. J. R. Newton	31/8/18
2nd-Lieut. P. W. Salmon	1/9/18
2336—Pte. W. G. Bull	3/9/18
5561—L.-Cpl. W. L. Colclough	29/8/18
2nd-Lieut. P. T. McCarty	1/9/18
6761—Pte. L. J. Adams	1/9/18
6452—Pte. E. B. Errey	3/9/18
239—Pte. N. McGuiness	2/9/18
6853a—Pte. A. Murray	1/9/18
4397—Pte. P. Dash	2/9/18
5373—Pte. J. L. G. Makin	1/9/18
241—L.-Cpl. J. A. W. McKenzie	1/9/18
1770—L.-Cpl. J. J. Smith	24/9/18
6804a—Pte. H. Gibson	23/9/18
6026—Pte. C. V. Andrews	1/9/18
6141—Pte. J. Taylor	31/8/18
3946—Pte. H. A. Anderson, M.M.	1/9/18
4352—Cpl. R. J. Andrew	1/9/18
6276—L.-Cpl. W. J. Armstrong	31/8/18
2101—Pte. F. A. Atkins	31/8/18
4067—Pte. W. H. Bell (M.M.)	28/8/18
6774a—Pte. S. Booth	1/9/18
2350—L.-Cpl. J. R. F. Byrne	1/9/18
2868—Sgt. A. C. Cooper (M.M.)	28/8/18
6801—Pte. P. J. Corboy	2/9/18
6291—Pte. W. J. Coulson	2/9/18
6785—Pte. R. E. Cross	28/8/18
2232—Sgt. J. Cumming	2/9/18
1523a—Cpl. D. Dearth	1/9/18
5570—Pte. H. F. Degering	29/8/18
340—Pte. C. L. Doble	31/8/18
6307—Pte. T. M. Ellen	31/8/18
190—Cpl. S. C. Fishwick	1/9/18
1504—Sgt. H. Fromer	1/9/18
6803a—Pte. W. E. Garrett	1/9/18
4111—Pte. T. G. Gonzalez	1/9/18
3538—Pte. E. E. Hart	1/9/18
55—Pte. T. Hollins	1/9/18
6818—Pte. T. A. James	1/9/18
312—C.Q.M.-S. V. J. Jolly	31/8/18
4129—Pte. J. King	1/9/18
6831a—C.S.M. W. Love	31/8/18
1537—Pte. C. L. Mackay (M.M.)	1/9/18
6951—L.-Cpl. R. L. M. Maddisson	1/9/18
5860—Pte. S. W. Maddox	1/9/18
4723—Cpl. H. W. Martin	31/8/18

	Date of Death.
5118—L.-Cpl. E. L. Mitchell	1/9/18
1702a—Pte. A. E. Morris	1/9/18
4754—Pte. A. S. Quelch	1/9/18
4762—Cpl. R. Roff (M.M.)	1/9/18
4767—Cpl. C. Ryan	1/9/18
5133—Pte. G. Schlyder	1/9/18
4197—Pte. W. C. Smith	2/9/18
236—Pte. D. F. Sullivan	2/9/18
6404—Pte. T. W. Turnbull	1/9/18
6910—Pte. G. F. Urquahart	1/9/18
6915—Pte. W. A. Whitney	1/9/18
4218—L.-Cpl. S. Wood	1/9/18
5488/4385—L.-Cpl. R. Zimmer	1/9/18
2704—Pte. A. G. Moss	15/9/18
974—Pte. D. Wilson	11/9/18
1930—Sgt. M. T. McGillicuddy	3/10/18
656—Cpl. G. L. Lipton	3/10/18
6426—Pte. H. F. Withers	5/10/18
6794—Pte. U. H. Brown	5/10/18
3193a—Pte. A. Miles	7/10/18
5102—Pte. W. J. Walsh	5/10/18
471n—Pte. H. J. Beach	5/10/18
6069—Pte. W. Hours	5/10/18
6097—Pte. R. A. McGill	5/10/18
4487—Pte. W. R. O'Neill	4/10/18
6103—Pte. E. H. Owens	5/10/18
6158—Pte. J. M. Wood	5/10/18
647a—Pte. W. Allan	5/10/18
6275—Pte. W. J. Anderson	5/10/18
2nd-Lieut. W. D. Baldie	5/10/18
4363—Pte. J. W. Blankenberg (M.M.)	5/10/18
6782a—Pte. H. C. Chamberlain	5/10/18
3980—Pte. B. M. Connelly	5/10/18
2354—C.S.M. G. H. Cumming (M.M.)	5/10/18
4400—L.-Cpl. J. M. Dempsey	5/10/18
6808—Pte. V. M. Duffy	4/10/18
Capt. J. H. Fletcher	5/10/18
6309—Cpl. F. L. Ford (D.C.M.)	5/10/18
6799a—Pte. A. J. Fraser	5/10/18
Lieut. J. F. Gear (M.C.)	5/10/18
763a—Pte. A. G. Graham	5/10/18
967—Cpl. N. A. Grant	5/10/18
5831—Pte. H. Grove	5/10/18
6831a—Pte. H. M. Hellier	5/10/18
4435—Pte. A. Henderson	5/10/18
(Alias A. H. Roberts.)	
5926—T.-Sgt. J. G. Hewitt	5/10/18
5034—Pte. E. E. Holt	5/10/18
5504—Pte. E. H. L. Ireland	5/10/18
3555—Pte. A. Jeffrey	5/10/18
6827—Pte. R. V. Leggett	5/10/18
655—T.-Sgt. L. W. Lyons	5/10/18
318—Pte. A. B. Mackay	5/10/18
Capt. J. A. Mahony (M.C.)	5/10/18
6838a—Pte. H. B. Miller	5/10/18

APPENDIX.

	Date of Death.		Date of Death.
5863—Pte. A. P. Missen	5/10/18	5835—Pte. C. W. Hall	5/10/18
5647—Pte. D. R. O'Dowd	5/10/18	51395—Pte. K. T. Knight	5/10/18
4750—Pte. A. W. Pennant	5/10/18	3947—Pte. J. J. Lavery	5/10/18
6867a—Pte. H. Powell	5/10/18	2352—Pte. J. A. Clancy	5/10/18
1807—Sgt. L. S. Ranson	5/10/18	6835—Pte. J. L. Maxwell	5/10/18
2208—Cpl. J. D. Rowlands	5/10/18	Lieut. P. S. Carne (M.S.M.)	25/10/18
1780—Pte. W. H. Scholtz	5/10/18	6397—Pte. S. T. Tipping	29/10/18
1735—Pte. S. H. Stirling	5/10/18	1546a—Pte. A. O'Connell	1/11/18
2799—Pte. F. C. Titus	5/10/18	6281—Pte. R. J. G. Bennett	17/11/18
6908—Pte. A. M. Tornroos	5/10/18	6943a—Pte. W. A. Letts	12/11/18
2217—Pte. W. Walsh	5/10/18	5126—Pte. J. W. Tuck	14/11/18
2478—Sgt. W. Watson	5/10/18	5821—Pte. J. Dalglish	3/12/18
6914a—Pte. W. G. Wheeler	5/10/18	6947—Pte. R. G. Jenkins	1/12/18
1748a—Pte. J. T. White	5/10/18	5639—Pte. W. T. Law	1/12/18
1301—Pte. T. G. Wright	5/10/18	5954—Pte. A. Taylor	10/11/18
6777a—Pte. T. E. Burrows	5/10/18	51331—Pte. J. M. Campbell	5/10/18
1521—Pte. E. W. Cunningham	6/10/18	744—Pte. A. C. Neale (M.M.)	10/5/19
890—Pte. H. F. Hardy	5/10/18	4266—Pte. L. Williams	1/12/19
5127—Pte. H. R. Chattin	5/10/18		

Wholly set up and printed in Australia, by The McCubbin—James Press, Pty., Ltd., Bourke Street, Melbourne.

www.ingramcontent.com/pod-product-compliance
Lightning Source LLC
Chambersburg PA
CBHW021828220426
43663CB00005B/174